November 1, 2006

Perry, happy 49th birthday !!!

I hope that I am the lucky person to show you around Paris on your 50th birthday ... to share the delicious eating, fabulous shopping, awing art and architecture, and romantic walking (and sleeping)!

Love, Peter

(I would say more, but others may read it, and some words are only for your mind, heart and spirit.)

Paris
e>>guide

Paris
e>>guide

In style • In the know • Online

www.eparis.dk.com

LONDON, NEW YORK,
MELBOURNE, MUNICH AND DELHI
www.dk.com

Produced by
Departure Lounge

Contributors
Maryanne Blacker, Rosa Jackson, Katherine Spenley, Julie Street, Richard Woodruff

Photographer
Britta Jaschinski

Reproduced in Singapore by Colourscan
Printed and bound in Singapore by Tien Wah Press

First American Edition, 2005
05 06 07 08 10 9 8 7 6 5 4 3 2 1

Published in the United States by
DK Publishing, Inc.,
375 Hudson Street, New York, New York 10014

US ISBN 0-7566-0897-X

The information in this e>>guide is checked annually.
This guide is supported by a dedicated website which provides the very latest information for visitors to
Paris; please see pages 6–7 for the web address and password. Some information, however, is liable to
change, and the publishers cannot accept responsibility for any consequences arising from the use of this
book, nor for any material on third party websites, and cannot guarantee that any website address in this
book will be a suitable source of travel information.
We value the views and suggestions of our readers very highly. Please write to:
Publisher, DK Eyewitness Travel Guides,
Dorling Kindersley, 80 Strand, London WC2R 0RL, Great Britain.

Contents

The only guidebook that's always up-to-date

Written by people who know Paris inside out, this guide provides in-depth information and reviews of the best the city has to offer. Listings are packed with great ideas and accompanied by stylish photographs, for a tantalizing foretaste of what's in store. Detailed practical information for each entry – including map references to the Street Finder at the back of the guide – take you directly to the heart of the action. So whether you live in Paris or are just visiting, to experience the real soul and pace of the city, you need this guide. Now visit the website...

top choice

- Spend the morning at a food or flea market
- Stroll in one of the city's parks or gardens
- Explore the city on rollerblades
- Go clubbing in Bastille
- Gain a new perspective on the classic sights
- Find a bar to match your mood, be it mellow or loud
- Take your pick of restaurants, from crêperies to African

listings

features

The one-stop website for all the city has to offer

Click onto eparis.dk.com for the latest, most complete news from and about places listed in the guide, plus travellers' reviews, features on hot topics, and an up-to-the-minute shortlist of Paris's most useful service providers, from the tourist board to ticket agents. The website is only available to purchasers of e>>guide Paris (the unique password given below allows you access). And it's constantly updated. Every time you visit, you bring your guidebook bang up to date!

• Get the latest travel news and miss the crowds

• Check out the weather forecast and catch a cheap flight

• Book a hotel room that suits your budget and style

• Tap into what's on at the cinema and who's in at the clubs

• Browse reviews of the latest productions and secure tickets online

• Reserve a top table or seek out the best cheap eats

• Plan your shopping trip online

password for access to website: **paris93581**

top choices

How to spend your time in Paris? Whatever your interests – dining in fine restaurants or local bistros, exploring cultural attractions, checking out the social scene or shopping in designer boutiques – Paris will deliver. This guide is full of the best things to see, do, eat and drink, and opens with the top choices of what to do at any particular time of the year or day in this perennially exciting city.

TOP CHOICES – *the year*

Celebration is a year-round affair in Paris, with the French ever ready for a party. The Champs-Elysées is packed with happy revellers on New Year's Eve as people congregate to ring out the old and ring in the new. The annual Fête de la Musique kicks off summer on 21 June, when both seasoned and amateur performers take to the streets. Then come outdoor jazz and classical music festivals, and dance and theatre performances. And next, because it's summer, a sandy beach materializes beside the Seine. In mid-July, the Champs-Elysées is swamped again during the Bastille Day parade and the climax of the Tour de France. Finally, in early October Paris officially becomes the city that never sleeps as museums, swimming pools and clubs stay open all night for La Nuit Blanche.

SPRING

Foire du Trône
Pelouse de Reuilly, 12ème • Ⓜ Liberté/Porte Dorée/Porte de Charenton Open 11:45am–11pm daily (to 1am Fri & Sat)

This colossal fun fair began in AD 957, when merchants first met up with farmers to trade grain and wine. Today at this site to the east of the city, instead of wheat sacks and wine barrels, there are 350 attractions, including a giant Ferris wheel, gravity-defying rides and carousels, and clouds of candy floss. **End Mar–end May**

Portes Ouvertes
Ateliers d'Artistes de Belleville (AAB), 32 rue de la Mare, 20ème; www.ateliers-artistes-belleville.org

There's more to the Paris art scene than majestic museums and pricey private galleries, as the annual Belleville Artists Open Studios confirms. For four days, more than 250 artists in this multi-ethnic quartier (Map 12 F2) open their doors to the public. Pick up a map from the AAB and set about discovering the neighbourhood's cornucopia of painters, photographers and jewellers, along with the bistros, funky cafés and shops. **Mid-May**

SUMMER

La Fête des Tuileries
Jardin des Tuileries, 1er
Open 11am–midnight daily (to 1am Fri & Sat)

After the spring Foire du Trône, a similar array of rides and attractions springs up around the rue de Rivoli boundary of the Jardin des Tuileries (Map 9 D4). **Aug–Sep**

Summer Music Festivals
Festival de St-Denis, 01 49 33 66 66, www.festival-saint-denis.fr; Paris Jazz Festival & Festival Classique au Vert, esplanade du Château de Vincennes, 12ème • Ⓜ Chateau de Vincennes; Fête de la Musique, www.fetedelamusique.culture.fr

Throughout the summer, Paris is alive with the sound of all kinds of music. St-Denis' Gothic basilica *(see p108)* is the glorious backdrop to a month-long classical- and world-music festival starting in June. Inside the building, renowned performers belt out Brahms or Beethoven, and jazz, world, urban and folk music also reverberate both inside and out. At the same time, as part of the Paris Jazz Festival (Jun–Jul), both big-name and experimental jazz artists strike up in the Bois de Vincennes in a series of open-air afternoon concerts. Noise-pollution laws are in abeyance at the Fête de la Musique's all-day and all-night extravaganza on 21 June. The summer solstice is fêted by appreciative crowds as international and world-music acts, serious professionals, one-man bands and musical wannabes play their kind of music in varied locations all over the city. To round off the summer, classical music wafts over the lawns of the Bois de Vincennes during the Festival Classique au Vert (Aug–Sep). **Jun–Sep**

La Marche des Fiertés LGBT (Gay Pride)
www.fiertes-lgbt.org
This vivacious and flamboyant celebration of gay, lesbian, bi- and transsexual culture attracts around 650,000 onlookers and performers. A week of exhibitions, events and parties climaxes in the parade, which kicks off at 2pm and dances its way to place de la Bastille. It's fabulous fun, but the underlying message of tolerance, education and equality is serious. **End Jun**

Le Quatorze Juillet (Bastille Day)
France's national holiday recalls the storming of the Bastille in 1789 and the beginning of the republic. By 10am, hordes pack the Champs-Elysées for a glimpse of French military might and the president reviewing the troops. Later that night, thousands gather under the Tour Eiffel to watch the fireworks at Trocadéro, as others head off for more partying at the *bals des pompiers* (firemen's balls) held in stations all over the city. Some of these kick off the previous night, when Parisians can also dance their heart out on place de la Bastille. **14 Jul**

Le Tour de France
See the action at www.letour.fr
The world's best road cyclists descend on Paris each year for the final stage of the Tour de France. Riders loop past place de la Bastille before completing nine laps around the Champs-Elysées, place de la Concorde and rue de Rivoli, including a final sprint up the Champs Elysées to the finish line. **End Jul**

AUTUMN

Festival d'Automne
01 53 45 17 00, www.festival-automne.com
Parisians are jolted out of their summer slumber with the arrival of this forward-looking, city-wide arts festival, showcasing new talent from around the world. It's all about music, opera, theatre and dance not previously shown in France; the kind of productions that make you sit up and pay attention. **Sep–Dec**

Jazz à la Villette
www.cite-musique.fr • Ⓜ Porte de Pantin
La Villette's annual week-long jazz festival spills out into the Cité de la Musique *(see p108)*, local bars and the

park (scene of free open-air concerts). There's a penchant for innovative and experimental music, with appearances by big names such as Herbie Hancock, as well as a host of local favourites such as Baptiste Trotignon. **Sep**

La Nuit Blanche
Check out all the activities at www.paris.fr
The brainchild of Mayor Delanoë, "Sleepless Night" is designed to keep Parisians up all night with a hefty dose of culture. And, it's all free, from nocturnal swimming sessions and a 3am art crawl through the Centre Pompidou, to techno concerts. A must for the culturally curious, night owls and insomniacs. **Early Oct**

WINTER

Paris sur Glace
place Hôtel de Ville, 4ème; place Raoul Dautry, 15ème
Both open noon–10pm Mon–Thu, noon–midnight Fri, 9am–midnight Sat, 9am–10pm Sun
It might not be a frozen lake in the Alps, but in the depth of winter, an open-air Paris ice rink can be equally enchanting. Two rinks are open to the public free of charge – the one in front of the grandiose Hôtel de Ville is the largest and perhaps the prettiest, ringed with fir trees and twinkling lights when night falls. Skates are available for hire. **Early Dec–early Mar**

Le Réveillon (New Year's Eve)
While some Parisians prefer to spend their Réveillon (or Fête de St-Sylvestre) sitting around the table supping oysters and reminiscing, more spirited folk take to the streets. Crowds throng the Champs-Elysées, bars around Bastille teem and the Quartier Latin is alive with people throwing their arms around each other and screeching "*Bonne année!*". **31 Dec**

>> *For listings magazines with information on events and programmes in Paris,* see p230

TOP CHOICES – *morning*

Parisians, in general, are not morning people. The city takes its time to wake up; so much so that early risers will often find that they have the streets virtually to themselves. Then, suddenly, it's frantic: shop and kiosk shutters rattle open, delivery vans unload, Métro stations pour forth commuters, cyclists and pedestrians dart through traffic, risking life and limb, and café counters fill and empty with alarming speed. One of the great joys is just to sit back and watch the scene unfold. But whatever your plans, mornings in Paris are worth getting up for. The major museums are less crowded and, at the other end of the cultural spectrum, there are the morning markets. No two are alike, and each stall has something tempting – from stacks of oozing cheeses to buckets of olives and piles of *saucisson*.

Traditional Markets

Markets, a centuries-old Parisian feature, offer endless variety – from fat Provençal cherries in spring to hairy boars' heads in autumn. There are over 80 in the city, including roving morning markets such as the Marché Iéna-President Wilson (Wed & Sun, Map 8 E3). Most start around 8am. Some, such as rue Mouffetard in the 5th (Tue–Sun, Map 20 H1), are all-day, open-air affairs, while others, such as the Marché Enfants Rouge (Map 11 C4), are covered. The daily flower market on the Ile de la Cité (Map 16 H1) turns into a squawking bird market on Sundays and is definitely worth a visit. At all day-long markets, the pace is more leisurely in the mornings.

Best Breakfasts

Café Marly, 93 rue de Rivoli, 1er, 01 49 26 06 60; Market, 15 avenue Matignon, 8ème, 01 56 43 40 90
Kick-start the day at the Café Marly (which opens at 8am) with a strong espresso and an uncluttered bird's-eye view of the Louvre's iconic glass pyramid before the crowds arrive. Or, pull up a chair at one of the cafés on rue Montorgueil (Map 10 H3) or rue de Buci (Map 16 F2) and watch the city wake up over a coffee and a croissant. Alternatively, begin any weekday morning in plenty of

style with breakfast at Market, chef Jean-Georges Vongerichten's fashionable restaurant *(see p40)*. The offerings by master pastry chef Pierre Hermé that are sold here – including his famous flavoured macaroons – are nothing short of life-enhancing.

Wheely Fun

For information on bike hire, *see p229*
Shoot along the banks of the Seine on Rollerblades or a bike on Sundays (or every day from mid-Jul to mid-Aug), when the riverside expressways are closed to traffic. Glide from the Tour Eiffel down to the Musée d'Orsay on the Left Bank, and from the Tuileries to Bercy on the Right Bank. Alternatively, the roads and tracks of the vast and pleasant Bois de Boulogne are perfect for pedalling or skating – by afternoon, however, the crowds descend.

Quiet Museums

See www.rmn.fr to check the national museums in Paris
A museum city *par excellence*, Paris is blessed with both blockbusting temporary exhibitions and stunning permanent collections. To beat the crowds, arrive early. Note that national treasures such as the Louvre, the Musée d'Orsay and the Centre Pompidou are free on the first Sunday of each month.

Morning Cinema

For more on Left Bank art-house cinemas, *see p120*

When the day dawns grey and cold or the rain begins to fall, slip into a cinema and cosy up with a good film. Chains such as the independent MK2 and the multinational UGC offer a reduced tariff for the first morning session. Look for *version originale* (VO) of foreign films if you don't want to suffer French-dubbed renderings.

Free Fashion Shows

No matter if you weren't on the invitation list for the Paris fashion shows. The Galeries Lafayette (Map 9 D1) parades the latest looks in a weekly 30-minute free fashion show (11am Tue). Get there when the store opens at 9:30am and admire the imposing glass dome and Art Nouveau staircase in relative calm before giving your credit card a thorough retail work-out.

Beauty Treatments

For more on beauty, *see pp162–7*

Beauty salons are brimful on Saturday mornings; that's when serious working girls book their facials, manicures and top-to-toe treatments. Join them to experience the buzz, or opt for a leisurely weekday morning at a snazzy salon with the ladies-who-lunch set, and sit back and enjoy the cosseting.

Sunbathing and Swimming

Piscine Butte-aux-Cailles, 6 place Paul Verlaine, 13ème, 01 45 89 60 05

Come mid-July, the Seine goes seaside for a month as palm trees, deck chairs, umbrellas, hammocks and vast amounts of sand appear along a 3-km (2-mile) stretch of the Right Bank, opposite Notre Dame. Every summer, a couple of million people visit, so get there early if you want some space to soak up the sun. There's even a swimming pool. Serious swimmers may prefer the vintage Piscine Butte-aux-Cailles (Map 21 A5), with its outdoor pools fed by artesian wells. A morning dip here is downright civilized.

Auction Action

Drouot Richelieu, 9 rue Drouot, 9ème, 01 48 00 20 20, www.gazette-drouot.com

There's nothing quite like an auction to get the blood pumping, and Drouot Richelieu (Map 4 F5) holds sales Mon–Sat in 16 different salesrooms – enough to sate a big bidding appetite. If you just like to look, auction items go on view from 11am the day before. Expect everything from Louis XV chairs to works by Matisse.

Cookery Courses

Ecole Ritz Escoffier, 38 rue Cambon, 1er, 01 43 16 30 50, www.ritzparis.com; Promenades Gourmandes, 187 rue du Temple, 3ème, 01 48 04 56 84, www.promenadesgourmandes.com

Acquire a souvenir of French cuisine that lasts longer than a wheel of Camembert – expertise! Cookery classes with chef Paule Caillat at Promenades Gourmandes (Map 11 C3) run 9am–3pm and include a market tour, a hands-on class and a three-course lunch. Alternatively, the illustrious Hotel Ritz's Ecole Escoffier (Map 9 D2) holds Saturday morning introductory workshops, focusing on seasonal produce (9am–1pm).

Hot Tickets

Place de la Madeleine, 8ème (Map 9 C2); Gare Montparnasse, 14ème (Map 19 B1)

Buy last-minute, cut-price theatre tickets for same-day shows from one of Paris's two Kiosque Théâtres (open daily). Savvy Parisian show-goers often choose this option, as French theatres and some concert halls have complicated booking systems – requests for tickets sometimes have to be put in writing months in advance.

TOP CHOICES – *afternoon*

Stroll around any Paris park in the afternoon and you'll find you're not alone. Afternoon promenades, particularly following the customary, long Sunday lunch, are *de rigueur*, and the wide-open, well-manicured public spaces are the place to be. Boules players, with furrowed brows and flicking wrists, take over the dusty paths, and tittering children line up for weekend puppet shows. In the afternoon, too, shopping areas are always buzzy, especially on Saturdays; and, at the smallest hint of sunshine, the cobblestoned quays of the Seine are awash with sunbathers and picnickers. Between lunch and the apéritif is also prime time for visiting private art galleries. Alternatively, Paris is a rewarding city to explore on foot, and an afternoon amble through the streets reveals myriad riches, from impressive architecture to inviting cafés.

Sunday Lunch

La Guinguette de l'Ile du Martin Pecheur, 41 quai Victor Hugo Champigny-sur-Marne, 01 49 83 02 03, www.guinguette.fr
Sunday lunch doesn't get much more quintessentially French than at La Guinguette de l'Ile du Martin Pecheur (just 20 minutes from central Paris on RER line A2), where they serve *chanson* with the *entrecôte à la Bordelaise* (Mar–Sep). Lazing at long tables (in the open air, weather permitting) beside the river Marne, enjoying a singalong – it's a scene straight out of a Renoir painting. Resolute foodies seeking a three-star bite on Sunday are, however, limited to lofty hotel establishments – haute-cuisine restaurants are all closed on Sundays.

Picnics

For other recommendations for food to go, *see p38*
The tastiest of titbits, from earthy terrines and exquisite patisseries to fragrant strawberries and cold champagne, can be found at the gourmet emporia Hediard or Fauchon (both are located on place de la Madeleine, Map 9 C2) or La Grande Epicerie de Paris (*see p80*). Then, settle on a bench by the Seine on the Ile de la

Cité, or alternatively, *déjeune sur l'herbe* (picnic) in place des Vosges (Map 17 C1). Sadly, the tempting expanses of unspoiled lawn in the Jardin du Luxembourg or the Tuileries are strictly *"pelouse interdit"* – keep off the grass – domains.

Hammam

Les Bains du Marais, 31–3 rue des Blancs Manteaux, 4ème, 01 44 61 02 02, www.lesbainsdumarais.com
Before a night of bar-hopping, unwind at a single-sex session in the Hammam at the Mosquée de Paris *(see p164)* or, at the more chic Les Bains du Marais (Map 11 B5). At both spots, the entry fee (5€ at the former, 30€ at the latter) buys you *hammam* (Turkish bath), sauna and lounging-room access and a feeling of having slipped into the pages of *1,001 Arabian Nights*; massages, *gommages* (scrubs) and facials are extra.

Brocantes

The appearance of fluttering street banners announces the onset of the season of *antiquitiés-brocantes* (bric-a-brac and antiques fairs). From Apr to May and Sep to Oct, dealers peddling country furniture, silverware, jewellery, linen, books and prints invade local streets and squares. Many sellers travel in from the provinces, and prices are often lower than those at the permanent city antiques markets. The weekly *La Vie du Collectioneur* (published every Thursday) lists *brocantes* all over France.

Games

Stop off at the Jardins des Luxembourg (Map 16 E4) for a spot of cerebral jousting with the chess devotees who huddle around board-topped tables and do battle throughout the afternoon. You can either watch or join the queue to play. Serious card-players also occupy a table or two. If you prefer a spot of *pétanque*, try the Arènes de Lutèce *(see p98)*. The other players might let you join in, otherwise, bring your own set and some friends.

Gallery-Hopping

La Maison Rouge, 10 boulevard de la Bastille, 12ème, 01 40 01 08 81, www.lamaisonrouge.org
St-Germain, with its maze of commercial art galleries, particularly along rue de Seine, rue des Beaux Arts and rue de Guénégaud, is the ultimate for an urbane afternoon wander. Artistic pickings on the Right Bank, though, can be a little more edgy; explore the art squat Les Frigos *(see p112)* and La Maison Rouge (Map 17 D4), a former factory specializing in exhibitions of contemporary art from private collections.

Shopping

For more on shopping in Paris, *see pp56–91*
Go with the flow and shop, shop, shop in the 6th and 7th arrondissements, where the fashion choice is second to none. Rue de Grenelle is the magic mile of designer shoes, with clothes to match. Rue du Cherche Midi also does a fine line in shoes, bags and bread – the famed Poilâne bakery is here – while rue des Sts-Pères is the place to stock up on sexy lingerie and glamorous outfits. Also, trawl rue du Bac, rue du Dragon, rue St-Sulpice and rue du Four before collapsing in a happy heap encircled by shopping bags.

Tea

For more suggestions on salons de thé, *see p55*
Take tea at Ladurée *(see p55)*, famed for the richest and thickest hot chocolate around and addictive macaroons. Alternatively, try a more exotic milieu and sample sticky baklava and mint tea in Le Ziryab, the restaurant with the Seine-side view on the top floor of the Institut du Monde Arabe *(see p98)*; or at funky Andy Wahloo *(see p137)*, where pop art meets Morocco. Or, just about every place on boulevard de Belleville *(see p159)* serves up palate-cleansing fresh mint tea.

Architectural Treasures

Passage de Retz, 9 rue Charlot, 3ème, 01 48 04 37 99; Pavillon de l'Arsenal, 21 boulevard Morland, 4ème, 01 42 76 33 97
Much of the cityscape was created between the 17th and 19th centuries, but you can also pay homage to some modern masters of architectural design. Le Corbusier's genius is on display at Villa La Roche *(see p105)*; and the 60s avant-garde French Communist Party HQ (2 place Colonel Fabien, 19ème, Map 6 E4) is the work of one of his contemporaries, Brazilian architect Oscar Niemeyer. Paris's first skyscraper – just 22 storeys high – was designed by Edouard Albert in the 50s, and is found at 33 rue de Croulebarbe in the 13th (Map 21 A3). If you've a head for heights, whizz up to the top of the colossal Grande Arche de la Défense – one of ex-President Mitterrand's *Grands Projets* – for spectacular views. A visit to the Pavillon de l'Arsenal (Map 17 C3), the museum dedicated to architecture and urban design, will then help explain what you've just surveyed. Wind down in the Passage de Retz, a former toy factory turned art gallery. This 17th-century *hôtel particulier* with a modern twist also features a boutique and café by the much sought-after designer Christian Blecher (Map 11 C4).

TOP CHOICES – *evening*

At 7pm, the city's tone shifts noticeably as people escape from the workplace and prepare to get on with the business of enjoying themselves. Given the emphasis the French place on eating, it comes as no surprise that apéritif time is filled with anticipation. Parisians head to their local bar or café in droves as a prelude to dinner, or to wind up before a big night out. Midweek is a popular time for locals to hit town, be it to dance the night away or take in the season's must-see show, so on Wednesdays and Thursdays, in particular, the atmosphere is charged with excitement. And clubbers who can't wait till late are well-catered for: the latest nightlife craze is for "after-work" clubs, which allow people to go straight from office to club and start – rather than end – their evenings with a boogie.

Salons Scene

Jim Haynes, 01 43 27 17 67, www.jim-haynes.com; Patricia Laplante-Collins, 01 43 26 12 88, parissoirees@noos.fr

Emulate Gertrude Stein at a *salon*, a kind of intellectual open-house. Maverick academic and philosopher Jim Haynes's Sunday evening gatherings are legendary. Up to 50 people who call ahead are invited to his home and a mix of ages, nationalities and professions is always on the cards – as well as good food and wine. Patricia Laplante-Collins's Paris Connections nights, also held on Sundays, are similarly full of interesting types and excellent food; each week has a different speaker and theme – such as tips on writing screenplays, or an introduction to shamanism. Book in advance.

Views over the Capital

Aeroparis ballon operates summer to 9:30pm, winter to 5:30pm, www.aeroparis.com

Take an unofficial tour of the City of Lights. When the streetlights are switched on, it's a thrill to stand on the open platform at the back of the No. 29 bus and check

out the sights from the Gare St-Lazare via the Marais to Bastille. Alternatively, for another great view of Paris at dusk, take the last trip up in the tethered balloon at the Parc Andre Citroën *(see p167)*.

Pre-Dinner Drinks

Les Apéros de Jeudis, www.aperodjeudis.com; Apollo, 3 place Denfert-Rochereau, 01 45 38 76 77; Hotel Raphael, 17 avenue Kléber 16ème, 01 53 64 32 00, www.raphael-hotel.com

To relax after a long day, grab a table at your favourite café around 7pm and enjoy a glass of champagne or a kir.

(Parisians consider Pastis to be a drink for old men in the South of France.) If it's sunny, stake out your territory on a terrace and catch the last rays along with your tipple. Trendy bar-restaurant Apollo is ideal, but Paris's chicest summer cocktail spot is the stunning rooftop terrace at the Hotel Raphael. In less accommodating weather, try Le Fumoir *(see p132)*, Kong *(see p134)* or Pershing Hall *(see p178)*. Or, every Thursday evening during summer, join the crowd at Les Apéros de Jeudi, when Parisians gather in different open-air locations to meet over apéritifs.

Open Lectures

For forthcoming events, see www.louvre.fr

Public lectures at the Louvre are an erudite way to expand your mind. They start at 7 or 8:30pm, are held in

French and are usually linked to current exhibitions. To make the most of it, visit the show before attending the lecture – and bring a dictionary. The atmosphere, while intellectual, is inclusive, and the speakers seem genuinely keen to share their insight with Joe Public.

Clubbing

For further details, check www.soiree.fr, www.sortiraparis.com, www.workinzecity.org. Seven 2 One, 161 rue Montmartre, 2ème
Early evening clubs (*l'after work* in French), catering to those who just can't wait to get a little bit of dance-floor action, are currently hugely popular in Paris. Seven 2 One, which kicks off at apéritif time on Wednesdays and Thursdays, is the largest; while Work in Ze City club nights (Thursdays) start a little later at 8pm and take place at various more upscale venues, such as the Etoile club, with a clientele to match.

Shopping for Love

For a singles scene with a difference, head to Galeries Lafayette's *(see p83)* singles' supermarket night (Thu), where you can pick up some gastronomic treats and perhaps a Parisian soulmate. Locals on the lookout choose a special purple basket to signal their single status. If it all seems too overwhelming, there's an excellent in-store wine bar to help break the ice.

Modern Soirées

Reservations on 01 42 18 56 72
The Fondation Cartier *(see p113)* hosts Soirées Nomades (Nomadic Evenings) for cool, arty types. These exceedingly hip events encompass anything that can be vaguely described as "the arts", from avant-garde electric-harp music to circus performances, storytelling evenings and brass-band jam sessions. The programme is nothing if not eclectic. If you have time, get there early to check out the building and the current exhibition before the soirée begins. It's essential to reserve ahead.

A Romantic Sunset

The Pont des Arts (Map 10 F5) is one of Paris's prettiest bridges, and certainly one of the most romantic. The views across the city are stunning, and couples clutching bottles of champagne and the makings of a picnic head here in droves. Note, though, that it's also where boisterous foreign exchange students and busking travellers with questionable musical talents hang out. It may be a little sentimental, but watching the sun set over the city from this vantage point is a real pleasure.

Early Dinner

Be one of the lucky few and reserve an early table at L'Atelier de Joel Robuchon *(see p37)*. The hugely popular gourmet restaurant run by the eponymous superstar chef only takes bookings for 6:30 or 11:30pm; anyone wishing to eat at a more usual hour has to turn up and queue. Outside. Even if it's raining. So it's a great idea to skip lunch and arrive early for a chance to try Robuchon's exquisite – if pricey – food. Seating is arranged in a long bar formation so expect to sit alongside your companion and don't be shy about talking to your neighbour.

Come Dancing

From June to October, usually on Sundays, people flock to dance on the banks of the Seine. In the early evening, the square Tino Rossi (Map 17 C4) – the site of an open-air sculpture park – comes alive with rhythm junkies doing the rumba, executing a mean tango and samba-ing as if their lives depended on it. Some of the dancers here are awe-inspiring, most are fairly average and absolute beginners are welcome too. All that's required is a little enthusiasm and a large grin.

TOP CHOICES – *night*

The twinkling Tour Eiffel is an appropriate metaphor for a night out in Paris: frivolous, fun and rather beautiful. Residents of the City of Lights really come to life after dark. The city looks stunning and, more often than not, its inhabitants dress up accordingly. Night-time pursuits are taken very seriously. There's even a cultural all-nighter – La Nuit Blanche *(see p11)* – organized each year by the Mairie (city council). Year-round, a surprising array of high- and low-brow cultural attractions vies for your attention, ranging from late-opening exhibitions to mass roller-blading events, back-to-back film shows and wild club nights. Wherever you end up, take a cab home – a drive along the expressways on the banks of the Seine or around the place de la Concorde in the early hours is not to be missed.

Balades
For further details, check www.parisroller.com

On Friday nights, police close off boulevards around the city to offer thousands of skaters a nocturnal adrenalin rush. The event starts at 10pm outside Gare Montparnasse (Map 19 B1), but beginners can turn up for free tuition (8–9pm). In order to join in the fun, you must be experienced enough to know how to stop! In order to reduce the spills, the parade is cancelled in wet weather. If you need to hire roller blades, check out the website for useful addresses.

Late-Night Food
Many restaurants across the city serve until 11pm but one of the best options for a late meal is to indulge in a special late menu, offered after 10:30pm, at brasseries such as La Coupole *(see p218)*. Two courses of classic brasserie fare *(see p29)*, a quarter bottle of wine and a terrific atmosphere will set you back a little over 20€. If hunger strikes in the early hours of the morning, head for Au Pied du Cochon *(see p24)* or La Tour de

Montlhéry, aka Chez Denise *(see p25)*, where you can order anything, from a bowl of onion soup to a full three-course meal – even at 5am.

Art Appreciation
Catch an exhibition at the devastatingly cool Palais de Toyko *(see p104)*, which is open until midnight. The shows are invariably interesting, offbeat and a hit with Paris's bright young things, who wander around the warehouse-like space as much to be seen as to be inspired. The shop has become a destination in itself and Tokyo Eat, the on-site restaurant, is currently one of the city's hippest places to go for a meal. Don't miss a trip to the toilets-for-two and take advantage of the human juke-box concept – the waiter presents you with a menu of songs that the DJ will work into his playlist.

Hitting the Shops
Elyfleur, 82 avenue Wagram, 17ème, 01 47 66 87 19; Pavillon Noura, 21 avenue Marceau, 16ème, 01 47 20 33 33

Most of the city's shops and stores close at 7pm, but until midnight (and sometimes even later) on the Champs-Elysées you can stock up on magazines at

Stay in touch with late-night Paris through ▶▶ www.eparis.dk.com

Publicis Drugstore *(see p83)*; music and videos at Virgin Megastore *(see p223); and* general supermarket provisions and beauty products at Monoprix *(see p220)*. It's even possible to get a free makeover at Sephora *(see p220)* – perfect for a pre-club transformation. Nearby, pick up delicious Lebanese titbits at Pavillon Noura and flowers at 24-hour Elyfleur. Over in the Marais, books and wine are on offer at La Belle Hortense *(see p139)*.

Exotic Pleasures

Les Jardins d'Alexandrie, 28 rue Marbeuf, 8ème, 01 42 25 14 48; Café Egyptien, 112 rue Mouffetard, 5ème, 01 43 31 11 35
Hook up with a hookah and smoke some shisha at an authentic Arabian spot. Les Jardins d'Alexandrie offers up-market lounging as you listen to Arabic music and drag on sweet tobacco in between sips of mint tea. It also serves delicious food. Over on the Left Bank, Café Egyptien is a more laid-back affair, and while the decor may be simple the shisha menu is extensive, and not even remotely expensive for the excellent quality. Both venues stay open until around 2am.

Dancing the Night Away

Check www.novaplanet.com, www.flyersweb.com and www. lemonsound.com for special club nights and one-off events; Latina Café, 114 avenue Champs-Elysées, 8ème, 01 42 89 98 89
From up-market *boîtes*, to totally unpretentious – if somewhat seedy – haunts, Paris has every aspect of the clubbing scene covered. Those chasing the latest big thing should check the listings for any night run by party collective La Johnson. Current darlings of the clubbing set, they specialize in running very cool parties in distinctly uncool clubs such as La Scala and Club Madeleine Plaza. Alternatively, hit perennial favourites such as Le Queen *(see p145)*, Le Cab *(see p132)*, Le

Rex *(see p135)* and Batofar *(see p151)*. Latino lovers should join a salsa session at the Latina Café (open daily), but if you prefer a little more of a multimedia approach, head to alternative club space Project 101 *(see p147)*.

Cinematic All-Nighters

Cinemas, in particular those on the Left Bank *(see p120)*, often run special directors' retrospectives at which three films are shown back-to-back starting at midnight on Saturday. Breakfast is included for the survivors. If an all-nighter is too much, several movie theatres run special midnight showings of headlining films (also on Saturday nights). Check listings magazines such as *Pariscope* for details.

Late Bars

Chao Ba, 22 boulevard Clichy, 18ème, 01 42 89 98 89
The city is full of places to suit drinkers who prefer to start late and end early, and this after-2am crowd tends to be more relaxed and friendly than cocktail Cinderellas who start at a reasonable hour. Fortunately, late bars don't charge entry. Unfortunately, drinks tend to be pricey. But when only an all-nighter will do, head to one of these bars, which really get going after midnight: Le Connetable *(see p137)* is perfect for a *très* French session that often lasts until dawn; the Highlander pub *(see p212)* is open earlier but is absolutley jammed after hours; Le Bar *(see p135)* is a quiet place for a late tipple; Le Crocodile *(see p141)* is a prime spot for cocktails; and the Chao Ba is a rather classy drinking den in Pigalle.

restaurants

Restaurants alone are reason enough to come to Paris, whether you're seeking a slice of history, a dash of panache or a pinch of perfection. What sets French chefs apart is their mastery of technique, which has filtered down to a young generation of bistro chefs whose creative cuisine highlights seasonal ingredients. The current trend is for "tapas" – elegant food served in tiny portions.

GREAT VIEWS	DESIGNER	ALFRESCO
Le Vieux Bistro 14 rue du Cloître Notre-Dame, 4ème Like Notre Dame, its imposing near neighbour, this bistro is a Parisian classic. A table on the terrace guarantees relaxing views. *(See p30)*	**Le Cristal Room** 11 place des Etats-Unis, 16ème Actually the Baccarat store's in-house restaurant, this Philippe Starck-designed dining room is a stunning location for lunch. *(See p40)*	**Kastoori** 4 place Gustave Toudouze, 9ème Of all the terraces in this part of town, Kastoori's is the most in demand – for its great-value lunch menu and thalis. *(See p44)*
Au Bon Accueil 14 rue de Montessuy, 7ème The terrace view can't be beaten as the Tour Eiffel soars to dizzying heights just metres away. *(See p38)*	**Market** 15 avenue Matignon, 8ème The place to be during Fashion Week, Market always puts on a great break-fast, with goodies by star pâtissier Pierre Hermé. *(See p40)*	**Le Square Trousseau** 1 rue Antoine-Vollon, 12ème The early 20th-century dining room is full of charm, and in summer the pavement tables of this popular bistro can't be beaten. *(See p52)*
	R'Aliment 57 rue Charlot, 3ème The bright, modern interior of this Marais eatery cuts a creative dash; the healthy dishes follow suit. *(See p28)*	**L'Iode** 48 rue d'Argout, 2ème This Breton outpost serves beau-tifully fresh fish and seafood and has outside tables on a pleasant, traffic-free street. *(See p26)*
La Tour d'Argent 15–17 quai de la Tournelle, 5ème In addition to a lofty gourmet repu-tation, this restaurant has amazing views over the Seine. *(See p33)*		**Café Noir** 15 rue St-Blaise, 20ème Well off the beaten track, in summer Café Noir makes the most of the tranquil location on a pedestrian street with outside tables. *(See p49)*
Maison Blanche 15 avenue Montaigne, 8ème Perched on top of the Théâtre des Champs Elysées, the dining room overlooks dusky rooftops and the meandering Seine. *(See p40)*		**Restaurant du Palais Royal** 110 galerie Valois, 1er With tables in the Palais Royal gar-dens, this restaurant has an enviable setting. Fortunately, the food is equally fine. *(See p24)*

ROMANTIC	LATE NIGHT	GLOBAL

Velly
52 rue Lamartine, 9ème
A local bistro can be just the place for a tête-à-tête. In this time-worn dining room, the updated bistro food is a sensual pleasure. *(See p45)*

Au Pied de Cochon
6 rue Coquillière, 1er
Don't be put off by the name – this buzzy round-the-clock spot does serve pig's feet, but there's also less challenging fare on offer. *(See p24)*

Chez Vong
10 rue de la Grande Truanderie, 1er
In a city where convincing Chinese cuisine is all too rare, Chez Vong is a real find, with tasteful decor and stunning food. *(See p25)*

L'Ambroisie
9 place des Vosges, 4ème
Posh frocks and suave suits are *de rigueur* at this elegant restaurant, with its exquisite setting and luxury food. *(See p29)*

Le Tour de Montlhéry
5 rue des Prouvaires, 1er
A remnant of Les Halles' market days, this is a great spot for a vast steak in the small hours. *(See p25)*

Abazu
3 rue André-Mazet, 6ème
Freshness is key at this Japanese restaurant, where Parisians go to chill out and enjoy the theatrical *teppanaki* experience. *(See p34)*

Fogon St-Julien
10 rue St-Julien-le-Pauvre, 5ème
Find first-class Spanish food at this address near Notre Dame. Their six different paellas will have you stamping your feet for more. *(See p32)*

Le Souk
1 rue Keller, 11ème
Less extravagant than a trip to Morocco, Le Souk is just as exotic, with its spiced tagines, mood lighting and attentive service. *(See p51)*

>> *Brasseries are a good choice for a late dinner; most remain open until midnight or later.*

Sardegna a Tavola
1 rue de Cotte, 12ème
This sunny Sardinian restaurant has established itself as the best of its kind in Paris, thanks to the quality of its ingredients and cooking. *(See p52)*

Aux Lyonnais
32 rue St-Marc, 2ème
This traditional bistro with vintage decor, charming service and fragrant Lyonnais food will deliver a perfect Paris moment. *(See p25)*

L'As du Fallafel
34 rue des Rosiers, 4ème
There are falafal joints galore on this street, but few can match this one. "Often imitated, never equalled", says the sign. *(See p29)*

Restaurants

Au Pied de Cochon *former market eatery* `10 G4`
6 rue Coquillière, 1er • 01 40 13 77 00
≫ www.pieddecochon.com Open 24/7

The signature dish of humble grilled pig's trotter with Béarnaise sauce is one to try at this jolly 24-hour brasserie in the heart of Les Halles, the city's former central food market. It's great for a meal of onion soup and briny oysters, too, and gets lively after 2am, when theatre folk and clubbers tend to drop by. **Moderate**

L'Ardoise *seasonal menus* `9 C3`
28 rue du Mont Thabor, 1er • 01 42 96 28 18
Open lunch & dinner Tue–Fri, dinner only Sat & Sun

Pierre Jay's bistro is one of the few in Paris to open on Sundays, but that's only one reason to visit. Local office workers and Parisians in the know congregate here for the great-value food, ranging from pig's trotters to pan-fried scallops with oyster mushrooms. Desserts are not their strong point though. **Moderate**

Restaurant du Palais Royal *real class* `10 F3`
110 galerie Valois, 1er • 01 40 20 00 27
Open lunch & dinner Mon–Sat (Mon–Thu in winter)

In summer, a table on the terrace here is hotly sought-after, so book ahead. In winter the jewel-toned dining room is a treat, and the Mediterranean-inspired food is consistently delicious. (The chef claims to make the best risotto in Paris.) For dessert, try *millefeuilles* filled with fruit and crème Chantilly. **Moderate**

L'Espadon *luxury lunching* `9 D2`
Hôtel Ritz, 15 place Vendôme, 1er • 01 43 16 30 80
≫ www.ritzparis.com Open lunch & dinner daily

L'Espadon delivers everything you'd expect of the Ritz: sumptuous surroundings, smooth (and surprisingly unsnooty) service and simply fabulous food. The lunch menu (68€) is a bargain, entitling diners to a lavish four-course feast, including a stunning cheese trolley and coffee with *mignardises* (tiny cakes). **Expensive**

Chez Vong *flavourful Oriental* `10 H4`
10 rue de la Grande Truanderie, 1er • 01 40 26 09 36
>> www.chez-vong.com Open lunch & dinner Mon–Sat

Those who despair of ever finding great Chinese food
in Paris are relieved to discover this discreet Les
Halles restaurant. Among the plants and chinoiserie,
discriminating diners savour authentic steamed fish,
Peking duck and prawns in lotus leaf. Not cheap, but
the freshness and flavour justify the price. **Moderate**

La Tour de Montlhéry *late-night joint* `10 G4`
5 rue des Prouvaires, 1er • 01 42 36 21 82
Open lunch & dinner Mon–Fri

Hearty food (mutton chops, stuffed cabbage) and a
noisy, smoke-filled atmosphere are the order of the
day at this round-the-clock haunt in Les Halles.
Closely packed tables mean that there is often cross-
table chat; luckily, the flowing wine helps make
conversation a breeze. **Moderate**

Café Moderne *creative cuisine* `10 G2`
40 rue Notre-Dame-des-Victoires, 2ème • 01 53 40 84 10
Open lunch & dinner Mon–Fri, dinner only Sat

Achieving a balance between hip and inviting isn't
easy, but Café Moderne proves that it can be done –
and well. The cosy red banquettes accommodate a
cosmopolitan bunch who contentedly polish off
dishes such as thyme-flavoured lamb in filo pastry,
and squid filled with Parmesan. **Moderate**

Le Meurice *heavenly hotel dining* `9 D3`
Hotel Meurice, 228 rue de Rivoli, 1er • 01 44 58 10 10
Open lunch & dinner daily

The cloud-painted ceiling, gilt galore and cushy chairs
put you in just the right relaxed frame of mind to appreciate the subtle tastes of Yannick Alleno's understated
creations. Try a lightly smoked salmon chunk wrapped
in paper-thin crisp potato, John Dory dotted with cumin
or the most delicate lemon meringue tart. **Expensive**

Aux Lyonnais *revitalized bistro* `10 F2`
32 rue St-Marc, 2ème • 01 42 96 65 04
Open lunch & dinner Tue–Fri, dinner Sat

French super-chef Alain Ducasse has rejuvenated an
1890s restaurant into a classic bistro complete with
burnished red façade, zinc bar, tiles and majestic
mirrors. This is updated regional food at its finest –
sabodet (pork sausage), eggs poached in red wine,
and irresistible Saint-Marcellin cheese. **Moderate**

>> *Cheap: under 13€ for a main course; moderate: 13–20€; expensive: over 20€*

Restaurants

L'Iode *piscatorial delights*
10 G3
48 rue d'Argout, 2ème • 01 42 36 46 45
Open lunch & dinner Mon–Fri, dinner Sat

In the busy shopping area of the *2ème*, this cheerful seafood stop sticks to a mantra of keeping things simple. Expect treats such as grilled sole or crispy deep-fried baby squid; nothing flashy or too fancy, just fresh produce, relaxed service and lots of locals, especially in the airy upstairs room. **Moderate**

Chez Georges *quintessential bistro*
10 G3
1 rue du Mail, 2ème • 01 42 60 07 11
Open lunch & dinner Mon–Sat

On this quiet corner, the glorious old Paris bistro of film and fiction is alive and well and full to the rafters every night. Its success rides on the winning combination of a worn but grand interior, maternal waitresses and good, honest food such as duck with ceps and plump profiteroles doused in chocolate. **Moderate**

Le Petit Dakar *African chic*
11 C5
6 rue Elzévir, 3ème • 01 44 59 34 74
Open lunch & dinner daily

Thanks to its link with the shop opposite selling African art and *objets*, Le Petit Dakar would look right at home on the pages of *Marie Claire Maison*. Its menu is limited to just a few reliably tasty Senegalese classics such as *thieb'oudjen* (fish stew) or *maffé* (meat in peanut sauce). **Cheap**

Rue Ste-Anne *noodle central*
10 E2
Demand from Japanese ex-pats has created many great noodle shops in the *10ème*, particularly on rue Ste-Anne. Higuma (at No. 32bis), with an army of dextrous wok-handlers in the open kitchen, is a favourite. Try a giant bowl of ramen topped with grilled pork, rice with tempura, or *yakisoba* (stir-fried noodles). Nearby, Laï Laï Ken (at No. 7) is equally popular with a young clientele who comes for more of the same. **Cheap**

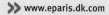

Anahi *South American hideaway* `11 B3`
49 rue Volta, 3ème • 01 48 87 88 24
Open dinner only daily

Sisters Carminia and Pilat brought a little bit of Latin America to this old Parisian deli almost 20 years ago. Since then, they've converted a stylish crowd, including the occasional celeb, to the joys of Argentinian beef, Mexican stews and assorted South American titbits. The snug atmosphere is appealing, too. **Moderate**

Les Enfants Rouges *winning wine bar* `11 C4`
9 rue de Beauce, 3ème • 01 48 87 80 61
Closed Sun & Mon; closed dinner Tue, Wed, & Sat

Run by the couple behind the legendary Montmartre bistro Le Moulin à Vins – now Café Burq (*see p46*) – this intimate wine bar guarantees a serious selection of wines from both well-known and up-and-coming producers. Also on the menu is simple but robust French grub and a festive atmosphere. **Moderate**

L'Ambassade d'Auvergne *hearty fare* `11 A4`
22 rue du Grenier St-Lazare, 3ème • 01 42 72 31 22
» www.ambassade-auvergne.com Open lunch & dinner daily

This two-storey tavern with heavy oak beams and dangling hams has a well-earned reputation for serving up Auvergne on a plate. That means sturdy farmhouse food that's perfect for an icy winter's evening (if slightly less appealing in the height of summer). Pork and cabbage are menu staples, from cabbage soup with Roquefort cheese to braised pork with cabbage and white beans. Also on offer is the famed regional Salers beef, as well as lamb and fish dishes. The highlight, however, has to be the *aligot*, a creamy potato and Tomme cheese mixture, delivered to the table in a large copper dish, that is then teased into long ribbons by deft waiters and served as a side dish. Admittedly, you've got to be in the mood for an intense cholesterol hit. There's also a great selection of regional cheeses, and *eau de vie* (fruit-based brandy) to round things off. **Moderate**

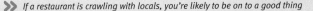

Les Petits Marseillais *southern comfort* `11 B5`
72 rue Vieille du Temple, 3ème • 01 42 78 91 59
Open lunch & dinner daily

A trendy crowd frequents this lively bistro run by two friends from Marseille – they're the nice guys behind the bar. Food has a southern bent: pasta with baby squid and saffron, duck with polenta and Parmesan. As quarters are close, getting into a conversation with your neighbours is also on the menu. **Moderate**

R'Aliment *trendy organic quick bites* `11 C4`
57 rue Charlot, 3ème • 01 48 04 88 28
>> www.resodesign.com
Open lunch & dinner Tue–Sat, dinner only Mon

Plenty of colour makes this funky organic eatery popular with a design-conscious set. Soups, quiches and daily changing hot dishes – such as vegetable gratin with squash seeds, and fried grouper with roasted potatoes – are prepared behind the bar, filling the room with wholesome smells. Bring a book or a friend as service can be slow. **Moderate**

Le Potager du Marais *vegetarian food* `11 A5`
22 rue Rambuteau, 3ème • 01 42 74 24 66
Open lunch & dinner daily

It may be vegetarian and organic, but that doesn't mean it's all tofu and sprouts. Instead, tuck into tasty dishes such as meat-free pasta carbonara with chanterelles, minestrone and chunky tarts. No incense and batik throws either, just a galley-style room with pared-back decor and an emphasis on healthy eating. **Cheap**

Le Pamphlet *quick-change menu* `11 C4`
38 rue Debelleyme, 3ème • 01 42 72 39 24
Open lunch & dinner Tue–Fri, dinner only Sat & Mon

The menu at this Pyrenees bistro takes its lead from seasonally available produce and changes several times a week; one day, rack of Pyrenean lamb, the next, glazed suckling pig. Owner-chef Alain Carrère – an aficionado of butter and cream – can be gruff, but generally a friendly atmosphere reigns. **Moderate**

L'As du Fallafel   *Middle-Eastern mecca*   `17 B1`

34 rue des Rosiers, 4ème • 01 48 87 63 60
Open all day Sun–Fri

One of many falafel joints on the bustling rue des Rosiers, but undoubtedly the best. The "special", with crunchy chickpea balls cooked to order, fried aubergine, shredded cabbage, hummus and spicy sauces will convert non-believers. This is the epitome of fast food, so don't expect to linger. **Cheap**

L'Ambroisie   *classy cuisine*   `17 C1`

9 place des Vosges, 4ème • 01 42 78 51 45
Open lunch & dinner Tue–Sat

Bernard Pacaud's food is sedate and sophisticated, just like the interior of this 17th-century townhouse with high ceilings and gilt flourishes. High-end dining means polished cooking, artistic presentation and deluxe ingredients (lobster, foie gras, truffles). Service is efficient but sometimes frosty. **Expensive**

Brasseries

When you want a vintage setting, straightforward food, professional waiters and great atmosphere, nothing can beat a Parisian brasserie. Many of the city's most historic examples belong to the Flo group, whose owner Jean-Paul Bucher founded the empire in 1968 with the purchase of **Brasserie Flo**, which resembles a hunting lodge but still has the feel of an Alsatian tavern. Nearby, another Flo flagship, **Julien**, brings a dash of class to this gritty part of town, near the Gare de l'Est, with its glitzy Art-Nouveau interior. Perhaps the most beloved Flo brasseries, however, are the Art-Deco **La Coupole** – no longer a bona fide literary haunt, but still a great venue — and the more intimate **Le Balzar**, whose purchase by the group sparked an outcry among its intellectual habitués. The typical brasserie fare of *choucroute* (shredded, fermented cabbage, also known as *sauerkraut*), enormous seafood platters, steaks and sole *meunière* is generally good enough in Flo brasseries to prevent the regulars from grumbling, and the desserts, such as giant ice-cream sundaes and parfaits, can be spectacular.

Among the independent brasseries, the **Brasserie de l'Isle St-Louis** is a favourite for its tavern-like interior and view of Notre Dame's elegant rear. Near the Gare St-Lazare, **Garnier** is known for its outstanding seafood and rather glamorous setting, while the down-to-earth **Le Grand Colbert**, next to the Palais Royal, may have the oldest interior – part of the dining room dates from the 17th century.

Whatever the brasserie, try not to be tempted by the more complex dishes – the kitchens can get overwhelmed at peak times, resulting in slapdash preparations. For contact details, *see p218.*

Restaurants

Café de la Poste *grandmother's cooking* `17 D2`
13 rue Castex, 4ème • 01 42 72 95 35
Open lunch & dinner Mon–Fri, dinner only Sat

One might suspect that a white-haired *grandmère* was lurking in the kitchen of this budget gem, given the timeless food: steak with fried potatoes, rabbit with mustard sauce, buttery, sugary desserts at down-to-earth prices, in a homely bistro.... No, you're not hallucinating, this is still Paris. **Cheap**

L'Enoteca *Italian know-how* `17 C2`
25 rue Charles V, 4ème • 01 42 78 91 44
Open lunch & dinner daily

This welcoming wine bar is *the* place to try both Italian wine (there are some 30,000 bottles in the cellar) and choice Italian food. Dishes such as swordfish *carpaccio* with pesto, risotto with asparagus, and *bunet* (chocolate flan), together with unpretentious service and decor, mean reservations are advisable. **Moderate**

Georget *rustic bliss* `11 B5`
64 rue Vieille du Temple, 4ème • 01 42 78 55 89
Open lunch & dinner Mon–Fri, dinner only Sat

More like a country kitchen than a Paris restaurant, this is the kind of place where you get to watch your steak being chopped off an enormous side of beef and thrown on to the wood-fire griddle to sizzle. The atmosphere might be smoky and the staff can be rude, but the food is good and filling. **Moderate**

Le Vieux Bistro *timeless attraction* `16 H2`
14 rue du Cloître Notre Dame, 4ème • 01 43 54 18 95
Open lunch & dinner daily

Despite its touristy address, The Old Bistro retains an authentic feel, including a dining room that looks as if it hasn't changed in decades, and a cache of regulars who never tire of dishes such as Lyonnais sausage with potatoes, *boeuf bourguignon* and *tarte tatin*. Portions are generous; the service likewise. **Moderate**

For the secrets of services charges and tipping, check ➤➤ www.eparis.dk.com

Mon Vieil Ami *modest inventiveness* `17 A2`
69 rue St-Louis-en-l'Ile, 4ème • 01 40 46 01 35
Open lunch & dinner Wed–Sun

Distinguished French chef Antoine Westerman's take on Alsatian cuisine bears no hint of pedestrian pork and cabbage. Instead, it's all about innovative food combinations to match the unmistakably modern interior of his one Paris bistro. Westerman's culinary mastery lurks behind a demure, easily missed façade; in fact, compared to many eateries on the tiny Ile St-Louis, Mon Vieil Ami seems very low-key indeed. All the action is inside and on the plate: generous servings of chicken with caramelized *sauerkraut* and potato purée, and roast cod with carrots, raisins and dates. It's lighter and more varied than traditional Alsatian fare, but that's because a Michelin three-star chef devised the menu. Westerman might not be flinging the pans out back, but he's there in spirit, and that means that the bistro is fast becoming an old friend to many. **Moderate**

L'Osteria *risotto central* `17 C1`
10 rue de Sévigné, 4ème • 01 42 71 37 08
Open lunch & dinner Tue–Fri, dinner only Mon

Toni Vianello is the risotto maestro; he's even written a cookbook on the subject, and his risottos are simply sensational – especially the one with pheasant and black truffles. This is some of the finest Italian food around and, as a result, tables are jam-packed, often with designers and political gurus. **Moderate**

Anahuacalli *a trip down Mexico way* `16 H3`
30 rue des Bernardins, 5ème • 01 43 26 10 20
Open dinner only daily

Cooking from south of the border doesn't come much better than this; forget runny guacamole and dry taco shells, this is *mole poblano* (turkey cooked with chocolate) territory. It's serious regional Mexican food with very good margaritas served up by charming staff, albeit in a rather subdued atmosphere. **Moderate**

Restaurants

Fogon St-Julien *Spanish class* `16 H2`
10 rue St-Julien-le-Pauvre, 5ème • 01 43 54 31 33
Open lunch & dinner Sat & Sun, dinner only Tue–Fri

Owner-chef Alberto Herraiz dishes up some of the best Spanish food in Paris in this sunny dining room on one of the city's oldest streets. His quest for quality ingredients is evident in his elegant tapas and superb paella Valenciana: saffron-stained rice topped with plump chicken, rabbit, snails and vegetables. **Moderate**

Le Cosi *rugged cuisine* `16 G4`
9 rue Cujas, 5ème • 01 43 29 20 20
Open lunch & dinner Mon–Sat

Corsica has its own mountain cuisine featuring unusual cheeses, outstanding charcuterie and long-simmered stews, and the red walls of this bistro create a suitably warm setting for this hot-blooded food. Expect a sophisticated spin on rustic ingredients, with pulses, *brocciu* (a ricotta-like cheese) and *cabri* (kid) featuring large on the menu. If you've room for dessert, do try the delicious *fiadone* cheesecake. **Moderate**

Les Délices d'Aphrodite *Greek odyssey* `20 H1`
4 rue de Candolle, 5ème • 01 43 31 40 39
» www.mavrommatis.fr Open lunch & dinner Mon–Sat

With a dining room done out in cool Mediterranean blue, a ceiling of trellised ivy, and good-quality Greek food, from *dolmades* to spit-roasted lamb, this is the perfect antidote to a grey day in Paris. The service is typically Greek too – it can be slow but it comes with a smile, so relax. **Moderate**

Le Reminet *sugar and spice* `16 H3`
3 rue des Grands-Degrés, 5ème • 01 44 07 04 24
Open lunch & dinner Thu–Mon

This romantic little bistro just gets better and better, thanks to chef Hugues Gournay's passion for food. His interest in spices results in dishes such as lamb chops with a cumin-and-red-pepper crust. Desserts are outstanding and service couldn't be more helpful. A 13€ lunch menu is available (Mon, Thu and Fri). **Moderate**

La Tour d'Argent *fine food with a view* `17 A3`
15–17 quai de la Tournelle, 5ème • 01 43 54 23 31
➤➤ **www.tourdargent.com** Closed Mon & lunch only Tue

Views don't get much more Parisian than this, and the cuisine doesn't get more ageless: the restaurant has been serving the same pressed-duck recipe since 1890. It's kid-glove treatment all the way, but you don't have to blow the budget. The lunch menu is great value and the view's the same. **Expensive**

Restaurant Marty *Art Deco dining* `21 A2`
20 avenue des Gobelins, 5ème • 01 43 31 39 51
➤➤ **www.marty-restaurant.com** Open lunch & dinner daily

The Marty stands out among Parisian brasseries on two counts: it is independent, and chef Thierry Colas has an *haute cuisine* pedigree. As a result, the food goes beyond brasserie classics. Try salmon sautéed with grapes and served with a celeriac purée, or veal with herb butter and violet mustard. **Moderate**

Le Pré Verre *a modern twist on the classic* `16 G3`
8 rue Thénard, 5ème • 01 43 54 59 47
Open lunch & dinner Tue–Sat, dinner only Mon

The Delacourcelle brothers do French classics with a nod to the modern. Chef Philippe is a fan of herbs and spices, and it shows in his pairing of rabbit with cumin, adding ginger to shallot sauce, showering squid with sesame vinaigrette or popping parsley in the strawberry dessert. The cuisine is slightly fusion, but with an emphasis on good, sustaining food (such as mashed potato with foie gras). Perched on a corner in the scholarly Quartier Latin, this *bistrot à vins* is very much a neighbourhood favourite, attracting cooing couples, conversing academics, serious suits and curious visitors. It's casual and friendly, with a wooden floor and walls dotted with vintage jazz LPs. *Très* cool – especially in summer, when the doors are flung back and the tables spill on to the street. The wine list is worthy, and the lunch menu is a bargain.
Moderate

Restaurants

Abazu *Japanese cool* `16 F2`
3 rue André-Mazet, 6ème • 01 46 33 72 05
Open lunch & dinner Tue–Sat, dinner only Sun

Teppanaki restaurants are rare in Paris, so it's surprising to find this Zen oasis in the heart of bustling St-Germain. On the main floor you can watch the sharp-knifed chefs at work, grilling fresh, raw ingredients before the customers' eyes, while the downstairs room feels calmer thanks to a small fountain. **Moderate**

Allard *old timer* `16 F2`
41 rue St-André-des-Arts, 6ème • 01 43 26 48 23
Open lunch & dinner Mon–Sat

Allard doesn't seem to have changed much since the 1940s, and that's just the way its regulars like it. Against a backdrop of weathered wallpaper, visitors mix with the neighbourhood's bourgeois, who flock here for hearty dishes such as Bresse chicken with mushrooms and the *canard aux olives*. **Moderate**

L'Epi Dupin *creative cooking* `15 C3`
11 rue Dupin, 6ème • 01 42 22 64 56
Open lunch & dinner Tue–Fri, dinner only Mon

Chef François Pasteau's bistro is full day and night thanks to a mix of imaginative cooking (mackerel in a hazelnut-and-fennel crust and pigeon with braised onions), fast, friendly service and a cosy old dining room. Blackboard specials reflect the best produce the seasons have to offer. **Moderate**

Yen *a slice of Tokyo* `16 E2`
22 rue St-Benoît, 6ème • 01 45 44 11 18
Open lunch & dinner Tue–Sat

If you have a yen for noodles, this is the place to satisfy your craving. The neighbourhood couldn't be more Parisian, but once in the wood dining room you could easily be in Tokyo. At lunchtime, try a bento box; at dinner, the speciality is *soba* – buckwheat noodles served with a delicious dipping sauce. **Moderate**

Le Timbre *a modern touch* `15 D5`
3 rue Ste-Beuve, 6ème • 01 45 49 10 40
Open lunch & dinner Mon–Fri, dinner only Sat

Garret-like Le Timbre serves refined French food (roast pigeon with mango and ginger chutney, Jerusalem artichoke purée with truffle oil) with a dash of the British, thanks to its Mancunian owner. Cleverly arranged around the long counter, the dining room encourages conviviality. **Moderate**

La Table d'Aude *country helpings* `16 F3`
8 rue de Vaugirard, 6ème • 01 43 26 36 36
>> www.latabledaude.com
Open lunch & dinner Tue–Fri, dinner only Sat, lunch only Mon

Bernard Pautou's welcome is as warm as his *cassoulet* – a robust duck, pork and bean stew for which the Aude, a region in Languedoc-Roussillion, is renowned. This is no-nonsense country food – just the thing to keep winter chills at bay. **Moderate**

Le Salon d'Hélène *southwest-side story* `15 D3`
4 rue d'Assas, 6ème • 01 42 22 00 11
Open lunch & dinner Wed–Sat, dinner only Tue

French chefs in general don't tend to stray too far from formality – but there are exceptions, and Hélène Darroze is one of them. In an effort to make her south-western cooking more accessible, she opened Le Salon d'Hélène, a more reasonably priced, more casual eatery on the floor below her Michelin two-star restaurant. Rather than a three-course-plus-cheese meal, Darroze took to tapas – she hails from France's Basque country, and the Spanish influence is evident in her cooking. Graze on a range of beautifully presented small dishes (oyster with foie gras 'ice cream', langoustine tempura, duck liver with dried fruit) from the comfort of a plush pink sofa, bar-style high chairs with raised tables or a banquette loaded with cushions. Darroze comes from a family of chefs and also spent time in Alain Ducasse's restaurant in Monte Carlo, so diners are in capable, and creative, hands. **Expensive**

L'Ami Jean *Basque is best* 8 G5

27 rue Malar, 7ème • 01 47 05 86 89
Open lunch & dinner Tue–Sat

Some of the best bistro chefs in Paris come from the French Basque region, and Stéphane Jégo, who owns this tavern-like bistro, is one of them. Jégo cooks up specialities such as *axoa* (veal stew) alongside more modern inventions like marinated scallops with shaved ewe's-milk cheese. **Moderate**

Bellota-Bellota *simple Spanish pleasures* 8 G5

18 rue Jean-Nicot, 7ème • 01 53 59 96 96
Open lunch & dinner Mon–Sat

This breezy, tiled bar-cum-grocery is devoted to Spain's finest ham: ruby-red meat from black-footed Iberian pigs that graze on acorns (*bellotas*). And it's the acorns that give the ham its wonderful flavour. Excellent manchego cheese, anchovies, olives and tuna are also on offer. Perfect for lunch or a late supper. **Moderate**

L'Arpège *art appreciation* 15 A1

84 rue de Varenne, 7ème • 01 45 51 47 33
Open lunch & dinner Mon–Fri

Chef Alain Passard caters for the serious food connoisseur. His food is close to art, which seems appropriate given that the Musée Rodin *(see p101)* is just opposite. The wine list is almost as long as *War and Peace*, the decor is discreetly modern and the prices are rather steep. In recent times, Passard has shunned red meat, preferring instead to serve fish, shellfish, poultry and – his overriding passion of late – vegetables. In L'Arpège's kitchen at least, *légumes* have finally been granted their rightful place alongside fish and meat as diet staples. Passard prides himself on retaining the unique colours and flavours of his ingredients; consequently, his food looks as if it has escaped the pages of a glossy art mag. Tender lobster braised in Jura wine and his signature dessert, a candied 12-flavour tomato filled with dried and fresh fruit, nuts and spices, are beautiful to look at and even better to eat. **Expensive**

L'Atelier de Joël Robuchon *hot spot* `15 D1`

5 rue de Montalembert, 7ème • 01 42 22 56 56
Open lunch & dinner daily

He might not be a household name outside France, but in Paris Joël Robuchon stands for French cuisine at its most refined. Gastronomes were devastated when he announced his retirement from the restaurant world at the age of 51, and his comeback was the subject of rumours for years. Now in his late 50s, Robuchon has not only opened what is probably the most modern restaurant in Paris (with a twin establishment in Tokyo), but he is also planning other projects, including one in the 16th arrondissement. What is all the fuss about? Well, his potato purée for one, made from the flavourful *ratte* variety and with nearly as much butter as potato. At L'Atelier, diners sit around two bars in the compact, red-and-black lacquered dining room (there are no individual chairs and tables), while cooks toil in the open kitchen, slightly removed from the communal counters. You can order a little – from a selection of about 20 small plates inspired by Asia, Spain and offerings from the best Parisian chefs – or a lot, as it is also possible to have a blow-out three-course meal of full-sized offerings without feeling rushed. Some of the most outstanding dishes are *spaghetti à notre façon* (an Alsatian take on carbonara), turbot with the famous potato purée and, among the smaller plates, clams stuffed with garlic and a crisp mackerel tart with Parmesan cheese. Desserts, such as the chartreuse soufflé, are served in small portions to allow for grazing. Telephone reservations are possible only for 11:30am and 6:30pm; otherwise, be prepared to queue alongside Left Bank lawyers and publishers who are willing to swallow their pride for extraordinarily good food. **Expensive**

Au Bon Accueil *a success story*   `8 F5`
14 rue de Monttessuy, 7ème • 01 47 05 46 11
Open lunch & dinner Mon–Fri

Lying in the shadow of the Eiffel Tower, this bistro is teeming most days and nights (often with out-of-towners in the tourist season). Owner Jacques Lacipière has refurbished it to give it a trendier edge and better lighting, but the seasonal menu remains good quality and the service is always agreeable. **Moderate**

Café Constant *simply delicious*   `8 F5`
139 rue St-Dominique, 7ème • 01 48 04 88 28
Open lunch & dinner Tue–Sat

As head chef at the luxury hotel Le Crillon *(see p177)*, Christian Constant trained many of the best bistro chefs in Paris today, including Christian Etchebest of Le Troquet *(see p55)*. Constant is gradually colonizing the rue St-Dominique with this eponymous café; his classic restaurant, Le Violon d'Ingres; and most recently, La Table de la Fontaine, an affordable fish house. But Café Constant is the locals' favourite, and it's here that the chef can express his casual side (he is often seen having lunch here, which shows how comfortable he is with this simpler style of cooking). The menu is something of a nostalgia trip – *oeufs mimosa*, pumpkin soup with Gruyère, veal Cordon Bleu, profiteroles and *île flottante*, all prepared just as they should be. Like the food, the setting doesn't put on airs – white walls, old tile floors and red banquettes – and the staff are exceptionally friendly. **Moderate**

Best Places to Buy Food to Go

Long limited to a sandwich or a quiche, takeaway food in Paris is growing more varied by the minute. For salads, hot dishes and perhaps a slice of pâté, stop by any neighbourhood *charcutier/traiteur*, where you will be charged according to the weight of your order. The gourmet counters at Le Bon Marché's **Grande Epicerie** offer more exotic options, as do those at **Galeries Lafayette**. British-style sandwiches are sold at the popular **Cojean**, while top chef Alain Ducasse and *à la mode* baker Eric Kayser provide high-class sandwiches at **Be**. Perhaps the best meal to go, though, is the fat falafel sandwich at **L'As du Fallafel**, the pick of Lenny Kravitz and other discriminating chickpea fans. For 5€, it's heaven on a plastic plate. For contact details, *see p219*.

Flora *provincial elegance* `8 F2`
36 avenue George V, 8ème • 01 40 70 10 49
Open lunch & dinner Mon–Fri, dinner only Sat

This stylish restaurant's menu is influenced by southern France (chef Flora Mikula was born in Provence), but also dips into even sunnier lands, such as Turkey, Morocco and India. Mikula has a sure touch with produce and lots of finesse, as dishes such as lobster with wild mushrooms in coral vinaigrette attest. **Moderate**

Garnier *a fishy business* `3 C5`
111 rue St-Lazare, 8ème • 01 43 87 50 40
Open lunch & dinner daily

Sup on freshly shucked oysters at the bijou oyster bar just inside the door, or take an impeccably laid table near the window and watch the commuters from nearby Gare St-Lazare grind by. The setting is elegant, waiters are considerate and the seafood is a cut well above that of most Paris brasseries. **Expensive**

L'Angle du Faubourg *cornering success* `2 G5`
195 rue du Faubourg St-Honoré, 8ème • 01 40 74 20 20
≫ www.taillevent.com Open lunch & dinner Mon–Fri

Boosted by the success of his Michelin three-star restaurant, Taillevent, owner Jean-Claude Vrinat opened this more cost-conscious bistro. Contemporary in look, it combines both the classical and the modern in the kitchen, sending out attractive dishes such as braised veal cheeks to an up-market clientele. **Moderate**

Le Bistrot Napolitain *perfect pizza* `8 H1`
18 avenue Franklin D Roosevelt, 8ème • 01 45 62 08 37
Open lunch & dinner Mon–Fri, dinner only Sat

Down-to-earth bistros are thin on the ground in these parts, which explains the popularity of this Italian *trattoria*. It's hard to resist the crisp-crusted classic pizzas, such as Margherita, but the *carpaccio*, fish and pasta are equally tempting. Perfect for a quick bite after the cinema, but book ahead. **Moderate**

Restaurants

Maison Blanche *a drop of the Med* `8 G3`
15 avenue Montaigne, 8ème • 01 47 23 55 99
>> www.maison-blanche.fr
Open lunch & dinner Mon–Fri, dinner only Sat & Sun

The Pourcel twins just love the Mediterranean and it shows in their inventive menu. A plate of roast pigeon fillets with pan-fried peaches and *cacao* accompanied by a penthouse view of Paris might not come cheap, but extravagance has its rewards. **Expensive**

Market *exemplary innovations* `9 A2`
15 avenue Matignon, 8ème • 01 56 43 40 90
>> www.jean-georges.com Open breakfast, lunch & dinner daily

Jean-Georges Vongerichten, the whizz kid behind New York's Mercer Kitchen and Vong, has returned to his French roots with this fashionable spot. Celebrities and local suits can't get enough of his clever food, such as raw-tuna spring roll or "burnt" foie gras with a dried fruit compote. **Expensive**

Le Cristal Room *glass act* `8 E2`
La Maison Baccarat, 11 place des Etats-Unis, 16ème
01 40 22 11 10 Open breakfast, lunch & dinner Mon–Sat

A giant chandelier immersed in an aquarium gives a clue as to who was in charge of decorating the new Baccarat museum and boutique: the daring and witty Philippe Starck. Formerly a private residence, this mansion is now, literally, a crystal palace, with glass and mirrors creating dizzying optical effects. The in-store restaurant, a showcase for Baccarat's crystal and porcelain, has become a huge hit thanks to its ironic-but-chic decor and simple, yet deliciously prepared, food. What can you expect to eat? Most of the modish folk who come here probably don't care all that much, but dishes such as a frothy soup of *potimarron* (a type of pumpkin that tastes like chestnut) and the very good club sandwich show that the kitchen is far from careless. If you have any money left over, you can pick up a jewel or accessory as a souvenir. Be sure to book ahead. **Expensive**

Lucas Carton *haute cuisine* `9 C2`
9 place de la Madeleine, 8ème • 01 42 65 22 90
>> www.lucascarton.com
Open lunch & dinner Tue–Fri; dinner only Sat & Mon

Alain Senderens believes passionately that fine food merits fine wine: he looks for hints of dried fruit, herbs or toasted nuts in wine and then marries them with the real thing. Thus, each dish here is accompanied by a wine that harmonizes perfectly with it; a late-harvest Gewurztraminer with its rose-lychee bouquet teamed with roasted foie gras in an exotic fruit vinaigrette is a match made in heaven. The food is the perfect partner for one of the most lavish dining rooms in Paris – boasting curved Art-Nouveau wood partitions with glass-encased butterflies and rich, merlot-coloured banquettes. Senderens bought the restaurant in 1985, perhaps as a nostalgic nod to the time he spent here as a young *saucier* for the renowned chef Soustelle. Twenty years later, the apprentice is now the acclaimed master. **Expensive**

Savy *regional traditions* `8 G3`
23 rue Bayard, 8ème • 01 47 23 46 98
Open lunch & dinner Mon–Fri

An old-fashioned bistro, both in decor and disposition, that provides welcome relief from the 24-carat designer shops and salons of nearby avenue Montaigne. Comfort food, from coddled eggs to rib steak with bone marrow and matchstick potatoes, is served up in comfortable surroundings. **Moderate**

A Toutes Vapeurs *all steamed up* `3 C5`
7 rue de l'Isly, 8ème • 01 44 90 95 75
Open until 11pm Mon–Sat

Waistline-watchers and the health conscious love the little *paniers* (baskets) of vegetable, fish and meat combinations at this self-service eating house – all cooked while you wait. Choose a pre-prepared basket, a flavoured oil and, presto, it's in and out of the chrome "dry" steamer in minutes. **Cheap**

>> *A three-course* prix fixe *menu, though often limited in choice, is much cheaper than eating à la carte*

L'Astrance *top tables*

`7 C5`

4 rue Beethoven, 16ème • 01 40 50 84 40
Open lunch & dinner Mon–Fri

This three-year-old, 25-seat dining room near Trocadéro is arguably the most exciting restaurant to have opened in Paris this century (though Joël Robuchon's Atelier *(see p37)* is a close rival). Pascal Barbot and Christophe Rohat (who runs the dining room) worked with Alain Passard at L'Arpège *(see p36)* before branching out on their own with a style that reflects Barbot's time as a chef in Sydney. Asian spices turn up in all sorts of unexpected places, but never shock the palate. Minimalist names on the menu create an element of suspense, but first come surprise nibbles: soup made with nearly burnt bread (much more intriguing than it sounds) or an avocado and crab *millefeuille* flavoured with almond oil and a tiny Granny Smith julienne. Then comes "The Pea", a frothy green cream topped with crisp, golden-brown shavings of baked Tomme d'Auvergne cheese and a fresh pea pod lined with plump, tender peas. "The Mackerel" shows what Barbot can do with a humble fish: boneless fillets come coated in spiced crumbs, on a bed of Asian-style spinach with sesame. More *amuse-gueules*, such as herb-infused sorbets and an eggshell filled with eggy cream, pave the way for inventive desserts combining fruits and spices. The sober – but not off-puttingly so – grey dining room, its walls decorated with gilt-framed mirrors, puts the spotlight on the food. So cherished are reservations here (you must book exactly one month ahead) that foodies congratulate each other on their success in securing a table. **Expensive**

Locate Paris's vegetarian restaurants through ➤➤ www.eparis.dk.com

La Grande Armée *modern classic* `7 E1`
3 avenue de la Grande Armée, 16ème • 01 45 00 24 77
Open breakfast, lunch & dinner daily

Jointly owned by the Costes brothers and designer Jacques Garcia, this contemporary take on the classic brasserie is more bordello red and leopard skin than beer and brass. Count on dependable food (duck shepherd's pie), a stylish crowd and a surprisingly cosy atmosphere. Great for breakfast, too. **Moderate**

Jamin *cooking with class* `7 D3`
32 rue de Longchamp, 16ème • 01 45 53 00 07
Open lunch & dinner Mon–Fri

Benoit Guichard, longtime second-in-command to master chef Joël Robuchon *(see p37)*, is a traditionalist at heart as his pigeon sausage with foie gras exemplifies, but his menu reveals some contemporary thinking, too. And while the staid green-and-pink decor doesn't have many fans, the food does. The lunch menu is an excellent (and relatively economical) way to sample his culinary prowess. **Expensive**

Le Petit Rétro *trad French* `7 C2`
5 rue Mesnil, 16ème • 01 44 05 06 05
≫ www.petitretro.fr
Open lunch & dinner Mon–Fri, dinner only Sat

In keeping with its authentic Belle Epoque decor, Le Petit Rétro is a bastion of traditional French cooking. Melt-in-your mouth duck liver pâté and creamy veal stew never go out of fashion, which is precisely why this not-so-little bistro is always brimful. **Moderate**

L'Entredgeu *packed-out bistro* `1 D2`
83 rue Laugier, 17ème • 01 40 54 97 24
Open lunch & dinner Tue–Sat

Does Paris need another bistro? Of course it does, when it's as good as this one. The space is cramped and smoky, but locals crowd in nonetheless for the daily changing menu, which might include spot-on dishes such as veal *en cocotte* with new potatoes or rack of lamb with a salsify *jus*. **Moderate**

Restaurants

La Table de Lucullus *net benefits* `3 C1`
129 rue Legendre, 17ème • 01 40 25 02 68
Open lunch & dinner Tue–Sat

Self-taught chef Nicolas Vagnon doesn't compromise on quality, to the extent that his menu now focuses entirely on wild fish caught off France's Ile d'Yeu. His Tuesday-night tasting menu presents a single sea creature, such as eel or scallops, in different guises. The modest dining room is non-smoking. **Expensive**

Le Bistrot d'à Côte Flaubert *a treat* `2 F3`
10 rue Gustave Flaubert, 17ème • 01 42 67 05 81
» www.michelrostang.fr Open lunch & dinner daily

It's no surprise that *haute cuisine* chef Michel Rostang's first bistro turned out to be more sophisticated than many of its genre. The period interior, and walls of kaleidoscopic majolica ceramics and old Michelin guides, provide a convivial setting in which to sample consistently good bistro cooking. **Moderate**

Casa Olympe *fixed-menu finesse* `4 F5`
48 rue St-Georges, 9ème • 01 42 85 26 01
Open lunch & dinner Mon–Fri

Dominique Versini, aka Olympe, is a diva of the Paris restaurant scene. The compact, ochre-painted dining room showcases her fine cooking, which draws on her Corsican roots. The three-course, 34€ menu offers simple dishes, like potato salad with truffle shavings, that highlight the quality of the ingredients. **Moderate**

Kastoori *Indian idyll* `4 F4`
4 place Gustave Toudouze, 9ème • 01 44 53 06 10
Open lunch & dinner Tue–Sun, dinner only Mon

There aren't many Indian restaurants in Paris where you can enjoy a fairly authentic meal in warm, tasteful surroundings, or on a quiet pavement terrace. Hence the popularity of Kastoori, with its carefully spiced – if not chilli-potent – food. The 8€ lunch menu is one of the city's best bargains. **Cheap**

Rose Bakery *daytime distraction* `4 F4`
46 rue des Martyrs, 9ème • 01 42 82 12 80
Open during the day Tue–Sun

This café is dedicated to typically British products (from baked beans to sausages), many of them organic. Quiches, soups and snack-sized pizzas satisfy the lunch crowd, but the big draw is the childhood-fantasy cakes, from tangy lemon tarts to sticky toffee pudding. The decor is as simple as the food. **Cheap**

Velly *down-to-earth bistro* `4 F5`
52 rue Lamartine, 9ème • 01 48 78 60 05
Open lunch & dinner Mon–Fri

Just off the old-fashioned rue des Martyrs, Velly is the kind of bistro everyone hopes to find in Paris. In a no-frills setting, the real star is the food, prepared with seasonal ingredients and attention to presentation. Regulars love the *oeuf cocotte* with foie gras, and meaty mains like *onglet de veau* with salsify fritters. **Moderate**

Chez Dom *funky West African* `6 E5`
34 rue Sambre et Meuse, 10ème • 01 42 01 59 80
Open lunch & dinner Mon–Fri, dinner only Sat & Sun

Typical of the *quartier*, Chez Dom serves authentic Senegalese food. Flower-printed tablecloths set the cheerful tone, and a glass of potent *ti ponch* arrives even before you've asked for it. Boldly spiced meat and fish stews will have you licking the plate, but try to save room for the "sexy chocolate" dessert. **Moderate**

Martel *trendy French-Algerian* `11 A1`
3 rue Martel, 10ème • 01 47 70 67 56
Open lunch & dinner Mon–Fri, dinner only Sat

The latest haunt of couscous-loving fashionistas is this bistro in the interesting and up-and-coming 10th. Among the most popular dishes are the "lovers' arti-choke" a spiky treat to be shared, and lamb tagine with almonds, prunes and apricots, but it's hard for the food to compete with the glamorous crowd. **Moderate**

Restaurants

Café Burq *fashionable French* `4 E2`
6 rue Burq, 18ème • 01 42 52 81 27
Open dinner only Tue–Sun

Formerly a sepia-toned wine bar, the Moulin à Vins, this bistro has been reborn as a slick hang-out for Montmartre's young artists, film-makers and media folk. The mostly classic French food is decent enough, but what people really come for is the joyous, if smoky, atmosphere. **Moderate**

Terminus Nord *classy destination* `5 A4`
23 rue de Dunkerque, 10ème • 01 42 85 05 15
Open lunch & dinner daily

Despite its position opposite the busy northern railway station, the august Terminus Nord is no tourist trap, just one of the city's most handsome brasseries. Refuel post-journey on onion soup and fresh seafood served by white-suited waiters under the gaze of huge frescoes and turn-of-the-20th-century posters. **Moderate**

Chez Michel *from Brittany with love* `5 A4`
10 rue de Belzunce, 10ème • 01 44 53 06 20
Open lunch & dinner Tue–Fri, dinner only Mon

There's no mistaking Thierry Breton's roots: the menu is piled high with hearty seasonal offerings from his native Brittany. And to quash any doubt, he also sports the Breton flag on his chef's whites. While the area isn't very chic, the restaurant, with its red velvet banquettes and farmhouse-style seating in the basement, is nicely perched behind the imposing St-Vincent-de-Paul church, and the food is very smart indeed. The blackboard specials echo the seasons and carry an additional cost but they're worth it – game-lovers are well catered for in the cooler months with pigeon, wild boar and venison. At other times, try plump, fresh scallops with velvety celeriac purée. Breton's Paris-Brest, choux pastry filled with hazelnut butter cream, is pure dessert happiness. The service can be excruciatingly slow, but the staff are affable, and if there's any tension it melts when the food appears. **Moderate**

Chez Toinette *neighbourhood bistro* `4 E2`
20 rue Germain-Pilon, 18ème • 01 42 54 44 36
Open lunch & dinner Tue–Sat

You don't expect to find a discreet, candle-lit jewel like this one around the corner from bawdy Pigalle, so it's all the more surprising to discover that Chez Toinette also has seriously good food. You'll often find Provençal dishes on the menu, such as *daube de boeuf*; game is a speciality in winter. **Moderate**

Le Poulbot Gourmet *trad French food* `4 F1`
39 rue Lamarck, 18ème • 01 46 06 86 00
Open lunch & dinner Mon–Sat; closed Sun Jun–Sep; lunch Sun Oct–May

It's a little out of the way, but this Montmartre restaurant has a loyal following thanks to the sincerity of its owner and of its cooking. The small dining room is the perfect place to savour hearty dishes such as veal kidney with morel mushrooms. **Moderate**

Lao Siam *Southeast Asian offerings* `12 G1`
49 rue de Belleville, 19ème • 01 40 40 09 68
Open lunch & dinner daily

Neither service nor decor are particularly charming, but Lao Siam is almost always packed thanks to the lip-smacking flavours of its Thai and Laotian dishes. Squid salad is a good bet to start, followed by coconut-milk curry and a giant, juicy mango. The separate non-smoking dining room is less busy. **Cheap**

La Cave Gourmande *hidden talent*
10 rue du Général-Brunet, 19ème • 01 40 40 03 30 • Ⓜ Botzaris
Open lunch & dinner Mon–Fri

This sedate neighbourhood near the Butte Chaumont park is not where you'd expect to find an up-and-coming US chef, but Paris has a few such secret eating destinations. Mark Singer puts a modern spin on traditional French dishes, so you might find escargots, but not bathed in the usual garlic butter. **Moderate**

La Famille *globe-trotting hit* `4 F2`

41 rue des Trois-Frères, 18ème • 01 42 52 11 12
Open dinner only Tue–Sat, dinner 1st Sun of each month,
brunch 2nd–4th Sun of each month

Few Paris chefs have come to grips with fusion food, which is why La Famille, in newly fashionable Montmartre, has become such a hit. Young Basque chef Inaki Aizpitarte has had his passport stamped around the world, particularly in Latin America and Morocco, and also worked with the inventive Gilles Choukroun at Le Café des Délices before opening this restaurant with his cousin (he's the one in charge of the bar and the hip music). The short, constantly changing menu combines French (and especially Basque) ingredients with more tropical flavours, resulting in dishes such as pan-fried foie gras with miso sauce, gambas pan-fried with passion fruit, and chocolate custard with Espelette chilli pepper. Not everything works all the time but any culinary near-misses are easily compensated for by the fact that dinner here is guaranteed fun. This is especially true of the first Sunday of each month, when the entire menu is served in tapas-like portions so that you can really do Aizpitarte's creative endeavours justice and graze your way through every dish. A help-yourself all-day brunch of French pastries and egg dishes is served on the other Sundays, making customers feel that they are really part of the family. Since the spare space is rather limited and word has already been out for a while, it's essential to book. **Moderate**

La Mascotte *old Montmartre* `4 E2`
52 rue des Abbesses, 18ème • 01 46 06 28 15
Open lunch & dinner daily

At this old-fashioned neighbourhood institution, diners can choose from the extensive seafood selection or satisfy serious hunger pangs with the good-value 26€ menu. This might include a salad of green beans and endive, chicken with potato purée, and an almond cake with Berthillon ice cream. **Moderate**

Café Noir *eccentric surprise*
15 rue St-Blaise, 20ème • 01 40 09 75 80 • Ⓜ Porte de Bagnolet
Open dinner only daily

A thriving bar scene has put this *quartier* on the map, but if it's a good meal you're seeking here, this quirky bistro is the place to go. Located on a pedestrianized street, the restaurant's terrace tables are irresistible in summer; inside you can admire the coffee pot and hat collections while tucking into unusual dishes such as tandoori prawns with chicken livers. **Moderate**

Benisti *North African pit-stop* `12 F1`
108 boulevard de Belleville, 20ème • no phone
Open lunch & dinner Tue–Sun

Jewish, Arab and Chinese communities comfortably co-exist in Belleville, as a walk down the main boulevard will testify. One of the most popular places to stop and refuel is this Tunisian snack and pastry shop, where you can order a gargantuan grilled-meat sandwich or sip mint tea with a plate of sticky pastries. **Cheap**

Astier *fashionably shabby chic* `12 E3`
44 rue Jean-Pierre Timbaud, 11ème • 01 43 57 16 35
Open lunch & dinner Mon–Fri

Resolutely old-fashioned, Astier is as much loved for its worn decor and overrun tables as for its great-value four-course menu. That doesn't imply second-rate food: the cooking is classy and finely balanced between traditional dishes and seasonal specials. The wine list is long and worthy. **Moderate**

Restaurants

Dong Huong *Vietnamese canteen* `12 F1`
14 rue Louis-Bonnet, 11ème • 01 43 57 18 88
Open lunch & dinner Wed–Mon

When you can't face another multi-course meal, a bowl of Vietnamese noodles can be just the thing to revive your appetite. Dong Huong stands out for the quality of its *pho* (noodle soups) and grilled meats and for its large non-smoking room – a rarity in Paris. The crunchy imperial rolls are also exceptionally good. **Cheap**

Jacques Mélac *no-frills wine bar*
42 rue Léon-Frot, 11ème • 01 43 70 59 27 • Ⓜ Charonne
Open lunch & dinner Tue–Sat

There's nothing complicated about moustachioed Jacques' wine bar: cheese is hacked off a giant hunk, charcuterie is sliced before your eyes and the non-smoking room is reached through the tiny kitchen, where the day's specials such as *porc aligot* (sausage and cheesy potato mash) are prepared. **Moderate**

L'Homme Bleu *North African local* `12 E3`
55bis rue Jean-Pierre Timbaud, 11ème • 01 48 07 05 63
Open dinner only Mon–Sat

The queue out the door attests to L'Homme Bleu's popularity (they don't take reservations, so show up early). The main floor is more atmospheric thanks to its open kitchen, but those lucky enough to get a table anywhere won't complain. Delicious couscous and fragrant tagines are the stars. **Moderate**

Crêperie Bretonne Fleurie *pancakes* `18 F2`
67 rue de Charonne, 11ème • 01 43 55 62 29
Open lunch & dinner daily

Two steps from the booming Bastille bar scene, this crêperie shows the *quartier's* flip-side, with real Breton specialities. Proof of its authenticity is the crêpe filled with *andouille* (tripe sausage), but you can also stick to the more conventional ham, cheese and egg variations, washed down with cider. **Cheap**

50

www.eparis.dk.com

Le Petit Keller *retro home cooking* `18 F1`
13bis rue Keller, 11ème • 01 47 00 12 97
Open lunch & dinner Tue–Sat

This little 1950s-vintage restaurant is popular for its great-value set menu — 10€ at lunch and 15€ in the evening. The food is more like decent home cooking than ambitious restaurant fare, which is fine with the locals who can't be bothered to whip up salmon with sorrel sauce, duck *magret* or apple crumble. **Cheap**

Le Souk *spice-scented haven* `18 F2`
1 rue Keller, 11ème • 01 49 29 05 08
Open lunch & dinner Sat & Sun, dinner only Tue–Fri

Though it's run by chatty Algerians, Le Souk's food is totally Moroccan, with sweet and fragrant tagines and *pastillas* (poultry wrapped in crisp pastry, sprinkled with sugar) featuring alongside couscous. Tables are so sought after that there are two fixed dinner sittings, for which bookings are essential. **Moderate**

Le Bistrot Paul Bert *seasonal food*
18 rue Paul-Bert, 11ème • 01 43 72 24 01 • Ⓜ Faidherbe-Chaligny
Open lunch & dinner Mon–Sat

This place seems to have it all: an atmospheric setting, genuinely friendly service, a hip, festive crowd, intriguing (organic) wines and, best of all, great food that follows the seasons to the extent that the blackboard menu changes every day. It's a little out of the way, but you're unlikely to regret the effort. **Moderate**

Le Train Bleu *vintage dining* `18 E5`
Gare de Lyon, place Louis-Armand, 12ème • 01 43 43 09 06
≫ www.le-train-bleu.com Open lunch & dinner daily

With its stockpile of cherubs, gilt and big oak benches, Le Train Bleu is a glamorously vintage experience amid the hubbub of the Gare de Lyon train station. As you'd expect from a Belle Epoque dame, the food is a lofty take on French classics (lobster salad, veal chops) and there's a bar, too, for a quiet drink. **Moderate**

Restaurants

Au Trou Gascon *regional refinement*
40 rue Taine, 12ème • 01 43 44 34 26 • Ⓜ Daumesnil
Open lunch & dinner Mon–Fri

Devotees of serious, French southwestern cooking
hunt out this contemporary restaurant overseen by
Michelin two-star chef Alain Dutournier. Dishes
such as the surprisingly light *cassoulet* and the gutsy
regional Madiran wine make the trek to this outpost
more than worthwhile. **Expensive**

Le Square Trousseau *outstanding bistro* `18 F3`
1 rue Antoine-Vollon, 12ème • 01 43 43 06 00
Open lunch & dinner Tue–Sat

Thanks to its setting next to a leafy square, its beautifully weathered 1900s interior and the charismatic
and friendly staff, Le Square Trousseau oozes charm.
Wines from small producers complement modern
bistro fare, such as green asparagus with melon and
lamb shank in a syrupy sauce. **Moderate**

Sardegna a Tavola *authentic Italian* `18 F3`
1 rue de Cotte, 12ème • 01 44 75 03 28
Open lunch & dinner Tue–Sat, dinner only Mon

It's rare to find an authentic Italian restaurant in Paris,
let alone a Sardinian one that gives you a flavour of
this rocky, sun-baked isle. No compromises here:
both ingredients and dishes are genuine, from the
robust Sardinian wines to the pasta dishes, often
flavoured with almonds, mint or orange. **Moderate**

L'Avant Goût *top-quality bistro fare* `21 A4`
26 rue Bobillot, 13ème • 01 53 80 24 00
Open lunch & dinner Tue–Fri

Just a taste of Christophe Beaufront's creative fare and
it becomes patently clear why landing a table in here
without a reservation is impossible. The *pot-au-feu de
cochon* (pork simmered with fennel, carrot and spices),
accompanied by ginger chips, onion in cider, gherkins
and horseradish purée, is exceptional. **Moderate**

Les Cailloux *casual yet classy* `20 H5`
58 rue des Cinq-Diamants, 13ème • 01 45 80 15 08
Open lunch & dinner Tue–Sat

The owners of Les Cailloux are on to a winning formula with this Italian wine bar-restaurant located in the villagey Butte-aux-Cailles *(see p159)*. Some 40 wines are available, half of them Italian and a few by the glass, and the food (linguine with crab, roasted pepper with mozzarella) is simple but satisfying. **Moderate**

Tricotin *Oriental roundup*
15 ave de Choisy, 13ème • 01 45 84 74 44 • Ⓜ Porte de Choisy
Open lunch & dinner daily

It won't win any prizes for decor or location, but Tricotin wins out with its steaming display of Chinese, Cambodian, Thai and Vietnamese dishes. It's frantic, canteen-style eating, but the food is fresh and very affordable: *pho*, the Vietnamese meal-in-a-bowl soup, is the bargain deal. **Cheap**

Natacha *family values* `19 E1`
17bis rue Campagne-Première, 14ème • 01 43 20 79 27
Open lunch & dinner Mon–Sat, lunch only Sun

Long a fashion haunt, Natacha is a family affair, with young chef Alain Cirelli running the kitchen while his mother is front of house. And following a home-cooking tradition, many dishes are served in their casseroles: a roasted pheasant nestles in a copper pot and *hachis parmentier* (shepherd's pie) comes in a cast-iron dish. Desserts are similarly comforting. **Moderate**

Au Petit Marguery *timeless bistro* `20 H2`
9 boulevard de Port-Royal, 13ème • 01 43 31 58 59
Open lunch & dinner Tue–Sat

This bistro is famous for its game, and in winter it serves up the classic dish *lièvre à la royale*, a complex creation involving hare, foie gras, wine and blood. Service can be grumpy, but the clientele of local gourmands tucking into pâtés and partridge creates an atmosphere of pure enjoyment nonetheless. **Moderate**

Restaurants

L'Assiette *market leader*

19 C3

181 rue du Château, 14ème • 01 43 22 64 86
Open lunch & dinner Wed–Sun

Unquestionably elitist, L'Assiette attracts bourgeois diners who find it amusing to pay through the nose for bistro cooking in a bare-wood setting. The fact remains, however, that chef Lulu draws on the finest ingredients and her food is delicious. The puddings are the kind *maman* might make. **Expensive**

Le Père Claude *excellent grill*

14 F3

51 avenue de la Motte-Piquet, 15ème • 01 47 34 03 05
Open lunch & dinner daily

Meat-lovers are well catered for in Paris but nowhere more so than at this caramel-coloured local with its glassed-in grill bar. The protein-strong mixed grill comes with steak, black pudding, lamb and chicken, and golden gratinéed potatoes. A perennial favourite with omnivorous French politicians. **Moderate**

L'Os à Moëlle &
La Cave de l'Os à Moëlle *local heroes*

3 rue Vasco de Gama, 15ème • 01 45 57 27 27;
181 rue Lourmel, 15ème • 01 45 57 28 28 • Ⓜ Lourmel
Open lunch & dinner Tue–Sat

Chef Thierry Faucher produces food that is consistently attractive, satisfying and reasonably priced. Lunch and dinner are a pre-fixed (32€) blackboard affair, and might include velvety cauliflower soup ladled over roasted thyme and crispy croutons, foie gras coated in gingerbread crumbs, or roast pigeon with chestnuts. The four-course lunch menu offers several choices, while the indulgent six-course dinner menu is pre set.

In contrast, the casual and cheaper La Cave de l'Os à Moëlle, opposite, features three communal tables and a 20€buffet (you can have seconds and thirds) of robust fare. Terrines, bowls of olives and sea snails, a tureen of steaming soup and one main-course choice, such as pheasant with lentils, plus cheese, desserts and good-value wine are all included. **Moderate**

Le Troquet *upscale Basque* `14 G5`
21 rue François-Bonvin, 15ème • 01 45 66 89 00
Open lunch & dinner Tue–Sat

While this bistro in a nondescript street appears intensely old-fashioned, looks can be deceiving. Christian Etchebest's menu, while brief, is strictly seasonal and contemporary, often displaying the chef's Basque bias (fish wrapped in Bayonne ham with liberal sprinklings of Espelette pepper). **Moderate**

Chez Foong *Malay peninsula* `14 F4`
32 rue de Frémicourt, 15ème • 01 45 67 36 99
Open lunch & dinner Mon–Sat

Chez Foong offers a welcome taste of Malaysia's little-known (certainly in Paris) cuisine. The *prix-fixe* menus are great value; light, tasty starters such as omelette with ginger-peanut sauce are followed by steamed spiced fish and curries or grilled meats flavoured with lemongrass and coconut. **Moderate**

Le Suffren *neighbourhood favourite* `14 F3`
84 avenue de Suffren, 15ème • 01 45 66 97 86
Open breakfast, lunch & dinner daily

The timber and maritime theme may have given way to fashionable shades of black and orange and clubby fabric chairs, but the menu at this adored neighbourhood brasserie escaped unscathed. You'll find all the classics, from seafood platters and steaks to *choucroute*. **Moderate**

Salons de Thé
Coffee might be the brew of choice when it comes to dunking a croissant, but tea has caught on in Paris in a big way. The deservedly famous **Ladurée**, dating back to 1862, is excellent for lemon tea and multi-flavoured macaroons – they sell one of these every 25 seconds! Fuel up on a cup of strong Darjeeling and a fruit-crammed crumble at **A Priori Thé** in the glitzy Galerie Vivienne, or calm down after a serious Left Bank shopping spree with a pot of Celestial Empire at **La Maison de la Chine**. Stop by **Angelina** for mud-thick hot chocolate and gooey cakes in elegant surroundings, or, take a seat under a shady fig tree on the serene terrace of the **Grande Mosquée**'s Café Maure and sup on mint tea and honey-drizzled baklava. For contact details, *see p220*.

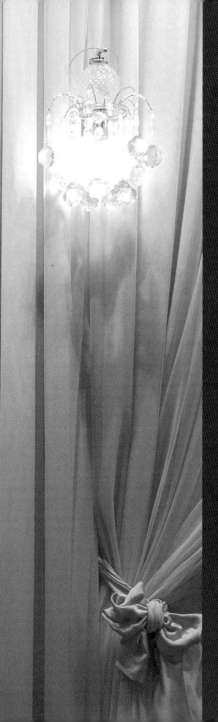

shopping

The capital of style, Paris has all the retail opportunities that a shopaholic might crave. The city's 20 arrondissements house a dazzling and diverse array, from tiny glamour-puss boutiques on serpentine streets to venerable department stores on sweeping boulevards. Trawl for luxury labels, pore over silky lingerie, search out one-off handbags or stock up on deliciously French homewares.

FOR THE HOME	VINTAGE & RETRO	BOUTIQUES

Thomas Boog
52 rue de Bourgogne, 7ème
Boog's fanciful creations are covered in shells, from chandeliers encased in white *coquilles* to mirrors ringed with mother-of-pearl. *(See p82)*

Catherine Arigoni
14 rue Beaune, 7ème
Fans of vintage clothing are wowed by Arigoni's well-selected couture cache, including items by names such as Pucci and YSL. *(See p82)*

AB33
33 rue Charlot, 3ème
This homely boutique offers an expertly put-together selection of women's fashion and accessories. *(See p69)*

Christian Tortu
6 carrefour de l'Odéon, 6ème
Tortu believes that all plants were created equal. His chic arrangements often fuse fruit with branches, buds or blooms. *(See p79)*

Yukiko
97 rue Vieille du Temple, 4ème
This pint-sized shop sells excellent-quality vintage clothing. Some items have been given a modern twist. *(See p71)*

Isabel Marant
16 rue de Charonne, 11ème
Marant puts a unique bohemian-style spin on ethnic chic, weaving multicultural influences into her ultra-wearable clothes. *(See p90)*

Coin Canal
1 rue de Marseille, 10ème
Groovy 60s lamps, chunky 50s furniture and dainty old glassware are just some of the retro treasures in this light-filled shop. *(See p89)*

>> Paris's flea markets (puces) *aren't as well-stocked as they used to be, but it's still possible to unearth some great vintage finds.*

Stella Cadente
93 quai de Valmy, 10ème
The name is Italian for "falling star", and this designer's creations certainly sparkle. Pretty colours are the norm here. *(See p87)*

>> The city's most design-conscious department stores – Printemps (see p83) and Le Bon Marché (see p83) – both sell a range of stylish homewares. Galeries Lafayettes (see p83) has four entire floors dedicated to the home.

Vanessa Bruno
25 rue de St-Sulpice, 6ème
Bruno's clothes are fresh, well-cut and easy to wear. Women of all ages will find something that suits them here. *(See p77)*

Sentou Gallery
18 & 24 rue Pont Louis-Philippe, 4ème
If you like contemporary style, you'll love Sentou's homewares, which are designed by international names as well an in-house team. *(See p73)*

Antik Batik
18 rue de Turenne, 4ème
This store attracts trendsetters who are keen to snap up garments and accessories from all over the world. *(See p67)*

SHOES & BAGS	FOR MEN	DESIGNER FASHION
Pierre Hardy 156 galerie de Valois, 1er The city's most cutting-edge foot-wear for women, and sharp shoes for men. Pierre Hardy designs shoes to make an entrance in. *(See p61)*	**Madelios** 23 boulevard de la Madeleine, 1er Almost a male service station, Madelios stocks all manner of gar-ments and accessories, and also has a men's beauty salon. *(See p61)*	**Helmut Lang** 29 rue St-Honoré, 1er Branded as a minimalist, a decon-structionist and even a futurist, the achingly hip Lang is always ahead of the fashion pack. *(See p61)*
Charles Jourdan 86 avenue des Champs-Elysées, 8ème By injecting fun and colour into shoes, design director Patrick Cox has breathed new life into this august company. *(See p84)*	**Loft Design by** 56 rue de Rennes, 6ème This store's not about flashy style. It's known for its well-thought out basics for the urban man. *(See p78)*	**Martine Sitbon** 13 rue Grenelle, 7ème Sitbon's clothes are modern in style, but the secret of their success is that they're also comfortable to wear. *(See p81)*
Jamin Puech 43 rue Madame, 6ème The unique handbags of design duo Jamin Puech are perfect for women who want to stand out from the crowd. *(See p78)* 		**Martin Grant** 44 rue Vieille du Temple, 4ème Dramatically structured, elegant coats are Grant's trademark. He also turns out impeccably tailored dresses and skirts. *(See p72)*
>> *The 7th arrondissement's rue de Grenelle is lined with shoe shops, which range from design outlets, such as Iris (see p80) and Jean-Baptiste Rautureau (see p82), to those selling copycat styles at greatly reduced prices.*	**Paul & Joe** 40 rue du Four, 6ème Men who know about fashion are fans of Paul & Joe's retro-style shirts, contemporary jackets and modish accessories. *(See p77)*	**L'Eclaireur** 10 rue Hérold, 1er The world's most avant-garde mens- and womenswear – from rare Italian couture to underground Japanese labels – are collected here. *(See p63)*
Karine Dupont 22 rue Poitou, 3ème Ideal for women on the go, Dupont's sturdy, functional bags, in snappy colours and designs, are fancy enough to take anywhere. *(See p67)*	**Agnès b** 12 rue Vieux Colombier, 6ème Agnès b man likes to look good, and this designer makes it easy with her durable, modern pieces. *(See p76)* 	**Lagerfeld Gallery** 40 rue Seine, 6ème The boutique-cum-gallery of this perennially elegant designer offers his signature Lagerfeld line, as well as some Fendi titbits. *(See p77)*

Shopping

Fifi Chachnil *ultra-feminine frills* 9 D3
231 rue St-Honoré, 1er • 01 42 61 21 83
>> www.fifichachnil.com Open 11–7 Mon–Sat

Nobody does girly lingerie like Delphine Véron.
Think baby-doll dresses in soft candy colours,
G-strings with feathery pom-poms at the hips, lush
red bras with cute little bows — all guaranteed to
summon up the *femme fatale* in every woman. Just
browsing in this sugary pink boudoir is fun.

Christian Louboutin *fabulous footwear* 10 F4
19 rue Jean-Jacques Rousseau, 1er • 01 42 36 05 31
Open 10:30–7 Mon–Sat

Louboutin's extravagant red-soled shoes are extremely
glamorous. Displayed in a white wall set with red
alcoves, the styles veer from fantasy (bejewelled
velvet) to resolutely feminine (leather and spidery
lace). Shoes, claims Louboutin, are like faces: some
are extraordinary front-on, others are better in profile.

by Terry *couture cosmetics* 10 F4
21 galerie Véro-Dodat, 1er • 01 44 76 00 76
>> www.byterry.com Open 10:30–7 Mon–Sat

Terry de Gunzburg, a former make-up artist and
creative director of YSL's cosmetics line for 15 years,
knows a thing or two about beauty and luxury; for
instance, that women can't get enough of it. So, she
launched "by Terry", a line of made-to-order *haute
couleur* cosmetics. Simply book a consultation with
Terry, self-described *couturier pour le visage*, to
discover what she can do to make you radiant.

   The make-up, which boasts some of the most costly
pigments around, is mixed up by a team of chemists
and colourists in the lab upstairs and packaged into
silver containers, which can be personalized with
initials or a message. Each order will comprise a year's
supply of a unique product, albeit at a handsome price.
There's also a range of ready-to-wear cosmetics (a few
doors away at No. 36), but it's more interesting – and
much more Parisian – to go for the bespoke service.

Helmut Lang *master of minimalism*   `10 E4`
219 rue St-Honoré, 1er • 01 58 62 53 20
≫ www.helmutlang.com Open 11–7 Mon–Sat

Lang's gallery-cum-boutique features a concrete staircase flanked by two imposing, black monolithic boxes, black vinyl ottomans and art by names such as Louise Bourgeois. These clean lines are also evident in the men's and women's clothes: razor-sharp pants and jackets, figure-hugging dresses and skinny T-shirts.

Madelios *male domain*   `9 C2`
23 boulevard de la Madeleine, 1er • 01 53 45 00 00
≫ www.madelios.com Open 10–7 Mon–Sat

A one-stop shop for men's fashion, with two floors of stylish, if faintly conservative, clothing. This means sharp suits by Dior, Paul Smith and Givenchy; stylish casuals by the likes of Lacoste and Diesel; plus a large range of accessories and shoes. Also found in-store are expert tailors and a men's beauty salon.

Pierre Hardy *his-and-hers heels*   `10 F4`
156 galerie de Valois, 1er • 01 42 60 59 75
≫ www.pierrehardy.com Open 11–7 Tue–Sat

Former Hermès accessories designer Pierre Hardy has had a big hit with his sophisticated, own-brand range of shoes. His elegant boutique is located within the up-market arcades enclosing the Palais Royal gardens *(see p162)*: lit by a wall of coloured neon tubes, it has something of a gallery feel to it, an impression reinforced by the fact that the shoes are presented on one long black shelf running round the walls.

Hardy's women's collection revolves around vertiginous heels, daring foot "décolletés" and open-toed stilettos in nude pink and coral that fasten with lingerie straps. But fans of flatter styles are also well served with kitten heels, sexy gladiator sandals and cute ballerina shoes in candy colours. The designer's capsule men's collection includes stylish cowboy boots, kangaroo-skin lace-ups and white leather desert boots. Unusually for Paris, service is with a smile.

L'Artisan Parfumeur *evocative scents* `10 F5`
2 rue Amiral de Coligny, 1er • 01 44 88 27 50
Open 10:30–7:30 Mon–Sat

This boutique rekindles memories with its cleverly scented candles and perfumes. Premier Figuier (First Figs) is Provence on a hot summer's day, Je Me Souviens (I Remember) conjures up childhood cuddles, while Pour des Prunes (Plum Pudding) is reminiscent of a pie baking in the oven. Delicious.

Salons du Palais Royal *regal perfumes* `10 F3`
25 rue de Valois, 1er • 01 49 27 09 09
» www.salons-shiseido.com Open 10–7 Mon–Sat

Every year Serge Lutens, Shiseido's creative director, comes up with new fragrances that are added to the range and sold exclusively in this lavish shop. Best-sellers include Rahat Loukoum, with its bittersweet almond, honey and vanilla scent, and Amber Sultan, aromatic amber spiced with evergreen rock rose.

Martin Margiela *bold fashion statements* `10 F3`
25bis rue de Montpensier, 1er • 01 40 15 07 55
Open 11–7 Mon–Sat

The Belgian fashion maverick's first Paris boutique is a startling all-white space, which can be a little intimidating to enter. Margiela's avant-garde mens- and womenswear tends to be on the conceptual side, but everything – apart from the weird split-toed shoes – is actually very wearable.

Maria Luisa *always in fashion* `9 C3`
2 rue Cambon, 1er • 01 47 03 96 15
Open 10:30–7 Mon–Sat

Maria Luisa has impeccable taste and a discerning eye. Her boutiques are favoured by the fashion elite who come by each season for the latest by Gaultier, Olivier Theyskens, Ann Demeulemeester and Jean-Paul Knott, to name but a few. Whether you crave cutting-edge or classic, new or established, this is prime territory.

L'Eclaireur *directional fashion*
10 G3

10 rue Hérold, 1er • 01 40 41 09 89
>> www.leclaireur.com Open 11–7 Mon–Sat

It might be Paris's hippest multi-brand boutique, but with no shop window it's certainly not the city's most obvious. You'll have to press the buzzer to get in to the dimly lit cavernous space, where, despite the store's ultra-trendy reputation, the welcome is warm and the staff are genuinely enthusiastic about helping customers put an outfit together.

The store's focus is on innovative, international fashion, showcasing superbly tailored men's collections by Austrian designer Carol Christian Poell and avant-garde mens- and womenswear by Japanese label Undercover. Other highlights include tactile deconstructed sweaters in vintage cashmere by LA-based designer Koi, a great selection of Linda Farrow vintage sunglasses and a more classic collection of menswear designed by actor John Malkovich that is exclusive to L'Eclaireur in France.

Ventilo *effortless chic*
9 C2

13–15 boulevard de la Madeleine, 1er • 01 42 60 46 40
>> www.ventilo.fr Open 10:30–7 Mon–Sat

An upmarket concept store, Ventilo sells a small but sophisticated range of women's fashion and home accessories. The look is chic with a Moroccan/Indian twist; think gorgeous fabrics, floaty *djellebas* and lots of beading and embroidery. The in-store café serves a selection of Japanese teas and world food.

Odette & Zoe *handbags galore*
10 F3

4 rue des Petits Champs, 2ème • 01 42 61 48 75
Open 11–7 Mon–Sat

This pink boutique is packed with bags of every imaginable style, shape and colour. The focus is on fun and originality rather than famous designer labels: quirky finds include suitcases printed with Marilyn Monroe's face, practical foldaway bags by Bensimon and purses made from vintage saris.

Flavie Furst *real gems* `10 E3`

16 rue de la Soudière, 1er • 01 42 60 06 01
Open 11–7 Mon–Sat

Flavie Furst makes glorious jewellery, her husband Ronald makes gorgeous bags – and that means that their tiny boutique is one big temptation. Flavie, who designed accessories for Lanvin before turning to full-time jewellery-making, loves the colour and emotive qualities of precious stones, and is careful not to over-power them with extravagant designs. She creates pieces that are original, expressive and, above all, easy to wear: an effortlessly pretty pale-blue teardrop sapphire set off-centre on a silver band, a single plump Tahitian pearl draped on a delicate gold chain.

No less eye-catching are her partner's handbags, which run from totes to baguettes, all with matching make-up bags inside. The bags are made in a multitude of colours and textures, including stripes and rowdy floral prints, tweed and cowhide; few who enter can leave without buying at least one.

Lavinia *wine emporium* `9 D2`

3–5 boulevard de la Madeleine, 1er • 01 42 97 20 20
Open 10–8 Mon–Sat

If your wine-appreciation skills need some polishing, Lavinia is the place to go. With a selection of over 6,000 bottles (including 3,000 French wines, 2,000 foreign wines and 1,000 spirits), 500 books, a staff of 15 sommeliers, dozens of glasses and decanters as well as various other wine-related paraphernalia, it's Europe's largest wine shop. The slick three-level store is maintained like a traditional wine cellar, with a temperature of 19°C (68°F), though a special section for rare wines is kept at 14°C (58°F). Prices range from a few euros a bottle through to several thousand-plus.

The glossy 80-seat, in-store restaurant serves lunch only (shark steak and chardonnay are a winning combination), though the bar is open till 8pm. In either, you can sample any wine in the store and there's no extra mark-up in price. Lavinia also holds regular tastings and runs wine courses.

For information on tax refunds, check »» www.eparis.dk.com

Killiwatch *hip hand-me-downs* `10 G3`
64 rue Tiquetonne, 2ème • 01 42 21 17 37
Open 2–7 Mon, 11–7 Tue–Sat (to 7:30 Sat)

This store buys pre-worn clothing, cleans it up a treat and puts it back out on the rails. Not just any old rags, though – this is stylish stuff: from fur-trimmed coats to leather minis and swirly 70s shirts. There's also club-wear from their in-house label, non-vintage jeans and streetwear, plus magazines and the latest club flyers.

Barbara Bui *clean-cut style* `10 H4`
23 rue Etienne Marcel, 2ème • 01 40 26 43 65
>> www.barbarabui.com Open 10:30–7:30 Mon–Sat

Barbara Bui's designs can be described as clothes for style-conscious rebels: refined, with an offbeat femi-ninity. Born and raised in Paris in a Franco-Vietnamese family, Bui designs clothes that subtly reflect both cultures. Her exquisitely finished and flattering trousers are wardrobe must-haves; ditto, her leather jackets.

Robert Le Héros *arty decor* `11 C4`
13 rue de Saintonge, 3ème • 01 44 59 33 22
>> www.robertleheros.com Open 1–7 Tue–Sat

After much anticipation, this leading textile design agency set up by four art-school friends now has its own boutique. Step past the jaunty red façade and you'll find a veritable art and design laboratory with a seasonally changing decor. The foursome's eye-catching graphic designs in gorgeous colourways are reproduced on everything from cushions, curtains and wallpaper to handbags and diaries.

Erik & Lydie *jewels galore* `10 H3`
7 passage du Grand Cerf, 2ème • 01 40 26 52 59
Open 2 7 Tue–Sat

Seriously pretty jewellery is what Erik & Lydie do best; contemporary and gently artistic with a slight Victorian bent. Spidery necklaces draped with flower-shaped stones recall the delicate garlands favoured by a previous generation, while the slim metal chokers wouldn't be out of place in the coolest of clubs.

Shoe Bizz *fashion for feet* `11 A5`
48 rue Beaubourg, 3ème • 01 48 87 12 73
Open 10:30–7:30 Mon–Sat

Shoe Bizz zeroes in on the hottest footwear trends, reproduces the styles and sells them for a lot less than you'd pay elsewhere. Don't expect flawless finishes or sturdy quality, though. These shoes aren't meant to last forever, just as long as the style is *en vogue* – but that's more than enough.

Atelier Narakas *casual designer looks* `11 B4`
79 rue du Temple, 3ème • 01 44 54 88 80
>> www.ateliernarakas.com Open 11–7:30 Thu–Tue

This two-storey boutique stocks a range of designer fashion and urban sportswear. Highlights include Vivienne Westwood Red Label, Paris-based designer Udo Edling and edgy Italian labels Gas and Nolita. Charismatic designer Alexandre Narakas also offers made-to-measure classic designs (allow one week).

Goumanyat & Son Royaume *spices* `11 C3`
3 rue Charles-François Dupuis, 3ème • 01 44 78 96 74
Open 2–7 Tue–Fri, 11–7 Sat

A whiff of faraway lands emanates from this elegant little shop-cum-olfactory-museum run by Jean Marie Thiercelin, a sixth-generation spice merchant. His family started out dealing in saffron in 1809; today their business encompasses 180 spices, including pink peppercorns from Pondicherry, vanilla beans from Madagascar, black peppercorns from Kerala and sea salt and oils from around the world.

This is where Michelin-starred chefs, such as Alain Ducasse and Joel Robuchon, come to stock up on rare condiments. Poke your nose into the jars on *le bar à sniffer* to discover the vibrant aromas of star anise, cloves and nutmeg; get a lesson on spices from the gracious Monsieur Thiercelin himself; or browse the store for gifts of saffron-flavoured chocolate, caviar, fine linen aprons, plant-based bath and skincare products, kitchen utensils and heady spice mixes.

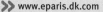

Karine Dupont *it's in the bag* `11 C4`
22 rue Poitou, 3ème • 01 40 27 84 94
>> www.karinedupont.com Open noon–7 Mon–Sat

Dupont makes practical, soft nylon bags in all shapes
and sizes, from roomy totes to shoulder slingers.
There are bags for every occasion, with names like
Kampus Lady, Kasual Travel and Klub. They come in
an array of modish colours and prints and many have
handy sections that can be detached as required.

Food *gourmet's hang-out* `11 C4`
58 rue Charlot, 3ème • 01 42 72 68 97
Open 11–7 Tue–Fri (closed lunch), 2–7 Sat

Much of the rue Charlot buzz was started by the opening of this intriguing bookstore-cum-gallery. With its
wall-to-wall bookshelves, it's a foodie's paradise,
where browsers linger over a range of mouthwatering
cookbooks in French, English and Japanese. Food also
stocks larder goodies and designer tableware.

Antik Batik *ethnic fusion* `17 C1`
18 rue de Turenne, 4ème • 01 44 78 02 00
Open 10:30–7 Tue–Sat, 2–7 Sun & Mon

Antik Batik sells globally inspired somethings that
follow the season's trends; from flowery headscarves
and crocheted bikinis for summer, to hand-knitted
hats, pullovers and bags for winter. Labels such as
Ordinary People, Laura Urbinati and Uniform can
also be found on the shelves.

Chic on the Cheap

Dépôt-ventes are where canny Parisians shop for
cut-price designer clothes. Try **Annexe des Créateurs**
(40–70 per cent off previous seasons' Versace,
Vivienne Westwood, Dolce & Gabbana and more),
Réciproque (six stores in one street selling womenswear, menswear and the biggest range of second-
hand Chanel in Paris) and **Dépôt-Vente de Buci** (two
neighbouring stores selling everything from YSL to
Yamamoto). Many stores have their own permanent
sales shops, the best of which are **APC Solde**, **Et
Vous**, **Cacharel** and **Kookaï**. At the cheap end of the
scale, **Guerrisol** has more of a whiffy jumble-sale
flavour. But this is where designers such as Gaultier
trawl for inspiration, and there are real bargains to
be had. For further details, *see pp221–2.*

Shopping

Abou d'Abi Bazar *affordable fashion* `17 C1`
10 rue des Francs Bourgeois, 3ème • 01 42 77 96 98
Open 2–7:15 Mon, 10:30–7 Tue–Sat, 2–7 Sun

Savvy shoppers pop in here regularly to pick up the season's must-have pieces. These include reasonably priced jeans, dresses and accessories from designers such as Vanessa Bruno, Stella Forest and Isabel Marant. Mixing and matching is a breeze, too, as the clothes on display are organized by colour.

La Chaise Longue *Marais institution* `17 C1`
20 rue des Francs Bourgeois, 3ème • 01 48 04 36 37
Open 11–7 Mon–Sat, 2–7 Sun

This tiny, two-storey home-decor boutique has become synonymous with design inventiveness and cheerful kitsch. Specializing in cheap and quirky accessories for bathrooms and kitchens – such as cocktail shakers, retro fans and miniature kitten-shaped frying-pans – LCL is the perfect hunting ground for novelty presents.

Galerie Simone *designers' creative lab* `11 C4`
124 rue Vieille du Temple, 3ème • 01 42 74 21 28
Open noon–7 Tue–Sat

The city's coolest boutique for fashion, furniture, jewellery and accessories, Galerie Simone showcases one-offs and limited editions by some of the edgiest new designers in Paris. Check out Michel Morellini's draped leather dresses, conceptual silver jewellery by Georges Tsak and origami-inspired handbags by Sanja.

French Chain Stores

Several international high-street stores are actually of French origin: the young of body and heart make a beeline for branches of **Morgan**, **Etam** and **Kookaï** (which now has a capsule up-market collection, Creative Lab). Basic, fashion-conscious footwear can be snapped up at **André** (which also regularly invites guest designers), while **Princesse** **Tam Tam** is good for bikinis and underwear (though bra sizes often stop at a B-cup). On the beauty front, **Sephora** is hard to beat, but **Yves Rocher** is also worth checking out for all-natural bath and beauty products. **Monoprix** supermarkets are great one-stop shops for (slightly older) fashion, bags, beauty products and home accessories. For further details, *see pp221–2.*

AB33 *affordable fashion*   `11 C4`

33 rue Charlot, 3ème • 01 42 71 02 82
Open 11–8 Tue–Sun

Located in the heart of the retail hub that has emerged in the northern Marais, AB33 has an appealing take both on women's fashion and the shopping experience. Dynamic young owner Agathe Buchotte (the AB of the store's name) revamped an old grocer's shop with the help of her architect father, giving the space a lived-in feel with rugs, a magazine-strewn coffee table and a scattering of velvet poufs.

You won't find snooty Parisian vendors here, though; Agathe is an upbeat Marseillaise with a laid-back attitude who extends a friendly welcome to all and encourages browsing and extended trying-on sessions. She takes a highly personal approach to her buying, putting collections together as if they were her own wardrobe. And while Agathe is keenly aware of what's out there on fashion's cutting-edge, she manages to mix the season's hottest catwalk looks with clothes that are fun, easy and wearable. These are all arranged on accessible, colour co-ordinated rails, offering an extensive selection of mainstream lines such as Vanessa Bruno, Isabel Marant, Cabane de Zucca and celebrity jeans of choice Notify, showcased alongside delicate Italian lingerie by Kristina Ti and designer knits by rising Belgian star Christian Wijnants.

AB33 accessories, which include original jewellery creations by Marine de Diesbach and luxury leather bags by up-and-coming Danish designer Malm Strecker, have an edgier look. Agathe also produces her own line of customized suede and leather shoulder bags; clients can choose their own colours and fabric combinations (thus giving them a stylish one-off creation for 260€). Allow five days for production.

Comptoir des Cotonniers   *basic needs*   `11 B5`

33 rue des Francs Bourgeois, 4ème • 01 42 76 95 33
» www.meresetfilles.com
Open 10–7 Mon–Sat, 1–7 Sun

French women who like stylish clothes but don't like paying high prices for them stock up on well-designed wardrobe basics here. The look is modern, casual and urban: easy-to-wear jackets in wool and flannel for winter, crisp shirts and cool dresses for summer.

Azzedine Alaïa   *a well-kept secret*   `17 A1`

7 rue de Moussy, 4ème • 01 42 72 19 19
Open 11–7 Mon–Sat

No tempting shop window here; just a discreet buzzer to gain admittance to this cool address. The Tunisian maestro's flattering cuts and curve-conscious women's clothing are showcased in a cavernous space decorated by US artist Julian Schnabel. Don't miss the permanent sale area of old stock and samples out back.

A-poc   *instant ready-to-wear*   `11 B5`

47 rue des Francs Bourgeois, 4ème • 01 44 54 07 05
Open 11–7:30 Mon–Sat

A-poc, which stands for "A Piece of Cloth", is the brainchild of Japanese designer Issey Miyake, and it works like this: simply cut a piece of cloth from a bolt of his revolutionary woven-knit, non-run fabric and *voilà*, a new top, dress or wrap. Staff in the gallery-style space will advise how best to wear your new "poc".

Brontibay   *bags of style*   `17 C1`

6 rue de Sévigné, 4ème • 01 42 76 90 80
Open 11–8 Mon–Sat, 1:30–7:30 Sun

The name might be inspired by two Australian coastal havens (Bronte Beach and Byron Bay), but there's not a single swimsuit in sight. Instead, it's wall-to-wall bags in classy flannel, felt, nylon or leather (sometimes with gloves to match). They also sell pampering MOR lotions, plus Neal's Yard Remedies creams.

Hervé Gambs *man-made flowers* `11 B5`
9bis rue des Blancs Manteaux, 4ème • 01 44 59 88 88
>> **www.hervegambs.fr** Open 11–7:30 Tue–Sat, 1:30–7:30 Sun

Hervé is *the* man when it comes to artificial flowers. In fact, his silky blooms are so convincing that it's hard to tell his white orchids, purple calla lilies or trailing bamboo leaves from the real thing. As befits their couture status, there are two collections a year that reflect the latest horticultural trends.

Calligrane *paper chase* `17 A2`
4–6 rue du Pont Louis-Philippe, 4ème • 01 48 04 31 89
Open 11–7 Tue–Sat

Calligrane's three adjoining shops are devoted to the art of calligraphy and paper products. One specializes only in Fabriano, an Italian paper favoured by Goya and Michelangelo; another sells up-market briefcase and desk essentials; the third stocks textured paper from India, Brazil, Japan, China and Mexico – and holds occasional shows by artists working with paper. Simply sublime gifts for writers and artists.

Yukiko *vintage passions* `11 C4`
97 rue Vieille du Temple, 4ème • 01 42 71 13 41
Open 1–7 Tue–Sun

Yukiko is mad about vintage clothes, particularly furs. She searches all over the place, uncovering rare pieces that she then customizes to sell in her snug and charming Marais boutique.

Set on the quieter end of a bustling thoroughfare, this hole in the wall is crammed with wonderful old things, though contemporary gear by Stella Cadente *(see p87)* is also stocked, as well as lesser-known designers with a penchant for making old things like new again. You might be lucky enough to stumble upon an original Dior vanity case, some funky leather bags from the 1970s, pristine 50s pumps or clingy knee-high *Barbarella*-style boots. There's lots of retro jewellery too, including flashy rings, overstated bracelets and shiny enamel brooches. It's hard to get out of the door without falling for at least one of Yukiko's treasures.

Martin Grant *ladylike elegance* `11 B5`

44 rue Vieille du Temple, 4ème • 01 42 71 39 49
≫ www.martingrantparis.com Open 10–6 Mon–Fri

Australian designer Martin Grant has been making clothes ever since his grandmother taught him to sew at the age of seven. Several years on, he's still stitching, but now it's in a white and airy showroom that overlooks a 17th-century flagstone courtyard on the other side of the world. During his years in Paris – he's been here since 1992 – the low-key Grant has built up a loyal clientele, including actress Cate Blanchett, model Lauren Hutton and socialite Lee Radziwill (sister of Jacqueline Kennedy Onassis), as well as hordes of modern girls all over the world.

His clothes are ladylike but sexy, timeless and undeniably elegant. His frocks (calling them dresses just isn't right) have a faint echo of the 1950s about them: a strapless gown with wavy chiffon ruffles, a belted black wool sheath with built-in cape, a brocade cocktail dress in which a young Lauren Bacall would look drop-dead gorgeous. Coats, though, are his trademark, and Grant cuts them with sculptural precision (a skill no doubt gained by a four-year stint studying the art). Recent designs have included a single-breasted pony-skin coat with leather trim, a retro-look three-quarter-length tweed and a black Lurex evening trench. Even in summer, there's always a super-smart coat or three in the collection. Grant's clothes are made to hug those feminine curves and there's just something about the way he does it that makes the wearer look *très, très* chic. And that's just the ticket when in Paris.

Sentou *cool, contemporary living* `17 B1`

18 & 24 rue du Pont Louis-Philippe, 4ème • 01 42 71 00 01
29 rue François Miron, 4ème • 01 42 78 50 60
>> www.sentou.fr Open 11–7 Tue–Sat (closed 2–3pm)

It describes itself as "the art of living" store and that pretty much sums it up. Opened in Paris in 1977 as an outlet for the work of furniture designer Robert Sentou, this Marais store (actually three separate shops) has morphed over the years into a quasi gallery that champions modern design. Today, Sentou carries a varied selection of contemporary designs, from the ethereal bamboo-and-paper lamps of Osamu Noguchi to the upright birch chairs of Alvar Aalto, with the supple vinyl containers of D-sign by O, quirky china salad servers by Tsé-Tsé and playful picture plates by 100Drine in between.

The shop at No. 24, the original boutique, is now a temple to tablewares, including colourful hand-blown glassware by Sugahara, classy Stelton cutlery, coolly elegant silver and gold enamel-dipped china bowls, plates and cups by French design duo Tsé-Tsé, plus salt and pepper shakers, scented candles, containers, lacquered trays and spring vases (old test tubes wired together into snaking shapes). No. 18, meanwhile, is awash with the designs of former newspaper illustrator and furniture fabric designer 100Drine: vividly coloured, hand-painted plates with smiling faces and stacks of storage tins and notebooks dominate the space. In addition, there are roomy plastic shopping baskets and cute things for kids. Objects are displayed for easy, hands-on inspection and staff are helpful and happy to offer advice. The largest store, a five-minute stroll away on rue François Miron, houses the striking, modern furniture of Swedish company David Design and Aalto's classic tables and chairs, as well as lamps, furniture and textiles from the Sentou line.

Bô *modish homewares* `11 A5`
8 rue St-Merri, 4ème • 01 42 72 84 64
>> www.boutiquebo.com Open 11:30–7:30 Mon–Sat, 2–7:30 Sun

Parisians love the contemporary lines of this store's well-crafted wares, which run from vases to chairs via Limoges crockery, table linen and candlesticks. Much is the work of young designers, including Katsuhiro Kinoshita (lacquer storage boxes), Gilles Caffier (sleek furniture) and Catherine Grandidier (unusual lights).

Hervé Van der Straeten *chic designs* `17 B1`
11 rue Ferdinand Duval, 4ème • 01 42 78 99 99
Open 9–1 & 2–6 Mon–Fri, noon–7 Sat

Once the creator of jewellery collections for Lacroix, YSL and Gaultier, Hervé Van der Straeten now designs his own furniture and jewellery. Almost exclusively produced in 24-carat gold-plated brass, the latter includes ornate necklaces and bracelets, and wafer-thin pendant earrings inspired by blades of grass.

A L'Olivier *gourmet oils* `17 B1`
23 rue de Rivoli, 4ème • 01 48 04 86 59
>> www.olivier-on-line.com Open 2–7 Mon, 10–7 Tue–Sat

Opened in 1822 by a Parisian pharmacist specializing in cod-liver oil, A L'Olivier was relaunched in 1978 as a gourmet food store. The beautiful packaging of the extensive selection of olive oils, flavoured oils and organic vinegars would grace any shelf, and hampers of Provençal specialities can be made up to order.

Diptyque *haute-couture candles* `17 A3`
34 boulevard St-Germain, 5ème • 01 43 26 45 27
>> www.diptyqueparis.com Open 10–7 Mon–Sat

In business for 41 years, Diptyque is the original and still the best when it comes to candles of distinction. Devotees include Kristin Scott-Thomas (who favours Shadow in the Water) and Donatella Versace (an admirer of Fig Tree). This elegant and highly fragrant store also sells scents and room sprays.

Tara Jamon *good-looking fashion* `16 E2`
18 rue du Four, 6ème • 01 46 33 26 60
Open 10:30–7:30 Mon–Sat

Stepping into Tara Jamon's sunny corner shop is like stepping into spring. A Canadian expat with a French heart, she specializes in sophisticated, reasonably priced clothes. Think pert sundresses, slim-fit sheath dresses with knee-length coats, pleated skirts and silk cardigans in ice-cream colours with bags to match.

Vannina Vesperini *outer underwear* `15 D2`
63 rue des Sts-Pères, 6ème • 01 42 84 37 62
➤ www.vesperini.com Open 10:30–12:30 & 2:30–7 Mon–Sat

Vannina Vesperini subscribes to the idea of *dessus-dessous*, putting underwear on top rather than hiding it beneath clothes. Her dot of a shop brims with silk, satin and lace, from a clingy black teddy with sheer lace sleeves, to a chartreuse petticoat with lacy black inset, plus silk bras and panties in every hue.

Sabbia Rosa *lush lingerie* `15 D2`
73 rue des Sts-Pères, 6ème • 01 45 48 88 37
Open 10–7 Mon–Sat

Mme Rosa is renowned for her sumptuous, hand-made and exotic-looking camisoles, corsetry, bras and knickers, all of which are coveted by the likes of Madonna, Naomi Campbell and Cindy Crawford. Settle into the seductive sofa, survey the silk, satin and chiffon, and splash out on something custom-made.

La Maison du Chocolat *choc therapy* `15 C3`
19 rue de Sèvres, 6ème • 01 45 44 20 40
➤ www.lamaisonduchocolat.com Open 10–7 Mon–Sat

For those who believe that chocolate is one of the basic food groups, La Maison du Chocolat is heaven on a plate. Indulge in the handmade ginger-flavoured *ganache*, the cocoa-covered truffles or the potent Andalousie (chocolate cake, with lemon cream and truffle) by *chocolatier* Robert Linx.

Les 3 Marches de Catherine B `16 E2`

1 & 3 rue Guisarde, 6ème • 01 43 54 74 18
» www.catherine-b.com Open 10–7:30 Tue–Sat, 2:30–7:30 Mon

Catherine B is a luxury vintage-clothes sleuth who specializes in tracking down old Hermès and Chanel bags. Her bijou boutique is packed to the medieval rafters with scarves, jewellery and sought-after Kelly bags. The sister store next door sells a small selection of equally pricey and exquisite vintage clothes.

APC *urban basics* `15 D4`

3 & 4 rue Fleurus, 6ème • 01 42 22 12 77
Open 10:30–7 Mon–Fri, 11–7:30 Sat

The Atelier de Production et Création is something of an institution among Parisian hipsters who like their denim dark, rigid and slightly industrial. The girls' line includes A-line skirts, sweet summer dresses and winter basics, while boys rule with those dark jeans, sober shirts and simple V-necked sweaters.

Agnès b *Parisian chic* `15 D2`

6 (women's) & 12 (men's) rue du Vieux Colombier, 6ème
01 45 49 02 60 (women's), 01 44 39 02 05 (men's)
» www.agnesb.fr Open 10–7 Mon–Sat

Agnès b is synonymous with quality fabrics, clean lines and quintessential French style. The modern yet classic designs – precisely tailored trousers, crisp shirts and must-have little black dresses – suit all ages and lifestyles and often work over a few seasons.

Free Lance *sharp shoes* `15 D2`

30 rue du Four, 6ème • 01 45 48 14 78
Open 10–7 daily

Whatever your footwear fancy – dainty, fur-covered, shiny or snakeskin – you'll find it, or its close kin, here. Free Lance, who have been in the business for more than 100 years, keep up with the shoe trends; often, they're creating them. Their strappy sandals and dominatrix heels are particularly hot.

For companies that deliver long-distance, check out » www.eparis.dk.com

Lagerfeld Gallery *art & women's fashion* `16 E1`
40 rue de Seine, 6ème • 01 55 42 75 51
Open 11–7 Tue–Sat

This sedate and rather masculine-looking store sells Karl's own Lagerfeld Gallery line, selected items from the Fendi collection, which he also designs, and his accessories, perfumes and fabulously glossy fashion magazines. There are also regular photo exhibitions, often of Lagerfeld's own graphic compositions.

Vanessa Bruno *cross-generational clothes* `16 E3`
25 rue St-Sulpice, 6ème • 01 43 54 41 04
Open 10:30–7:30 Mon–Sat

Bruno's minimalist yet feminine garments appeal to women of all ages. They are individual, usually trend-resistant (from shapely coats and jackets to flattering trousers), and have a good quality-price ratio. A huge success since it hit the shelves in 1998 is her tote bag in sequins, leather or canvas.

Paul & Joe *for modern men* `16 E2`
40 rue du Four, 6ème • 01 45 44 97 70
» www.paulandjoe.com Open 11–7:30 Mon–Sat

The shop is named after Sophie Albou's two young sons, who are going to have to wait a while to sport the groovy slimline trousers, see-through shirts and 1930s-style jackets that their mama turns out. Confident guys go wild for the African-print tracksuits and the flamboyant pineapple-printed shirts.

Woman *erotic pursuits* `15 D2`
4 rue de Grenelle, 6ème • 01 49 54 66 21
» www.soniarykiel.fr Open 10:30–7 Mon–Sat

Nathalie, daughter of renowned designer Sonia Rykiel, caused quite a stir when she opened her "temple of pleasure" in St-Germain. The boutique's three floors offer all manner of seductive treats, from black lace lingerie and pashmina dressing gowns to designer dildos and lipstick-shaped vibrators.

Marie Mercié *eccentric hatters*   16 E3

23 rue St-Sulpice, 6ème • 01 43 26 45 83
Open 11–7 Mon–Sat

Beautifully finished, handmade hats are the *raison d'être* of this boutique. Celebrities including Catherine Deneuve are among the fans of Marie's stylish headgear, which ranges from flamboyant wedding hats and cute felt cloches to skullcaps sprouting branches. Bespoke hats can be ordered (allow up to one month).

Onward *avant-garde trends*   16 E2

147 boulevard St-Germain, 6ème • 01 55 42 77 55
Open 11–7 Mon & Sat, 10:30–7 Tue–Fri

This Left-Bank institution has a reputation for showcasing experimental fashion. Clothing by maverick designers such as Bernhard Willhelm and quirky Dutch duo Viktor & Rolf are featured here as well as accessories that make bold fashion statements, such as teaspoon necklaces and jewelled handcuffs.

Jamin Puech *cheeky handbags*   16 E3

43 rue Madame, 6ème • 01 45 48 14 85
>> www.jaminpuech.com Open 11–7 Mon–Fri, noon–7 Sat

Do you crave a bag with beads, shells, embroidery, leather fringing or crocheted raffia? Designers Benoit Jamin and Isabelle Puech have that certain something to slip on to your wrist. This dramatic boutique (created by theatre designer Elisabeth Leriche) displays hundreds of their equally theatrical bags.

Loft Design by *comfortable chic*   16 E2

56 rue de Rennes, 6ème • 01 45 44 88 99
>> www.loft-design-by.com Open 11–7 Mon–Sat

With its wood floors, barely there shelves and brick walls, Loft looks more like its namesake than a clothes shop. In keeping with the minimalist surroundings, designer Patrick Frèche specializes in tasteful urban basics for men and women in grey, black and white, with the occasional splash of seasonal colour.

Christian Tortu *designer blooms* `16 F2`
6 carrefour de l'Odéon, 6ème • 01 43 26 02 56
Open 10–8 Mon–Sat

One of Paris's hottest floral designers, Tortu popularized purely seasonal arrangements utilizing fruits, grasses, flowers and twigs. He even created a chic, all-green bouquet way back in the showy 80s. His compact boutique now enjoys iconic status and people drop by just to see his arresting window displays.

Deyrolle *animal, vegetable and mineral* `15 C1`
46 rue du Bac, 7ème • 01 42 22 30 07
» www.princejardinier.fr Open 10–7 Mon–Sat (closed 1–2pm Mon)

In 1995, Prince Louis-Albert de Broglie traded banking for horticulture and opened his first Paris store (Le Prince Jardinier), selling tomato chutneys and preserves made at his Loire Valley château, plus gardening tools and clothes, soaps and seeds. At Deyrolle – Paris's most famous taxidermist, now also owned by the Prince – all of this is for sale, as well as stuffed animals and mounted butterflies for your walls.

Shadé *big on style* `15 D2`
63 rue des Sts-Pères, 6ème • 01 45 49 30 37
Open 11–7:30 Mon–Sat

Shadé is proof that size really doesn't matter. Despite its miniscule proportions, this shop packs quite a sartorial punch. Once inside – no easy task if there are more than four people already browsing – you'll be amazed at the array. Time passes quickly when you're picking through such items as fetching, heart-shaped silk bags with beaded appliqués and shimmery tassels, or handmade velvet pouches embroidered with silk flowers, many by imaginative Brazilian designer Roberta. But this place is not just about bags; with feathery hats, scarves, bustiers, frou-frou skirts, Joe jeans and Converse sneakers also on sale, women can pick up an entire outfit. Add an umbrella with a flouncy frill, some jewellery – a bracelet brimming with charms, a metallic heart on a leather band or a sparkly choker – and *voilà*, you're ready for any distraction that Paris has to offer.

La Grande Epicerie *culinary temptations* `15 C3`
Le Bon Marché, 22 rue de Sèvres, 7ème • 01 44 39 80 00
» www.lebonmarche.fr Open 8:30–9 Mon–Sat

At Bon Marché's epicurean grocery, you can peruse 100-plus varieties of cheese, countless olive oils and vinegars, and international foodstuffs (candy-coloured Italian pasta, Zulu chilli sauce). Alternatively, snap up take-away gourmet meals and pastries. All in all, a treat for the eyes as well as the taste buds.

Iris *Italian shoe box* `15 D2`
28 rue de Grenelle, 7ème • 01 42 22 89 81
Open 10:30–7 Mon–Sat

Rue de Grenelle is a hot spot for shoe shops; there are just so many places from which to choose, but this all-white store is *the* place to visit if Italian-made shoes are what your heart desires. Venice-based Iris manufactures shoes for Marc Jacobs, Alessandro Dell'Acqua, Chloé and Véronique Branquino. *Bellissimo*!

Carine Gilson *luscious lingerie* `15 C2`
36 rue de Varenne, 7ème • 01 42 22 60 20
» www.carinegilson.com Open 11–7 Tue–Sat, by appt Mon

French women pay attention to the little things in life and this store has plenty of them, from lacey garters to flimsy slips, vampy black satin bras and satin robes for sexy lounging. Gilson bases each collection around an artistic theme, for example the Russian ballet or Klimt; in her hands, lingerie is definitely an art form.

Editions de Parfums Frédéric Malle `15 C2`
37 rue de Grenelle, 7ème • 01 42 22 77 22
» www.editionsdeparfums.com Open 11–7 Tue–Sat, 1–7 Mon

Editions de Parfums offers scents composed by nine of France's most legendary "noses". In this dimly lit labyrinth, filled with books, leather chairs and portraits of the nine perfumers, you can stop and smell the roses... and the lilacs... from vast glass "sniffing tubes" that keep the perfumes unadulterated.

Paul Smith *English class* `15 D3`

22 & 24 boulevard Raspail, 7ème • 01 42 84 15 30
»www.paulsmith.co.uk Open 11–7 Mon, 10–7 Tue–Sat

The Brit with a penchant for craftsmanship, tradition and humour is a favourite on this side of the Channel, too. His Paris HQ is a magnet for men who are after a sharp suit, a kimono-print shirt or a silver-and-turquoise bracelet, while women pop in for printed scarves, shoes and expertly cut jackets and dresses.

Lucien Pellat-Finet *cashmere king* `15 D1`

1 rue Montalembert, 7ème • 01 42 22 22 77
»www.lucienpellat-finet.com Open 10–7 Mon–Fri, 11–7 Sat

Lucien Pellat-Finet is known for his contemporary luxury knits in instantly identifiable colours and idiosyncratic patterns. His playful boutique, designed by new-generation architect Christian Biecher, perfectly matches the mood of his hooded sweaters, barely-there tank tops, bikinis and homewares.

Martine Sitbon *original chic* `15 D2`

13 rue de Grenelle, 7ème • 01 44 39 84 44
Open 11–7 Mon–Sat

This slick, barn-like space, with its colour splashes on the ceiling, is a fitting backdrop for Sitbon's original, richly coloured clothes. Encompassing stark, angular tailoring as well as a softer, more romantic approach (panelled velvet and silk or fluttery chiffon dresses), Sitbon's designs fly off the shelves.

Record Shops

While the vast emporiums of **fnac** and **Virgin** will sate any musical craving (and are open until midnight), Paris possesses other disc dealers for specialist sounds. Sixties vinyl, particularly French *chanson*, reigns at **En Avant La Zizique**, while tiny **Afric' Music** shimmies to a different beat: CDs from the Congo to Togo, with a little Caribbean thrown in. Jazz aficionados browse stacks of vinyl, secondhand CDs and old jazz magazines at **Paris Jazz Corner**, while **Waves** on rue Keller (electronica) and nearby **Techno Import** (techno and trance) are more up to date. At the other end of the musical spectrum, **Papageno** is bliss for opera buffs, with more than 4,000 vinyl albums (pre- and post-war), and rare boxed sets and CDs. For further details, *see pp222–3*.

Catherine Arigoni *couture collectibles*   `15 D1`
14 rue Beaune, 7ème • 01 42 60 50 99
Open 2:30–7:30 Tue–Sat, by appt Mon

Former antiques dealer Arigoni is serious about vintage clothing, and couture riches abound in her wardrobe-sized shop. Try a 1960s Pierre Balmain evening dress of silk, satin and pearls, a 1930s beaded purse or 1940s black Chanel pumps in mint condition. Beware: opulent items command corresponding prices.

Jean-Baptiste Rautureau *flashy shoes*   `15 D2`
24 rue de Grenelle, 7ème • 01 45 49 95 83
Open 11–7 Mon–Sat

Men's shoes are anything but tedious in the hands of Rautureau, a member of the clan that designs ever-trendy Free Lance shoes *(see p76)*. This is footwear for guys who want to make a statement – usually a loud one. Shoes come in everything from python-print and suede to red-and-white stripes and gold, but if snakeskin mules are not for you, you can also pick up some loafers with a little less attitude.

Thomas Boog *shell-shocked*   `15 A1`
52 rue de Bourgogne, 7ème • 01 43 17 30 03
≫ www.thomasboog.com Open 11–7 Mon–Fri, noon–7 Sat

Former shoe designer Thomas Boog is wild about shells, and it shows. He began by adorning candle-sticks with them, but now he's moved on to bigger things: screens, mirror frames and chandeliers, as well as chairs made from driftwood. What's more, there's no hint of seaside kitsch in any of his creations.

The Best of the Galéries

The city's covered arcades were built in the 19th century as places for elegant ladies to promenade protected from the elements. These days, several are still attractive shopping havens. Stroll through the **Galérie Vivienne** (Map 10 F3), with its vaulted glass roof and mosaic floor, and shop for fashion at Jean-Paul Gaultier and Nathalie Garçon, or for artificial silk flowers at Emilio Robba. Nearby, the **Galérie Véro-Dodat** (Map 10 F4) houses art galleries, antiques dealers, Italian leatherware at Il Bisonte, and the purple headquarters of couture make-up queen by Terry *(see p60)*. Farther north, the **Passage du Grand Cerf** (Map 10 H3) is a hotbed of creativity boasting everything from hat- and jewellery-makers to ceramic artists and furniture designers.

To find markets from flea to gourmet, look up ≫ www.eparis.dk.com

Iunx *exclusive scents* `15 D1`

48–50 rue de l'Université, 7ème • 01 45 44 50 14
Open 10:30–7:30 Mon–Sat

Iunx is a high-tech perfumery with state-of-the art equipment. Despite the rather daunting, minimalist design, staff are approachable and knowledgeable. You'll soon be seduced by the store's range of creams, gels, scented candles and ten exclusive fragrances created by in-house "nose" Olivia Giacobetti.

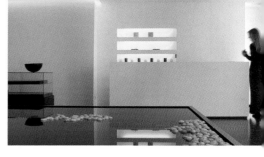

Publicis Drugstore *Champs-Elysées icon* `8 F1`

133 avenue des Champs-Elysées, 8ème • 01 44 43 77 64
>> www.publicisdrugstore.com
Open 8am–2am Mon–Fri, 10am–2am Sat & Sun

After a recent face-lift, this complex emerged encased in curved glass screens. Inside are restaurants, bars, a wine cellar, cinemas and stores, including a news kiosk (with international press), a gift shop and a pharmacy. It's the latest hip hang-out.

Renaud Pellegrino *handbag maestro* `9 B2`

14 rue du Faubourg-St-Honoré, 8ème • 01 42 65 35 31
Open 10–7 Mon–Sat

For over 20 years, Renaud Pellegrino has been mixing fabrics and techniques and turning out exceptional handbags: a silk bag in the shape of a matchbox, one dusted with Murano glass pearls, another in multi-coloured leather and linen. Many of his creations are inspired by the canvasses of Matisse and Braque.

Department Stores

From cutting-edge designs to must-have basics, the city's department stores cater to all needs and tastes. France's oldest is the swanky **Bon Marché**. With its serious men's and women's fashion, Paris's best lingerie selection, and photo and fashion exhibitions, it is ideal for a bout of relaxed retail therapy. Over on the Right Bank, **Galéries Lafayette** has bigger crowds but offers all the top designers, a water and champagne bar, and the chic Lafayette Maison for homewares. The largest beauty hall of all Parisian department stores belongs to **Printemps**: two floors and 200 brands of make-up, fragrances and skin care. They've also got a luxury fashion floor and a men's store with the Nickel spa *(see p163)*. For further details, *see pp220–21*.

Shopping

Charles Jourdan *British shoe flair* `8 G1`
86 avenue des Champs-Elysées, 8ème • 01 42 61 15 89
>> www.charles-jourdan.com Open 10–7 Mon–Sat

Long known for its elegant shoes, the 83-year-old French house decided to update and appointed Patrick Cox as design director in 2003. Cox's new look for Jourdan is sexy, shiny and graphic: a touch of the 60s (black patent) and the 70s (pink and perspex), while not forgetting the timeless designs.

Erès *make a splash* `9 C1`
2 rue Tronchet, 8ème • 01 47 42 28 82
>> www.eres.fr Open 10–7 Mon–Sat

If you cringe at the thought of donning a swimsuit, Erès is a must. This chi-chi shop is one reason why so many Frenchwomen look good on the beach: its perfectly cut bathing suits in appealing colours are flattering beyond belief, and bikini tops and bottoms are sold separately. They also do a range of underwear.

Galerie Noémie *face painting* `8 F1`
92 avenue des Champs-Elysées, 8ème • 01 45 62 78 27
>> www.galerienoemie.com Open 11–9 Mon–Sat, 1–8 Sun

Created by young painter Noémie Rocher, this make-up store puts an arty spin on cosmetics. Products are presented on artist's palettes and packaged in sweet little pots and paint tubes. Book in to have your face painted by a professional make-up artist or a bespoke shade of lip gloss specially mixed for you.

Zadig & Voltaire (de luxe) *eclectic* `8 G3`
18–20 rue François Premier, 8ème • 01 40 70 97 89
>> www.zadig-et-voltaire.com Open 10:30–7 Mon–Sat

Zadig & Voltaire – the French fashion and accessories line aimed at 20–45-year-olds – has boutiques all over the city, but this is their most up-market to date. In the light, airy space that is perfumed with the store's scented candles, label fans will find the design collective's own clothes mixed with choice items by Chloé, Diane von Furstenberg, Alberta Ferretti et al as well as sought-after jeans by Paper Denim.

Clothes are displayed on colour-coordinated rails and the staff have a good eye for putting together outfits. Accessories include Marc Jacobs shoes, Jamin Puech bags *(see p78)*, Kathy Korvin jewellery and gorgeous high-heeled sandals by hot designer Jean-Michel Cazabat. Downstairs, the Gaïa mini-spa offers a range of relaxing treatments from holistic massage with essential oils to *digitopuncture* (energizing crystals laid on acupuncture points).

La Parfumerie Générale *beauty central* `8 G2`

6 rue Robert-Estienne, 8ème • 01 43 59 10 62
Open 10–7 Mon–Sat

The brainchild of Victoire de Taillac (ex-publicist for Paris's mega-chic concept store Colette) and partner Ramdane Touhami, this is a beauty emporium specializing in state-of-the-art skin care and whatever your heart desires in cosmetics. The focus is on new and different products, most of them plant-based, as well as some classics. The store stocks the best beauty items – for men and women – from around the globe, including chocolate tea body scrub from Greece, lip balm from Egypt and essential oils from Morocco.

Beauty buffs can discover Doux Me, a skincare range made from organic essential oils that contains no fragrances, animal products or artificial colours. Kama Ayurveda is a similar range from India. For men, there are hard-to-find Anthony products, and an old-style barber, where *monsieur* can get a shave with products from legendary London barber Geo F Trumper.

Résonances *upscale home accessories* `9 C2`

3 & 5 boulevard Malesherbes, 8ème • 01 44 51 63 70
» www.resonances.fr Open 10–8 Mon–Sat

Walking into this bright and airy shop (one in a chain), with its aproned staff, is a bit like entering a time warp. However, while it might appear a little old-fashioned, Résonances is anything but. A cross between a bookshop, a DIY store and home-interiors shop, the store carries a wide range of traditional French wares updated for urban sophisticates.

There are accessories for every room: pint-sized cups for that first-of-the-day coffee, ceramic butter dishes and stainless-steel fruit presses for the kitchen; a multitude of soaps, lotions and towels for the bathroom; and cedar hangers and cushions for the bedroom. In addition to cookbooks, there are interior-design manuals that provide inspiration for renovations (as well as plenty of DIY gadgets to help them along), while wine buffs will appreciate a wall-mounted corkscrew that defies being misplaced.

Roger Vivier *footwear as art* `9 B2`

29 rue du Faubourg-St-Honoré, 8ème • 01 53 43 00 85
≫ www.rogervivier.com Open 10:30–7 Mon–Sat

Roger Vivier, the revered French shoe designer famous for his creations for Dior and YSL, died in 1998. But his legend lives on thanks to this boutique created by Italian shoe maestro Bruno Frisoni and his muse, Inès de la Fressange. Its upper floor resembles a chic Parisian apartment, where 18th-century antiques are cleverly mixed with futuristic furniture by Hervé Van der Straeten *(see p74)* and the walls are hung with art.

Rather than simply reproducing classic styles from the archives, Frisoni has updated the shoes by introducing contemporary twists. Vivier's famous curving Choc heel thus becomes the Choc-Choc, a vertiginous shoe in lime-green crocodile skin. Other revamped classics include Zorro, a shoe whose fine straps resemble the classic crusader's mask, and a more tapered version of the square-toed ballerinas Vivier created to go with YSL's famous Mondrian dress.

Stephane Kélian *fancy footwork* `9 C2`

5 rue du Faubourg-St-Honoré, 8ème • 01 44 51 64 19
≫ www.stephane-kelian.fr Open 10–7 Mon–Sat

Slip your just-pedicured feet into a pair of Kélian's top-of-the-line shoes if you plan to stroll the streets in style, before hitting that upscale bar. You'll find practical (but never boring) flatties, wedges and lofty stilettos; Kélian is a rare soul who can successfully create both the classic and the fabulously fashionable.

The Golden Triangle

Trawling the three main shopping arteries of the ultra-chic *8ème* is a quintessential Right Bank experience. Start at couture heartland on avenue Montaigne with a visit to **Dior**, **Chanel** and **Christian Lacroix** and perhaps a stop-off at **Louis Vuitton**. Alternatively, shop Italian-style, taking in **Prada**, **Emmanuel Ungaro**, **Valentino**, **Dolce & Gabbana**, **Marni** and the **Gucci** mega-store. Avenue George V is home to **Givenchy**, **Balenciaga** and **Jean-Paul Gaultier**'s new Starck-designed HQ. The vibe is trendier and less intimidating on rue du Faubourg-St-Honoré: after **Chloé**, **Lanvin** and **Bottega Veneta**, head down to rue St-Honoré for **John Galliano**'s outrageous fashions and the mother of Paris concept stores, **Colette**. For further details, *see pp221–2*.

Artazart *cult canal bookshop* `11 C1`
83 quai de Valmy, 10ème • 01 40 40 24 00
>> www.artazart.com Open 10:30–7:30 Mon–Fri, 2–8 Sat & Sun

Artazart is *the* place to stock up on books (mostly French) and international magazines that deal with everything from fashion and interiors to calligraphy. The interior of the store is decorated by French graffiti artist Miss Tic. Artazart is also a great spot to pick up the latest flyers for hot club nights and local events.

Ginger Lyly *funky designs* `11 C2`
33 rue Beaurepaire, 10ème • 01 42 06 07 73
Open 11:30–7:30 Tue & Thu–Sat, 2–7:30 Wed, 3–7:30 Sun

With its brightly painted frontage, Ginger Lyly draws a hip crowd on the look-out for groovy clothes and accessories. Vivid T-shirts and off-the-wall bags feature along with chintzy jewellery and raggedy hats. Walls host exhibitions by local artists and there is always some up-to-the-minute music in the air.

Antoine & Lili *colourful kitsch* `11 C1`
95 quai de Valmy, 10ème • 01 40 37 41 55
Open 11–8 Mon–Fri, 10–8 Sat

The brightly painted façades of these three adjoining boutiques give warning of their style. Young designs in vibrant colours are found in the pink house as well as quirky gifts; fresh flowers, plants, and homewares populate the green house; while the yellow house has a funky café with lip-smacking cheesecake.

E2 *everything old is new again* `11 A1`
15 rue Martel, 10ème • 01 47 70 15 14
Open by appt only

Husband-and-wife design team Michèle and Olivier Châtenet buy up classy vintage clothing (think Pucci, Hermès and Dior) and then transform it into modern must-haves. Imagine embroidered kilts, favoured by Gwyneth Paltrow and Madonna, or a whole new made-to-order outfit fashioned from a groovy old kimono.

Stella Cadente *canal style* `11 C1`
93 quai de Valmy, 10ème • 01 42 09 27 00
>> www.stella-cadente.com Open 11–7:30 daily

The boutique-cum-living-room of Stella Cadente, alias Ukranian-born designer Stanislassia Klein, was one of the first to appear on this street that fronts the now-trendy Canal St-Martin. Her dreamy, girly dresses, beaded cardigans and coats lined with flashy colours fit right in with the local, arty vibe.

Viveka Bergström *fantasy creations*   `5 D5`
23 rue de la Grange-aux-Belles, 10ème • 01 40 03 04 92
>> www.viveka-bergstrom.com Open 12–7 Tue–Sat

After honing her design skills at Paco Rabanne, innovative Swedish jeweller Viveka set up this cosy boutique, complete with home-from-home coffee tables and sofas. The designer, who works from a studio out back, is renowned for her pieces made from leather, precious metals and Swarovski crystals.

Coin Canal *retro heaven*   `11 C1`
1 rue de Marseille, 10ème • 01 42 38 00 30
>> www.coincanal.com Open 11–2 & 3–7:30 Tue–Sat

This corner shop is filled with lovingly selected pieces from the 1930s to the present day. Items are arranged in "rooms" and everything you see is for sale; from the Art-Deco drinks trolley to 1950s vases displayed on a 1960s wooden sideboard. Paintings by a Chinese artist, also for sale, add a contemporary touch.

Patricia Louisor *elegant bohemian*   `4 F3`
16 rue Houdon, 18ème • 01 42 62 10 42
>> www.patricialouisor.com Open noon–8 daily

One of the original boutiques that sparked the buzz about trendy Abbesses's alternative fashion scene. Louisor puts her own stylish spin on easy-to-wear garments, such as wide-legged trousers, flowing coats and jackets, and sweet *cache-coeurs* (wraparound tops) in delicate knits. Prices are very reasonable.

Lili Perpink *Japanese pick-and-mix*   `4 F2`
22 rue la Vieuville, 18ème • 01 42 52 37 24
Open 11:30–7:30 Tue–Sat (closed 1:30–2:30)

Scarcely bigger than a walk-in wardrobe, Lili's quirky little shop is a treasure trove of vintage fashion mixed with ultra-modern Japanese creations. Lili also keeps an eye out for up-and-coming European designers, stocking elaborate hand-knits by Irish designer No and feminine prints by French designer Julie Greux.

Spree *eclectic concept store* `4 F2`
16 rue la Vieuville, 18ème • 01 42 23 41 40
Open 11–7:30 Tue–Sat, Mon 2–7:30

When you first walk past Spree's window, it's hard to work out whether this is a retro furniture store, modern art gallery or cutting-edge fashion haven. The interior is punctuated with original Charles Eames and George Nelson chairs, and hung with Calder-like mobiles and 1960s Murano disc chandeliers, all of which can be bought. The warehouse-like space at the back of the store is devoted to fashion and boasts an excellent selection of international designers, including Comme des Garçons, Eley Kishimoto, Vanessa Bruno and Isabel Marant. Accessories scattered around the store include retro-style bags by Aurélie Mathigot, rings (designed to look as if they pierce your finger) by Pièces à Conviction and surreal silver jewellery by hip French label Lyie van Rycke. Spree is also the only place in Paris to find handmade ballerina shoes by E Porselli, otherwise available only in Italy.

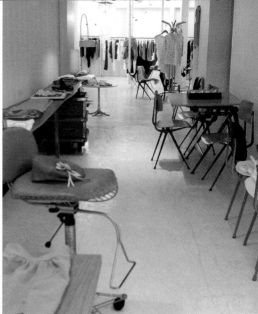

Shine *cutting-edge style* `18 F2`
30 rue de Charonne, 11ème • 01 48 05 80 10
Open 11–7:30 Mon–Sat

This trendy store (for women and men) stocks clothes from young designers mixed in with a sprinkling of urban sportswear and big-name labels, as well as unusual accessories. Highlights include Cacharel, See by Chloé and UK label Preen, and the delicate handknits of Macedonian designer Lidiya Georgieva.

Nuits de Satin *antique glamour* `11 D4`
9 rue Oberkampf, 11ème • 01 43 57 65 05
>> www.nuitsdesatin.com Open 12:30–7:30 Mon–Sat

An essential stop for anyone on the look-out for second-hand silk and satin lingerie. Choose from early 1900s corsets, pointy 1930s satin brassieres and sassy 50s swimsuits and suspenders. There's a good selection of groovy retro designer threads, too. No wonder this boutique is a favourite of stylists.

Isabel Marant *ethnic chic* `18 E2`
16 rue de Charonne, 11ème • 01 49 29 71 55
Open 10:30–7:30 Mon–Sat

Fashion hounds flock to this spacious Bastille boutique for Marant's youthful designs with an exotic edge. This is one designer who looks like she has some fun at her drawing board. Marant's imaginative designs favour natural fibres, often combined to create luxury items with a bohemian feel; a style that has made her one of Paris's top young designers. Clothes hang perfectly, especially fluid jersey dresses; flirty, floral tops and lots of silks and satin. When chilly winds blow, there's more substantial gear, including nubbly wool skirts cut on the bias, boiled wool coats with appliquéd or embroidered details, mohair jumpers and hippy-style bobble hats.

Recently, Marant has expanded to add accessories to her collection, in the shape of sassy bags and shoes, jewellery (delicate drop earrings and graceful silver necklaces) and perky singlets and shorts.

Alter Mundi *other worlds* `12 E5`
41 rue du Chemin Vert, 11ème • 01 40 21 06 65
>> www.altermundi.com Open 11–7:30 Tue–Sat, 2–8 Sun

This boutique-cum-gallery, housed in a vast loft-like space, operates on the principles of fair trade and showcases furniture and *objets d'art* from the developing world. Highlights include sandalwood vases from Mozambique, papier-maché sculptures from Burkina Faso and Mexican silver jewellery.

La Maison de la Fausse Fourrure `17 D1`
34 boulevard Beaumarchais, 11ème • 01 43 55 24 21
>> www.lamaisondelafaussefourrure.fr
Open 10–7 Mon–Sat (Mar–Aug: Mon–Fri)

Those who have qualms about following catwalk fur trends can ease their conscience by visiting this store. Stock up on everything from fake-fur fabric to imitation leopard-skin bags and tigerskin coats to furry lampshades and other household accessories.

Bastille Fashion Focus 18 F2

The 11ème tends to be associated with its nightlife buzz, but a daytime visit reveals a hive of independent fashion activity. One of the first young designers to move into the *quartier* and open her *atelier-boutique* on rue Keller was **Gaëlle Barré** *(see p221)*. This young woman turns out finely tailored collections based on mixing and matching prints. Indeed, her whimsical, feminine creations (50s-style dresses and tailored trench coats) frequently fuse polka-dots, stripes and floral patterns, all on the same garment.

Fellow rue Keller pioneer **Anne Willi** *(see p221)* works with a much more muted palette of colours, and natural fabrics such as linen and embroidered cotton. The simplicity of her style and her reversible clothes have been influenced by Japanese designers such as Yohji Yamamoto, but the charm of Willi's collections lies in the unusual details: halter-neck dresses tying with straps that dangle pebbles down the back or skirts decorated with criss-cross lacing up the side.

Continuing along the street, **Des Petits Hauts** *(see p222)* is just what its name says – a boutique specializing in "little tops" of every imaginable shape and colour. Styles range from casual khaki T-shirts and basic jumpers to strappy sorbet-coloured shift tops and sophisticated black evening-wear. On the rue de Charonne, which crosses rue Keller, **Catherine Magnan**'s *(see p221)* collections have more of an avant-garde feel – think striped men's shirts recycled into women's blouses and halter-neck patchwork tops. Her spacious tote bags made from recycled leather jackets are a sought-after Parisian fashion accessory.

art &
architecture

The city's great historic monuments have survived world wars intact, and its cultural treasures extend well beyond its enduring landmarks – many lesser known museums are set in stunning mansions. But Paris knows better than to rest on its laurels: new architectural and cultural projects sit next to the old, in harmonious juxtaposition.

Chez Robert Electron Libre *art house* `10 G5`

59 rue de Rivoli, 1er • no phone
»» www.59rivoli.org Open 1:30–7:30 Tue–Sun

Three artists first occupied this dilapidated, six-storey building in 1999. Today, the "squart" (a fusion of "squat" and "art") houses some 30 artists' studios and has become the city's third most visited centre of contemporary art, attracting around 40,000 fans of experimental art each year. Visitors can wander from studio to studio, watching artists at work alongside displays of their paintings, sculptures and installations. Most works are for sale. Despite its high profile, the place still has a ramshackle charm that makes a pleasant alternative to Paris's slick gallery scene and most artists are happy to chat about their work. Look out for Kalex's life-size figures – sculpted from old metal objects and rocks, and resembling abandoned extras from the *Lord of the Rings* film trilogy – and the work of Pascal Foucart, who drips bold, colourful paint on to canvas in hypnotic patterns.

Tour St-Jacques *medieval remnant* `16 H1`

Standing all alone on the place du Chatelet is a striking Gothic tower, the only remains of the 16th-century St-Jacques-La Boucherie church – a stopover point for pilgrims en route to Santiago de Compostela in Spain. Its gargoyle-covered summit witnessed the experiments into atmospheric pressure of French mathematician Blaise Pascal, whose statue stands outside. Aptly, the tower now serves as a weather station.

Ste-Chapelle *island chapel* `16 G1`

4 boulevard du Palais, 1er • 01 53 73 78 50
Open Mar–Oct 9:30–6 daily; Nov–Feb 9–5 daily

Hidden inside the Palais de Justice, this magical two-tiered Gothic chapel was built to house what Louis IX believed to be Christ's crown of thorns. Make straight for the upper level, which is spectacularly illuminated by huge, panoramic stained-glass windows, most of which date from the 13th century. **Adm**

Carte Musées-Monuments

Providing entry to 60 of the city's biggest sights and museums, including the Musée Picasso and Musée d'Orsay, this card lets culture aficionados cut costs and queues. Valid for one, three or five consecutive days, it is available from participating museums, branches of fnac *(see p222)*, tourist offices and major Métro stations.

Jeu de Paume *films and photos* `9 C3`
1 place de la Concorde, 1er • 01 47 03 12 52
Open noon–7 Tue–Fri, 10–7 Sat & Sun

Once an indoor court for real tennis, the Jeu de Paume is now an exhibition space concentrating exclusively on photography and the moving image. The temporary shows are either retrospective or thematic, and have included works by fashion photographer Guy Bourdin and experimental films from Jean-Luc Godard. **Adm**

Bibliothèque Nationale de France Richelieu *exhibition space* `10 F3`
58 rue de Richelieu, 2ème • 01 53 79 59 59
》 **www.bnf.fr** Galleries open 10–7 Tue–Sat, noon–7 Sun

Stripped of books since the new national library *(see p111)* opened in 1996, the original is still worth visiting for its breathtaking domed Salle Labrouse and for the frescoed galleries that host temporary exhibitions of mostly modern photography, drawings and engravings.

Musée Carnavalet *historical collection* `17 C1`
23 rue de Sevigné, 3ème • 01 42 72 21 13
Open 10–5:40 Tue–Sun

With a superb setting and exhibits that include paintings, furniture and personal artefacts, the Musée Carnavalet's colossal collection offers an authoritative and highly engaging history of Paris. Occupying two buildings, the museum was founded by Baron Haussmann, who had the foresight to preserve some of the Paris he was demolishing as he reshaped the city in the mid-1800s. The 16th-century Hôtel Carnavalet, one of the Marais' oldest *hôtels particuliers*, focuses on Paris from prehistoric times up until the 1700s. Its rooms are furnished with fabulous period furniture and paintings. The neighbouring *hôtel* picks up the story from 1789 to the present day and has France's biggest collection of Revolutionary exhibits. Check out the painting of Danton with his gargantuan head; in comparison, the portrait of fellow revolutionary Robespierre shows a far less powerful and rather prim leader. **Adm**

》 *Note that the Carte Musées-Monuments does not grant access to temporary exhibitions*

Musée National Picasso *100% Pablo* `11 C5`
5 rue de Thorigny, 3ème • 01 42 71 25 21
>> www.musee-picasso.fr Open 9:30–5:30 Wed–Mon

On Picasso's death in 1973, the French state waived the hefty inheritance taxes due in return for prime pickings from the artist's home and studio. Subsequent donations make this one of the most complete collections of Picasso's works, and one so popular that there are often long queues to get in.

The museum's exhibits – remarkable for their sheer diversity – are a chronological record of the artist's life. Visitors are taken from his simple but accomplished teenage sketches, through paintings of the famed Blue and Rose periods, to the massive, man-sized sculptures of Cubist heads. Must-sees include a series of little-known paper constructions; *Bull's Head* (a witty bronze that combines a bicycle saddle and handlebars to resemble the animal's head); and tribal masks from Picasso's personal collection which clearly inspired his work. **Adm**

Musée d'Art et d'Histoire `11 A5`
du Judaïsme *celebrating the Jewish diaspora*
71 rue du Temple, 3ème • 01 53 01 86 60
>> www.mahj.org Open 11–6 Mon–Fri, 10–6 Sun

In the heart of the Jewish area, the Marais, this absorbing museum traces the history and art of Judaism from the Middle Ages to the present day. Look out for Emile Zola's original *J'accuse!* article that denounced state anti-Semitism in the 19th-century Dreyfus affair. **Adm**

Les Galéries de Paris
In 19th-century Paris, the city's many *galeries* and *passages* served as fashionable meeting places as much as for shopping. With their attractive metal vaulting and glass roofs, they put most modern malls to shame. Galerie Vivienne (Map 10 F2) is the most up-market: Passages des Panoramas (Map 10 F3), built in 1800, is the oldest.

Musée de la Publicité *adverts as art* `10 E4`
107 rue de Rivoli, 1er • 01 44 55 57 50
>> www.museedelapub.org Open 11–6 Tue–Fri, 10–6 Sat & Sun

Temporary shows organized by theme (psychedelic posters), artist (Rene Gruau) or brand (Air France), and drawn from a fantastic array of posters, press ads and radio and TV commercials, are held within this wing of the Louvre. From the kitsch to the stylish, this collection acknowledges the power of persuasion. **Adm**

Patrimoine Photographique *photos* `17 C2`
62 rue St-Antoine, 4ème • 01 42 74 47 75
>> www.patrimoine-photo.org Open Tue–Sun 10–6.30

Hidden away in a peaceful garden at the back of
the 17th-century Hôtel de Sully, this intimate museum
is the public exhibition space for the vast national
photographic archives. The well-organized temporary
shows tend to revolve around historical themes or
individual photographers. **Adm**

Musée Cognacq-Jay *art museum* `17 C1`
8 rue Elzévir, 4ème • 01 40 27 07 21
Open 10–6 Tue–Sun

Founders of La Samaritaine department store,
Ernest Cognacq and his wife Louise Jay were also
keen collectors, notably of Rococo artists. Their
predilection for the 18th century is in evidence here,
with pieces that include gorgeous period furniture
and exquisite Saxe and Sèvres ceramics. **Adm**

Atelier Brancusi *reconstructed studio* `11 A5`
Place Centre Pompidou, 4ème • 01 44 78 12 33
>> www.cnac-gp.fr Open 2–6 Wed–Mon

Part of the Centre Pompidou *(see p99)*, this space
houses the reconstructed Parisian studio of influential
Romanian sculptor Constantin Brancusi (1876–1957).
Three cosy galleries display examples of his elegant,
abstract works, while another hosts temporary shows
by modern sculptors such as Richard Deacon. **Adm**

Eglise St-Eustache *city landmark* `10 G4`
Rue du Jour, 1er • 01 40 26 47 99
>> www.st-eustache.org
Open 9–7 Mon–Sat, 8:15–12:30, 2:30–7 Sun

The city's second-biggest church after Notre Dame,
St-Eustache (built 1532–1640) witnessed Louis XIV's
first Communion and holds the tomb of his influential
finance minister, Colbert. Its imposing exterior is
Gothic, while the interior is decidedly Renaissance.

>> *St-Eustache hosts regular free organ concerts*

Art & Architecture

Maison Européenne de la Photographie
picture perfect `17 B1`

5–7 rue de Fourcy, 4ème • 01 44 78 75 00

›› www.mep-fr.org Open 11–8 Wed–Sun

Of all the city's show spaces dedicated to photography, this one is possibly the best. The venue – with its vast, high-ceilinged rooms – usually organizes several simultaneous temporary exhibitions, drawing on its own and other collections. **Adm**

Institut du Monde Arabe
Arab centre `17 B3`

1 rue des Fossés St-Bernard, 5ème • 01 40 51 39 53

›› www.imarabe.org Museum open 10–6 Tue–Sun

Jean Nouvel's acclaimed building mixes modern steel and glass with traditional Arab architecture to stunning effect. The south-facing windows operate like a camera aperture, automatically regulating light. Inside, a museum houses a wide range of Arabic art and artefacts, as well as temporary exhibitions. **Adm**

Musée National du Moyen Age
`16 G3`

6 place Paul-Painlevé, 5ème • 01 53 73 78 00

›› www.musee-moyenage.fr Open 9–5:45 Wed–Mon

Built into the ruins of Roman baths, this handsome 15th-century mansion was formerly home to the Abbots of Cluny; it now houses a vast collection of medieval sculpture, ceramics, stained glass, furniture and tapestries. The baths themselves are a prime example of Gallo-Roman architecture: the frigidarium is spectacular, with its 15-m- (50-ft-) high vaults and traces of original mosaics. Key architectural finds from around Paris are displayed here, including the "Gallery of Kings": 21 carved stone heads, depicting the Kings of Judah, which were housed in Notre Dame for 500 years, but moved here just after the French Revolution. The museum's showpiece, however, is *The Lady and the Unicorn*, a series of six radiant Flemish tapestries. Don't overlook the museum's grounds, landscaped to echo gardening fashions of the Middle Ages. **Adm**

Check up on special opening days in Paris museums at ›› www.eparis.dk.com

Arènes de Lutèce *Roman recreation* `17 A5`
Entrances on 49 rue Monge & 7 rue de Navarre, 5ème • no phone
Open summer 8–10 daily; winter 8–5 daily

A rare remnant of the city's Roman past, this late 1st-century amphitheatre was unearthed in 1869. For 200 years, it welcomed up to 17,000 spectators at gladiatorial combats, until the Barbarians invaded Lutèce (Paris). Today, the games played here are less bloody; it's a favourite with *boules* players and skateboarders.

La Sorbonne *long-established centre of learning* `16 G3`
47 rue des Ecoles, 5ème • 01 40 46 20 15
➤➤ www.sorbonne.fr Visits by appointment: call 01 44 54 19 30

Founded as a theology college in the 1200s, La Sorbonne quickly gained a reputation as an intellectual stronghold. Classes were taught in Latin, giving rise to the area's name, Le Quartier Latin. The college was the hub of the student riots of 1968; if you want to get a taste of the more sedate student life of today, attend the free lectures open to the public or visit the the gold-domed 17th-century chapel.

Musèe de l'Assistance Publique `17 A3`
47 quai de la Tournelle, 5ème • 01 40 27 50 05
Open 10–6 Tue–Sun

This quirky museum traces the history of hospitals in Paris. Their social and religious roles are brought to life by paintings, manuscripts and a reconstructed pharmacy. Early surgical instruments also feature, including some oversized dental pliers that are a reassuring reminder of just how far medicine has come. **Adm**

Abbaye du Val-de-Grâce *museum* `20 F1`
227bis rue St-Jacques, 5ème • 01 40 27 50 05
Open noon–5 Tue–Wed, 1–5 Sat, 1:30–5 Sun

Built as a Benedictine abbey in the 17th century, this imposing complex includes a fine Baroque chapel and a museum on the history of the French military medical service. Gruesome exhibits include casts of the faces of disfigured soldiers who were the first subjects of maxilo-facial surgery during WWI. **Adm**

Musée du Luxembourg *art exhibitions* `16 E3`
19 rue de Vaugirard, 6ème • 01 42 34 25 95
»» www.museeduluxembourg.fr Open 11–7 daily

Situated within the grandiose Palais du Luxembourg, this museum hosts popular temporary shows. These are based around two themes: the Italian Renaissance (in tribute to the palace's founder, Marie de Médici) and 19th- and 20th-century art (a nod to the venue's previous incarnation as a modern-art museum). **Adm**

Eglise St-Sulpice *Left Bank church* `16 E3`
Place St-Sulpice, 6ème • 01 46 33 21 78
Open 7:30–7:30 daily

Similar in size and layout to Notre Dame, St-Sulpice demonstrates an intriguing mix of architectural styles because it took 120 years to build, starting in 1646. Its Italianate façade is topped by two famously uneven towers. Inside, there are three notable Delacroix frescoes in the Chapelle des Sts-Anges.

Musée National Eugène Delacroix `16 E2`
6 rue de Furstenberg, 6ème • 01 44 41 86 50
»» www.musee-delacroix.fr Open 9:30–5 Wed–Mon

The former apartment and studio of Romantic painter Delacroix (1798–1863) now house an intimate museum displaying his paintings and engravings, and tracing his life via photographs, personal belongings and letters. Drawings include studies for his celebrated murals inside nearby St-Sulpice. **Adm**

The Big Three
Justice cannot be done to the dauntingly large **Musée du Louvre** in a single visit, so stick to a specific period of art, or to the works of particular countries. Many of the smaller rooms contain gems, such as works by Dutch Masters that are often overlooked in the rush to see more famous exhibits. The **Musée d'Orsay** is synonymous with Impressionism, but the collection also includes major works by realist painter Gustave Courbet, Art Nouveau furniture and photographs – notably Man Ray's shot of Proust on his deathbed. Worth visiting for its stunning temporary exhibitions (as well as its architecture), the **Centre Pompidou** (aka the Centre Beaubourg) also has a splendid permanent collection of modern art. For details, *see p224.*

Musée Maillol –
Fondation Dina Vierny *muse's collection*

`15 D2`

59–61 rue de Grenelle, 7ème • 01 42 22 59 58
>> www.museemaillol.com Open 11–6 Wed–Mon

At the age of 15, Dina Vierny became the chief model
and creative muse of French sculptor Aristide Maillol
(1861–1944). Her subsequent collection of his work –
and that of his friends and contemporaries – is showcased in this grand *hôtel particulier*. Maillol's larger-
than-life marble sculptures dominate the entrance hall,
while his early years are well represented in rooms
dedicated to his drawings, Nabi-influenced paintings
and intricate tapestries. Other 20th-century artists
featured include Gauguin, a major influence on
Maillol, Pierre Bonnard and Maurice Denis *(see p106)*.
Works by Picasso, Degas, Cézanne and Odilon Redon
are illuminated in darkened drawing rooms, while
conceptual art gets a look in with Marcel Duchamp's
famed "Ready-Made" art. Note that the frequent
temporary exhibitions can attract long queues. **Adm**

Musée Rodin *the sculptor's former home*

`15 A1`

77 rue de Varenne, 7ème • 01 44 18 61 10
>> www.musee-rodin.fr
Open Apr–Sep 9:30–5:45 Tue–Sun (Oct–Mar to 4:45)

Along with artists Jean Cocteau and Henri Matisse,
sculptor Auguste Rodin rented rooms in this *hôtel
particulier* in 1908. Smitten with the state-owned pro-
perty, he donated all his work, personal archives and
belongings to the government in exchange for the
foundation of a museum here. Inside, the huge bronze
and marble sculptures include his famed *Kiss* and the
headless *Walking Man*, as well as a number of works
by Rodin's student and lover Camille Claudel. There
are also paintings by Monet, Renoir and van Gogh from
the artist's private collection, and furniture from his
house in Meudon. The museum's real charm, however,
lies outside in the spacious gardens, where *The
Thinker* is framed by the gold-domed Invalides. Nearby
are the triumphant *Burghers of Calais* and a masterful
monument to Balzac. One of Paris's real gems. **Adm**

Eglise de la Madeleine *Classical church* `9 C2`

Place de la Madeleine, 8ème • 01 44 51 69 00
Open 7:30–7 Mon–Sat; 9–1 & 3:30–7 Sun

Modelled on a Greek temple, the Madeleine church took almost 100 years to build. It was variously intended to be a stock exchange, a tribute to Napoleonic glory and a railway station before it was consecrated as a church in 1842. The magnificent marble-and-gilt interior features three stunning domes.

Eglise St-Augustin *high-rise church* `3 B5`

46 boulevard Malesherbes, 8ème • 01 45 22 23 12
Open 8:30–6:45 Mon–Fri; 8:30–1 & 2:30–6:45 Sat & Sun

Built in 1860–71, this was the city's first church to incorporate a metal frame, allowing its dome to rise to 50 m (164 ft). Architect Victor Baltard filled the triangular site by placing progressively larger chapels along the nave. The painted ceilings are the work of Classicist artist William Bougereau.

Musée Jacquemart-André *wealthy collectors' home* `2 H5`

158 boulevard Haussmann, 8ème • 01 45 62 11 59
>> www.musee-jacquemart-andre.com Open 10–6 daily

Dutch Masters, Italian Renaissance and 18th-century French art make the private collection of Edouard André and wife Nélie Jacquemart seem like a smaller, more manageable version of the Louvre. In addition, this purpose-built *hôtel particulier*'s opulent interior and contents create a fascinating record of 19th-century Parisian bourgeois life. **Adm**

Musée Galliéra *the story of style* `8 E3`

10 avenue Pierre 1er de Serbie, 16ème • 01 56 52 86 00
Open 10–6 Tue–Sun

This museum of sartorial style has a vast collection of clothing, accessories and photos with which to stage temporary exhibitions for followers of fashion. Shows range from displays of 18th-century waistcoats to the glitzy wardrobe of Marlene Dietrich. The museum is closed for two or three months a year. **Adm**

Along the Champs-Elysées 8 G2

It's been sung about, marched on, and plays host each year to the Bastille Day parade *(see p11)*, the Tour de France climax *(see p11)* and any other occasion for national celebration. Running from place de la Concorde up to Napoleon I's Arc de Triomphe, the 3-km- (2-mile-) long avenue, built by Baron Haussmann as part of his grand plan for a new Paris, still exudes a certain grandeur, even though it has suffered from an invasion of tacky, touristy shops and food outlets.

At its lower end, the expansive but traffic-heavy place de la Concorde is dominated by a 3,300-year-old granite obelisk, a gift from the Viceroy of Egypt. From here to the midway roundabout, the Champs-Elysées is bordered by gardens on both sides. The northern stretch of greenery backs on to the high-security 18th-century presidential residence, the Palais de l'Elysée, while the southern side is dominated by the colossal glass dome of the **Grand Palais** *(see p224)* and neighbouring **Petit Palais** *(see p224)*, both remnants of the 1900 Exposition Universelle. The former hosts diverse, crowd-pulling temporary shows, while the latter – usually home to the city's fine-arts collection – is undergoing a massive renovation programme (due to end autumn 2005) to improve lighting, increase exhibition space and generally restore its former glory.

At the back of the Grand Palais, the **Palais de la Découverte** *(see p225)* is a child-friendly science museum with a planetarium and an array of interactive exhibits relating to human biology, astronomy and meteorology. The hottest spot at the upper end of the avenue is the **Publicis Drugstore** *(see p83)*, reopened in 2004 after a daringly modern make-over by architect Michele Saee. The minimalist, curvaceous steel-and-glass-spiralled frontage sets it apart from its ornate, 19th-century neighbours.

>> *Some state buildings open to the public during the* Journées du Patrimoine *(3rd weekend in Sep)*

Art & Architecture »»

Musée d'Art Moderne de la Ville de Paris (MAMVP) *modern art* `8 E3`
11 avenue du Président Wilson, 16ème • 01 53 67 40 00
Open 10–6 Tue–Sun

The city's impressive 20th-century art collection occupies part of the Palais de Tokyo, a vast building that was originally built for the 1937 Exposition Universelle. Showpieces include diptychs by Henri Matisse and Raoul Dufy's *La Fée Electricité*. **Adm**

Palais de Tokyo *contemporary art* `8 E4`
13 avenue du Président Wilson, 16ème • 01 47 23 38 86
»» www.palaisdetokyo.com Open noon–midnight Tue–Sun

Complementing the adjoining MAMVP, this venue hosts cutting-edge art shows and installations. These are often site-specific, with artists creatively utilizing the vast proportions of the revamped interior. It's worth trying the basement restaurant, Tokyo Eat, for its designer good looks and food to match. **Adm**

Palais de Chaillot `7 C4`
17 place du Trocadéro, 16ème
Musée de l'Homme • 01 44 05 72 72
»» www.mnhn.fr
Open 9:45–5:15 Mon, Wed–Fri, 10–6:30 Sat & Sun
Musée de la Marine • 01 53 65 69 69
»» www.musee-marine.fr Open 10–6 Wed–Mon
Cité de l'Architecture et du Patrimoine • 01 58 51 52 00

The curved twin pavilions of the Palais de Chaillot are separated by a large terrace that offers spectacular views of the Tour Eiffel and beyond. In the west wing, the Musée de la Marine features a wealth of surprisingly interesting exhibits – such as Napoleon I's flamboyant imperial barge – that trace the glories of French maritime history. Major redevelopment of the Palais has seen the scaling down of the Musée de l'Homme (its amazing ethnographic collection is destined for the Musée du Quai Branly, due to open in early 2006). In its place, the Cité de l'Architecture et du Patrimoine, a museum of modern architecture, is due to open in early 2006. **Adm**

Musée Marmottan-Monet *Monets galore*

2 rue Louis Boilly, 16ème • 01 42 24 07 02 • Ⓜ Ranelagh
>> www.marmottan.com Open 10–6 Tue–Sun

The Musée Marmottan-Monet boasts the world's largest collection of works by Claude Monet – all thanks to a generous donation by the artist's son. Rich pickings include an early series of Le Havre caricatures and a flurry of watercolours from travels to London, Normandy and Norway. The famous series of paintings of Rouen cathedral at different times of the day is also on show here. Don't miss the purpose-built basement, which displays a number of vibrant water-lily paintings inspired by the artist's garden at Giverny. Complementing the Monets are major works from fellow Impressionists Berthe Morisot, Manet, Degas, Renoir, Gauguin and Alfred Sisley. Most recently, the museum has added a collection of over 300 wonderfully crafted, medieval illuminated manuscripts from the English, French, Italian and Flemish schools. **Adm**

Musée Guimet *oriental art* `8 E3`

6 place d'léna, 16ème • 01 45 05 00 98
>> www.museeguimet.fr Open 10–6 Wed–Mon

Recently renovated, the four floors of this excellent museum of Asian art contain *objets*, paintings and sculptures from most of the major Eastern cultures over five millennia. Highlights include exquisite Japanese wood-block prints, archaeological finds from Pondicherry, India, and Chinese ceramics. **Adm**

Fondation Le Corbusier *modern architecture*

Villa La Roche, 10 sq du Dr Blanche, 16ème • 01 42 88 41 53
>> www.fondationlecorbusier.asso.fr • Ⓜ Jasmin
Open 10–12:30 & 1:30–6 Mon–Fri (to 5pm Fri)

Modernist architect Le Corbusier designed this private house in 1923 for his fellow countryman, the Swiss art collector Raoul La Roche. The adjoining Villa Jeanneret was built for Le Corbusier's brother and is now home to the Foundation's offices. Originally conceived as part of a larger development, only these two houses were actually built. Pioneering his now-celebrated five points of architecture, Le Corbusier harnessed natural light and applied his Purist theory to the colour scheme. Villa La Roche itself, with its triple-height space, swooping curved gallery and blocks of colour, is the star of the show. Its rooms also feature small displays of the architect's paintings, furniture, drawings and sculpture. **Adm**

Château de St-Germain *notable château*
Place Charles de Gaulle, St-Germain-en-Laye • 01 39 10 13 00
»» www.musee-antiquitesnationales.fr
RER St-Germain-en-Laye Open May–Sep 9–5:15 Mon, Wed–Fri,
10–6:15 Sat & Sun, Oct–Apr 9–5:15 Wed–Mon

This imposing castle is set next to the River Seine, in gardens that were designed by Le Nôtre in the 1680s. Most of the building dates from the 1500s and now houses an outstanding archaeological collection. **Adm**

Musée Départemental Maurice Denis "Le Prieuré" *Nabi art*
2bis rue Maurice Denis, St-Germain-en-Laye • 01 39 73 77 87
»» www.musee-mauricedenis.fr • RER St-Germain-en-Laye
Open 10–5.30 Tue–Sun (to 6.30 Sat & Sun)

An exceptional collection tracing the birth of early 20th-century avant-garde art, the museum here includes works by Denis and his fellow Nabi painters. Don't miss the pretty sculpture-lined garden and chapel. **Adm**

Canal St-Martin Boat Trip *Paris from the water* `17 D3`
Linking the Seine with the Canal d'Ourcq, the Canal St-Martin offers the opportunity to cruise through northern Paris. Barges (www.canauxrama.com) depart from Bastille's Port de l'Arsenal (9:45 & 2:30) and take two-and-a-half hours to travel through attractive tree-lined alleys, tunnels (look out for Keiichi Tahara's entrancing art installations), locks, and under swing bridges before arriving at Parc de la Villette. This large, modern park is also home to the Cité de la Musique *(see p108)*, Le Zenith *(see p124)* and Cité des Sciences et de l'Industrie *(see p108)*. **Adm**

Musée de l'Erotisme *erotic assemblage* `4 E3`
72 boulevard de Clichy, 18ème • 01 42 58 28 73
Open 10am–2am daily

The city's only museum that's open until 2am is, perhaps unsurprisingly, dedicated to erotic art and located in the red-light district of Pigalle. Ignore the tacky window displays; this is actually an intriguing collection where sacred *objets d'art* sit next to temporary exhibits by artists such as comic-book artist Robert Crumb. **Adm**

Montmartre *elevated attractions* `4 F2`

The hill of Montmartre has become even more tourist-struck since the worldwide success of the 2001 film *Amélie*. Most visitors previously stuck to the place du Tertre, with its hordes of caricaturists and wannabe artists, and the landmark **Sacré Cœur** church *(see p223)*, from which there are magnificent views of the city. Now, the tourist trail includes homages to *Amélie*'s local greengrocers, re-named Maison Collignon as in the film, and to her favourite bar, the **Café des Deux Moulins** *(see p214)*, the interior of which is hung with pictures of the leading lady, Audrey Tautou.

However, the real charm of Montmartre lies in its romantic, village atmosphere. Reminders of its past as a working-class, rural community (until absorbed into Paris in the late 19th century) include two windmills, the **Moulin de Radet** *(see p224)* and **Moulin de la Galette** *(see p224)*. Even some vineyards remain here, like those on the rue des Saules (Map 4 F1), which produce around 1,000 bottles of perfectly drinkable wine each year.

From the 1880s, a bohemian boom attracted writers and artists aplenty: the Bateau-Lavoir (destroyed in the 70s) housed the studios of iconic painters Modigliani, Picasso and Braque; and the studios of Renoir and Dufy were located in what is now the **Musée de Montmartre** *(see p225)*. The museum offers an intriguing insight into the *quartier*'s artistic past and contains some original Toulouse-Lautrec posters. Nearby, the sculpture of a man apparently engulfed by the neighbouring wall is a tribute to Marcel Aymé's *Le Passe-Muraille*, a novel about a government worker who could walk through walls. A recent local addition is a fibre-optic lighting artwork installed in the stairs on rue du Chevalier de la Barre (Map 4 G1), which illuminates at night to form the shapes of different constellations.

Musée de la Musique *music matters*
Cité de la Musique, 221 avenue Jean Jaurès, 19ème
01 44 84 46 00 • Ⓜ Porte de Pantin
» www.cite-musique.fr Open noon–6 Tue–Sat, 10–6 Sun

With the benefit of infrared headsets, visitors can sample sounds from Venetian lutes, Flemish harpsichords and a host of other instruments on display. Each day on the free stage, musicians play everything from 17th-century horns to modern African pipes. **Adm**

Cité des Sciences et de l'Industrie
Parc de la Villette, 30 avenue Corentin Cariou, 19ème
01 40 05 80 00 • Ⓜ Porte de Pantin
» www.cite-sciences.fr Open 10–6 Tue–Sun (to 7 Sun)

This well-planned centre presents science and technology in their many forms via exhibits, audio-visual installations and interactive displays. The complex also contains the huge Géode dome cinema, a 3D film theatre with moving seats, and a 1950s submarine. **Adm**

Stade de France *stunning arena*
rue Francis de Pressensé, St-Denis • 01 55 93 00 45
Ⓜ St-Denis Porte de Paris
» www.stadefrance.fr Visits on the hour 10–5 daily

The spectacular oval stadium dominating the St-Denis skyline was built for the 1998 football World Cup. Even the cheapest of its 80,000 seats offers great visibility of major sports events and rock concerts. Tours take visitors into changing rooms and VIP boxes. **Adm**

Basilique St-Denis *royal mausoleum*
1 rue de la Légion d'Honneur, St-Denis • 01 48 09 83 54
Ⓜ Basilique de St-Denis
Open 10–7 Mon–Sat, noon–7 Sun (Oct–Mar to 5 daily)

An industrialized suburb it may be, but St-Denis, with its majestic church, is generally considered the birthplace of Gothic architecture. It is also the resting place for most the French kings. Look out for the ostentatious tombs of François I and Claude de France. **Adm**

Musée d'Art et d'Histoire de St-Denis *local history*

22bis rue Gabriel Péri, St-Denis • 01 42 43 37 57
Ⓜ St-Denis Porte de Paris
Open 10–5:30 Mon–Fri (to 8 Thu), 2:30–6:30 Sat & Sun

Set in a former Carmelite convent, this museum alone merits a trip out to St-Denis. Highlights include the cramped reconstructed nuns' cells and a unique collection of posters from the 1871 Paris Commune. **Adm**

Musée Gustave Moreau *artist's home* `4 E4`

14 rue de la Rochefoucauld, 9ème • 01 48 74 38 50
≫ www.musee-moreau.fr Open 10–12:40 & 2–5:15 Wed–Mon

Troubled by the thought of anonymity, the Symbolist painter Moreau (1825–98) established an autobiographical museum in the studio and apartment he shared with his parents just before his death. Thousands of Moreau's often mystical paintings and drawings are on show, as well as memorabilia. **Adm**

Porte St-Denis & Porte St-Martin `11 A2`

These towering twin gates, just yards apart, were intended to lend the city a Roman grandeur. They are particularly striking today, in what has become a rather seedy part of north Paris. The larger Porte St-Denis was erected in 1672 and depicts battle scenes marking the triumph of Louis XIV's armies along the Rhine, while the Porte St-Martin was constructed two years later to commemorate the capture of Besançon.

Last Resting Places

Tree-lined **Cimitière de Père-Lachaise** is the largest, best-known cemetery in Paris. After the remains of dramatist Molière and poet La Fontaine were transferred here in 1817, it began attracting famed "residents" and skilled sculptors. The most visited grave is that of singer Jim Morrison; the quirkiest is the statue of 19th-century journalist Victor Noir: women rub his now-faded crotch to increase their chances of getting pregnant. The famous dead of **Cimitière de Montmartre** include the writer Zola, painter Degas and film director François Truffaut. Meanwhile, the small **Cimitière de Passy** has the highest density of famous names. Look out for the painter Manet, composers Debussy and Fauré, and actor Fernandel. For details, *see p223*.

≫ *The Cité des Sciences et de l'Industrie (see p108) can be reached by boat along the Canal St-Martin (see p106)*

Art & Architecture

Opéra Garnier *lavish venue* 9 D1

Place de l'Opéra, 9ème • 08 92 89 90 90

>> www.opera-de-paris.fr Open 10–5 daily (except matinées)

Architect Charles Garnier's national opera house is a glorious monument to Second Empire opulence. The façade is magnificently decorated with friezes and sculptures, while the interior is no less impressively embellished. A museum traces opera history via paintings, photographs and set models. **Adm**

Gare du Nord *monumental railway station* 5 A4

Opened in 1864 to cope with the rapidly increasing traffic on the railways, architect Jacques Ignace Hittorff's station is a grandiose example of 19th-century iron-and-glass vaulting, often overlooked by rail travellers rushing from A to B. The vast interior is fronted by an imposing, Roman-inspired stone façade lined with statues that personify the north European towns served by the station.

Seine-side Attractions

Few people know that a scaled-down **Statue of Liberty** (Map 13 B3) stands guard on an island in the Seine in the west of Paris. Donated in 1885 by the American community in Paris, it also acts as a reminder that the New York original was a gift from the French. Towards the city centre, on the river's right bank by the Place d'Alma, the golden **Liberty Flame** (Map 8 F4) is a return gift from the city of New York. Its proximity to the tunnel where Princess Diana was killed has made it her unofficial memorial. Between these two stands Gustave Eiffel's world-famous tower, which has long survived its status as a temporary exhibit for the 1889 Exposition Universelle. The **Tour Eiffel**'s *(see p224)* recently added white lights sparkle on every nocturnal hour until 2am, and cause almost as much controversy today as the tower did when it was first erected.

Opposite the sculpture-filled **Jardin des Tuileries** *(see p165)*, the colonnaded **Assemblée Nationale** *(see p224)* is the French parliament, which can be visited on a guided tour. Further east lies the domed home to the **Académie Française** (Map 16 E1), protector of the French language. Beyond here, the Seine is divided by the **Ile de la Cité** (Map 16 G2), the largest of Paris's two central islands and home to the city's iconic Gothic cathedral, **Notre Dame** *(see p223)*. On the island's other side, the turreted **Conciergerie** *(see p224)* was a 14th-century palace and, more famously, the prison of Marie Antoinette and family. Visitors here can learn about the French Revolution and view the reconstructed royal cell.

Of the 37 Seine bridges, the most spectacular is the Art Nouveau **Pont Alexandre III** (Map 9 A4), lined with gilded lamps and cherubs. The **Pont des Arts** (Map 10 F5) is popular for romantic rendezvous.

Nemo's Murals *public art* `12 2H`

Graffiti artist Nemo has been stencilling his "Shadow Man" on building façades around Paris since 1990. The silhouetted figure with its trademark suitcase pops up in poorer districts, like the 20th arrondissement (most spectacularly at 36 rue Henri Chevreau). Such is Nemo's notoriety that he now receives commissions, including a project around rue Mouffetard in the 5ème to commemorate the Bièvre, Paris's underground river.

Ministère des Finances *landmark* `22 F1`

The new headquarters of the finance ministry is a dominating, three-building riverside complex that was completed in 1989. Architects Borja Huidobro and Paul Chemetov designed the spectacularly arched Colbert building – part of which overhangs the Seine to provide boat access for visiting officials – to echo the form of the nearby metro viaduct. The whole package is best viewed from the Pont de Bercy.

Musée du Cinéma *cinema heaven* `22 G2`

51 rue de Bercy, 12ème
>> www.51ruedebercy.com

The former home of the ill-fated American Center was designed by Frank Gehry and is being renovated to accommodate a mecca for cinephiles (due to open in 2006). The complex will include four cinemas, temporary exhibition space and a museum that looks back on a century of film-making. **Adm**

Bibliothèque Nationale de France `22 F3`
– François Mitterrand *modern library*

11 quai François Mauriac, 13ème • 01 53 79 53 79
>> www.bnf.fr Galleries open 10–7 Tue–Sat, noon–7 Sun

A hallmark of Mitterrand's presidency was his ambitious architectural *Grands Projets*. The last of these, a controversial library building, consists of four L-shaped towers, designed to look like half-open books. It hosts regular exhibitions of photographs and drawings.

Les Frigos *warehouse studios* `22 F4`
rue des Frigos, 13ème • 01 44 24 96 96
>> www.les-frigos.com

After years of struggle, this huge artists' community has won the right to stay in the old refrigerated warehouses of the SNCF. Call for details of the twice-yearly official open days, usually organized in May and September. Otherwise, impromptu individual visits are usually permitted.

Louise Weiss Galleries *art central* `21 D3`
The vibrant art scene on rue Louise Weiss has not looked back since 1997, when a project was hatched to group a number of galleries (mostly open 11–7 Tue– Sat) on this small street in the developing 13th arrondissement. Try Galerie Praz-Delavallade (www.praz-delavallade.com, at No. 28), with its focus on US artists, or Galerie Emmanuel Perrotin (at No. 30), a showcase for European and Japanese talent.

Cité Universitaire *campus buildings*
Boulevard Jourdan, 14ème • 01 43 13 65 96
>> www.ciup.fr • Ⓜ Cité Universitaire

These wildly eclectic residences were built from 1925, and still house foreign university students. The Asian and Armenian colleges follow their respective national architecture; the Swiss (by Le Corbusier) and Dutch (by Willem Dudok) express these notable architects' individual styles.

Manufacture des Gobelins *tapestries* `21A3`
42 avenue des Gobelins, 13ème • 01 44 08 52 00
Visits Tue–Thu at 2pm & 2:45pm

Founded in 1662 to supply Louis XIV with royal furnishings, the Gobelins factory still uses 17th-century techniques to produce tapestries that are now hung in state buildings and embassies. Conducted in French, guided visits take in the factory, the Beauvais tapestry and Savonnerie carpet workshops. **Adm**

Catacombes *underground Paris* `20 E3`
1 place Denfert Rochereau, 14ème • 01 43 22 47 63
Open 10–5 Tue–Sun

Illicit parties are sometimes held in the miles of tunnels beneath Paris, but the Catacombes, an ossuary since 1785, are easier to get into. Visitors stroll through subterranean corridors lined – often artistically – with bones and skulls moved here from overcrowded cemeteries of the period. **Adm**

Fondation Cartier pour l'Art Contemporain *modern exhibitions* `19 D2`
261 boulevard Raspail, 14ème • 01 42 18 56 72
» www.fondation.cartier.fr Open noon–8 Tue–Sun

Jean Nouvel's spectacular glass building houses regular exhibitions of relatively well-known contemporary artists, such as William Eggleston and Pierrick Sorin, with an emphasis on art installations, videos and photography. **Adm**

Fondation Henri Cartier-Bresson `19 B2`
2 impasse Lebouis, 14ème • 01 56 80 27 00
» www.henricartierbresson.org
Open 1–6:30 Wed–Fri & Sun (to 8:30 Wed), 11–6:45 Sat

Founder of the reputed Magnum photo agency, Henri Cartier-Bresson intended this centre to house the bulk of his work. At present, the affiliated museum hosts three shows a year, occasionally including Bresson's work, but mostly that of exciting younger artists. **Adm**

Mémorial du Maréchal Leclerc `19 B1`
23 allée de la Deuxième, 15ème • 01 40 64 39 44
Open 10–5:40 Tue–Sun

Actually two museums, the exhibits here focus on two French WWII heroes. Projected archive footage shows the Liberation of Paris under Leclercq, his Free France Forces and the Allies. Photographs and posters document the situation inside occupied France from the perspective of Resistance martyr Jean Moulin. **Adm**

» *For details of evening events at the Fondation Cartier pour l'Art Contemporain,* see p17

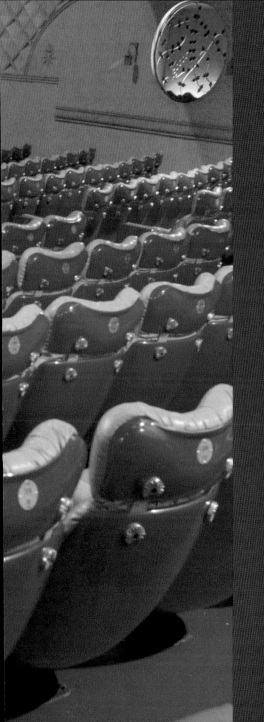

performance

From high-brow classical opera and theatre to radical circus acts and *chanson*, Paris offers a rich diversity of performance arts. Cinephiles are spoilt for choice by the city's numerous art-house cinemas, dance aficionados enjoy performances by both rising and well-established companies, and music fans can pick from leading classical orchestras and international acts.

TOP CHOICES – *performance*

TOURING BANDS	CUTTING-EDGE	FREE
Duc des Lombards 42 rue des Lombards, 1er This laid-back venue is famed for uniting exceptional exponents of modern jazz in exciting late-night jam sessions. *(See p118)*	**Bouffes du Nord** 37bis boulevard de la Chapelle, 10ème This famously shabby theatre stages an eclectic programme of plays and music, and is the HQ of innovative director Peter Brook. *(See p122)*	**Maison de la Radio France** 116 avenue Président Kennedy, 16ème The home of France's national radio station offers regular free concerts of classical music and big-name popular musicians. *(See p122)*
Bataclan 50 boulevard Voltaire, 11ème It's sweaty and it's smoky, but this well-loved spot just oozes atmosphere. Expect bands such as Sigur Ros and George Clinton. *(See p126)*	**Centre National de la Danse** 1 rue Victor Hugo, 93507 Pantin This acclaimed dance centre puts on public performances of new work by talented choreographers. *(See p124)*	**Cinéma en Plein Air** Parc de la Villette, 19ème Join the chilled-out crowds at these popular free film screenings in a park setting. There's a different theme each year. *(See p124)*
Le Zénith 211 avenue Jean Jaurès, 19ème Offering excellent visibility and acoustics, Le Zénith is a huge, hanger-like venue for blockbuster acts. *(See p124)*		>> *In the summer months, Paris hosts a string of festivals, many of which include free performances that span the musical spectrum (see pp10–11).*
Elysée Montmartre 72 boulevard Rochechouart, 18ème This former music hall hosts the kind of international bands (such as Travis and Marillion) that wouldn't quite fill Le Zénith. *(See p123)*	**Cartoucherie de Vincennes** route du Champ de Manœuvre, 12ème A five-theatre complex located in the Bois de Vincennes. Each venue has its own distinct character and artistic agenda. *(See p125)*	**La Flèche d'Or** 102 rue de Bagnolet, 20ème On weekdays, the early-evening music act at this quirky venue is free. Occasionally, evening gigs are too. *(See p126)*
New Morning 7–9 rue des Petites-Ecuries, 10ème An intimate jazz club that pulls the crowds for respected players such as Cuban pianist Omar Sosa. *(See p122)*		

Check what's on in music, theatre, sport and more at >> www.eparis.dk.com

HIGHBROW	ALTERNATIVE	FILM
Opéra Garnier Place de l'Opéra, 9ème Home to fiction's *Phantom of the Opera*, the sumptuous Garnier is best known for its excellent ballet performances. *(See p122)*	**Café de la Gare** 41 rue du Temple, 4ème Despite straying from its idealist roots, this legendary *café-théâtre* still offers quality short plays and one-man shows. *(See p119)*	**MK2 Bibliothèque** 128–62 avenue de France, 13ème A multiplex located in a classy Seine-side complex. The tall guy in front is never a problem thanks to well-spaced, comfortable seats. *(See p127)*
Comédie Française 2 rue de Richelieu, 1er Established by Louis XIV in 1680, this is still the city's prime venue for classical French theatre. *(See p119)*	**Cirque d'Hiver Bouglione** 110 rue Amelot, 11ème Traditional circus acts are given a modern spin here. Expect anything from contortionist choreography to tightrope acrobatics *(See p125)*	**Le Champo** 51 rue des Écoles, 5ème Director Claude Chabrol called this Left Bank cinema his "second university". The popular retrospectives often run for over a year. *(See p120)*
	Hôtel du Nord 102 quai de Jemmapes, 10ème The novelty of Anglophone stand-up comedy at a historic Paris landmark draws expats and Parisians alike. *(See p123)*	**La Pagode** 57bis rue de Babylone, 7ème Incongruously situated in a very bourgeois *quartier*, this Japanese pagoda is one of the city's most eccentric film venues. *(See p118)*
Théâtre du Châtelet 1 place du Châtelet, 1er The diverse programme here includes high-quality opera alongside progressive classical music and dance. *(See p119)*		**Studio 28** 10 rue Tholozé, 18ème Studio 28 claims to be the first-ever avant-garde cinema and upholds its reputation by screening around ten films per week. *(See p123)*
Opéra Bastille Place de la Bastille, 12ème The strikingly modern Opéra Bastille is Paris's main opera venue. Events range from the conservative to the avant-garde. *(See p122)*		**Le Grand Rex** 1 boulevard Poissonnière, 2ème Classified as a Historical Monument, this legendary 1930s cinema still hosts many a glitzy première. *(See p119)*
Théâtre des Champs-Elysées 15 avenue Montaigne, 8ème This venue earned its place in classical music history thanks to performances by such icons as Maria Callas and Debussy. *(See p121)*		>> *Many independent cinemas are cheaper on Wednesdays, and sometimes on Mondays too.*

La Pagode *oriental art-house cinema* `15 A2`
57bis rue de Babylone, 7ème
01 45 55 48 48 Film times vary: call for details

Shipped over brick-by-brick from Japan in 1895, this striking pagoda, complete with an ornamental Japanese garden, became a cinema in the 1930s. Jean Cocteau chose it for the premiere of his *Le Testament d'Orphée* in 1959. Now classified a historical monument, it has two screens and shows recent independent films.

Forum des Images *Paris on film* `10 G4`
Forum des Halles (Porte Eustache), 1er • 01 44 76 62 00
>> www.forumdesimages.net Research room open 1–9 daily

This centre archives films, documentaries, adverts and newsreels – anything connected with Paris. Visitors can search the database of some 6,500 films (from Lumière brothers shorts to *Superman II*) to watch on a personal screen. The cinema also screens several films a day in themed programmes. **Adm**

Le Point Virgule *small-scale comedy* `17 B1`
7 rue St-Croix de la Bretonnerie, 4ème
01 42 78 67 03 Performances at 8, 9:15 and 10:30pm daily

This tiny Marais *café-théâtre* organizes a prolific programme of one- and two-man comedy shows. From packed rows of slightly uncomfortable benches, spectators watch impromptu sketches, humour-spiced songs and surreal musical acts. Several shows a day are held during the popular summer Festival d'Humour.

Booking Tickets
Many venues have booking offices, but most people buy tickets at branches of **fnac** and **Virgin Megastores** or online at www.ticketnet.fr. Buy half-price theatre tickets in person on the day of performance from either of **Kiosque Théâtre**'s two outlets. For contact details, *see p13*. You can book cinema tickets at **Allociné** (08 92 89 28 92).

Duc des Lombards *hot jazz* `10 H5`
42 rue des Lombards, 1er
01 42 33 22 88 Open daily

Since opening in 1985, this respected jazz club has picked up several industry awards and maintained its ultra-cool reputation by attracting some of Europe's biggest names. Music ranges from free jazz to hard bop, and artists who have jammed here include trumpeter Eric Truffaz and bassist Henri Texier.

Comédie Française *classic theatre* `10 H4`
2 rue de Richelieu, 1er • 08 25 10 16 80
» www.comedie-francaise.fr Box office open 11–6 daily

Founded by Molière's troupe in 1680, this state
theatre is famed for its classical French productions
(Molière, Racine, Corneille), but an added draw is the
surprisingly intimate 896-seat Italianate auditorium.
Adventurous programming now sees regular forays
into established modern and foreign works.

Café de la Gare *rebel humour* `11 A5`
41 rue du Temple, 4ème • 01 42 78 52 51
» www.cafe-de-la-gare.fr.st

Born out of post-1968 populism, this, the original
café-théâtre, is still Paris's best for one-man shows,
comedy and short plays. The venue brought fame to
satirical comic Coluche, actor Patrick Dewaere and
writer/actor Sotha, all of whose works are still
performed to a mixed and enthusiastic audience.

Théâtre du Châtelet *historic venue* `16 H1`
1 place du Châtelet, 1er • 01 40 28 28 40
» www.chatelet-theatre.com Box office open 10–7 Mon–Sat

World-class ballet, opera and classical music
productions are the draw at this illustrious theatre. A
recent re-orientation in programming has given a more
contemporary direction (music by Pierre Boulez and
dance from Maurice Béjart). Excellent morning concerts
(Mon, Wed, Fri) are held in the foyer (entry charged).

Le Grand Rex *cinematic grandeur* `10 H2`
1 boulevard Poissonnière, 2ème • 01 45 08 93 58
» www.legrandrex.com Open daily, tours at regular intervals

Opened in 1932, the city's largest cinema has an
Art Deco façade and splendid Baroque-style decor.
Audiences of up to 2,650 come here for blockbuster
movies, concerts and the celebrated Christmas-time
son et lumière. Entertaining behind-the-scenes tours
feature Disney-esque special effects.

Left-Bank Cinemas *film buff's heaven* `16 G3`

Beyond the clusters of chain cinemas around Odéon and Montparnasse, the 5th and 6th arrondissements arguably offer the richest variety of art-house cinemas in the world. Some 20 – with a total of 39 screens between them – are located around boulevard St-Michel and form a cinephile's paradise. All films are shown in their original language (VO or *version originale*) with French subtitles where necessary, and the diversity is truly staggering. The tiny rue Champollion alone is home to three such cinemas. Film aficionados have a special affection for **Le Champo**, a regular haunt of *Nouvelle Vague* directors Jean-Luc Godard and François Truffaut, who nurtured their encyclopedic knowledge of cinema here. The entrance is adorned with memorabilia dedicated to Jacques Tati, while the main screen has Europe's only "periscope" projector, so-called because the projection room is situated below the screen. Known for its retrospective seasons (think Alain Resnais and Tim Burton), Le Champo also organizes debates in the presence of famed directors, as well as popular all-nighters. Just down the road, the **Reflet Medicis** specializes in major classics and retrospectives, while the **Quartier Latin** (which accommodates just 70 people) prides itself on exclusive premieres.

For classic American films, try the three Action cinemas. The **Grand Action** dreams up inventive seasons that span careers, themes and genres such as Love-Hate, Gangsters and The 100 Best Films. The **Action Ecoles** treats viewers to diverse retrospectives (from Buster Keaton to Blake Edwards), while the **Action Christine Odeon** favours 1950s movies. Other popular venues include **Images d'Ailleurs** (black cinema), **Racine Odeon** (legendary all-night sessions), **Studio Galande** (weekend screenings of *The Rocky Horror Picture Show*) and **St-André-des-Arts**, where contemporary *auteurs* are just as likely to be in the audience as they are to be screened.

Théâtre des Champs-Elysées 8 G3

15 avenue Montaigne, 8ème • 01 49 52 50 50
>> www.theatrechampselysees.fr
Box office open 10–noon & 2–6 Mon–Fri

Described by writer Marcel Proust as "a temple to music, architecture and painting", this theatre was where the infamous premiere of Stravinsky's *Rites of Spring* (1913) ended in riots and Joséphine Baker starred in her ground-breaking *Revue Nègre* in 1925.

Today, the historic 1913 theatre, with its dome painted by Maurice Denis *(see p106),* still hosts the *crème de la crème* of classical music. Concerts are almost unfailingly excellent: home of the Orchestre National de France and Orchestre Philharmonique de Radio-France, the venue also attracts top international orchestras (Vienna, Berlin), legendary singers (Luciano Pavarotti, Cecilia Bartoli) and renowned conductors (Pierre Boulez, Seiji Ozawa). Outstanding ballet productions have included turns by the New York City Ballet and the brilliant choreographer Maurice Béjart.

Lucernaire *one-stop entertainment* 15 D5

53 rue Notre-Dame-des-Champs, 6ème • 01 45 44 57 34
>> www.lucernaire.fr

Converted from an old factory, this vibrant Left Bank arts centre houses two theatres, three cinemas, an art gallery, a bar and a restaurant. The eclectic theatre programming favours new talent and innovative pieces, such as one-man condensed classics, while the cinemas show recent art-house releases.

Théâtre de la Ville *hip dance* 16 H1

2 place du Châtelet, 4ème • 01 42 74 22 77
>> www.theatredelaville-paris.com
Box office open 11–7 Mon–Sat, 11–8 Tue–Sat

This prestigious 1860s-built theatre has become the city's leading venue for contemporary dance. The 1,000-seat auditorium attracts innovative performers such as Pina Bausch and La La La Human Steps. World-music concerts and plays are also staged here.

Maison de la Radio France *concerts* `13 B2`
116 avenue Président Kennedy, 16ème
01 42 30 22 22

This distinctive circular building is home to French state radio. The Salle Olivier Messiaen hosts an eclectic repertoire of classical music, usually by one of two resident orchestras. Concerts are often free, including those in the music festival Présences (Jan–Feb) and one-off gigs by big names such as Peter Gabriel.

New Morning *no-frills club* `11 A1`
7–9 rue des Petites-Ecuries, 10ème • 01 45 23 51 41
≫ www.newmorning.com

Located on a run-down street with an all-but-hidden entrance, this is possibly the city's most famous jazz venue. Beloved of serious fans and musicians alike, the club was Chet Baker's favourite and, since opening in 1981, has attracted the key exponents of jazz, blues and Latin music from Roy Ayres to Taj Mahal.

Bouffes du Nord *dilapidated charm* `5 B2`
37bis boulevard de la Chapelle, 10ème • 01 46 07 34 50
≫ www.bouffesdunord.com Box office open 11–6 Mon–Sat

After years of neglect and with only minimal restoration, this legendary vaudeville theatre was reopened in 1974 by English director Peter Brook. The ramshackle interior provides a terrific backdrop for its often groundbreaking productions: an exciting menu of modern and reinvigorated classic plays, as well as jazz, opera and contemporary music. Performances here really benefit from the building's extraordinary acoustics.

A Night at the Opera
Crowned by Marc Chagall's gorgeous ceiling frescoes, the stunning auditorium of **Opéra Garnier** *(see p110)* is in fact used mostly for quality ballet productions and some lesser-known operas. The mainly classical repertoire is often given a modern slant in terms of design and choreography. The 2,700-capacity **Opéra Bastille** *(see p226)*, with its vast, curving glass façade, was commissioned by Mitterrand as an "opera for the people", but escalating construction costs have inflated the ticket prices (obscured views are, however, still available for just 5€). Classical opera is the mainstay here, with occasional ballet and classical-music concerts. Tickets are always in demand, so advance booking is well advised. Both venues offer daily guided tours.

Hotel du Nord *Anglo stand-up* `11 C1`
102 quai de Jemmapes, 10ème • 01 53 19 98 88
>> www.anythingmatters.com

Made famous by the eponymous 1938 Marcel Carné
film, this former hotel now showcases the best in
Anglophone stand-up comedy. With a decor that out-
classes that of most comedy joints, this intimate
venue attracts big-name performers (Daniel Kitson,
Boothby Graffoe) who often try out new material here.

Elysée Montmartre *concert venue* `4 G3`
72 boulevard Rochechouart, 18ème • 08 92 69 23 92
>> www.elyseemontmartre.com Box office open 9–7:30 Mon–Sat

This large Pigalle venue – now one of the city's best
for indie rock and trip-hop – stills bears vestiges of
its past life as a 19th-century music hall. Elaborate
carvings on the walls and ceiling add a certain grandeur to concerts, salsa nights and the popular twice-
monthly balls, which feature cover bands and DJs.

Studio 28 *quirky and convivial screenings* `4 E2`
10 rue Tholozé, 18ème • 01 46 06 36 07
>> www.cinemastudio28.com

Opened in the 1920s, this popular independent cinema
was once frequented by film icons Luis Buñuel and
Abel Gance and, more recently, fictional local resident
Amélie. Showing current art-house releases, classics
and pre-releases, it also holds monthly debates
featuring leading directors and well-known actors.

Cité de la Musique *modern music hall*
221 avenue Jean Jaurès, 19ème • 01 44 84 44 84
>> www.cite-musique.fr • Ⓜ Porte de Pantin

Designed by French architect Christian de Portzamparc,
this music-oriented complex at Parc de la Villette
includes a state-of-the-art oval auditorium that hosts
everything from classical to world music and contemporary jazz. Try to catch one of the classic silent-film
screenings that are accompanied by live music.

Cinema programmes change every Wednesday. Check www.allocine.fr or Pariscope for listings

Performance

Le Zénith *giant multipurpose venue*
211 avenue Jean Jaurès, 19ème • 01 42 08 60 00
» www.le-zenith.com/paris • Ⓜ Porte de Pantin

Purpose built by the state as a venue for popular music, Le Zénith benefits from great acoustics and an intimate atmosphere, despite its 6,400 capacity. The interior of the tent-like structure can be adapted as required, whether for French *chanson*, a big-name rock concert, ice-skating spectacle or sport event.

Cinéma en Plein Air *picnic and a movie*
Parc de la Villette, 19ème • 01 40 03 75 75 • Ⓜ Porte de Pantin
» www.villette.com Screenings Jul–Aug 10pm Tue–Sun

On fine summer evenings, the large lawn at Parc de la Villette is strewn with picnickers and cinephiles enjoying the night's free film. The huge inflatable screen shows recent blockbusters and classic foreign movies (all in original language) based around a different theme each year. Deck chairs are available for hire.

Centre National de la Danse *dance*
1 rue Victor Hugo, Pantin 93507 • 01 41 83 27 27
» www.cnd.fr • Ⓜ Hoche RER Pantin

This 1970s concrete office building on the banks of the Canal de l'Ourcq was refurbished in 2004 to house the HQ of the innovative National Dance Centre. Inside are no fewer than 11 dance studios; three serve as cosy spaces for cutting-edge shows by young choreographers from all over the world.

Come to the Cabaret

Cabaret is alive and kicking in the city where it first began, but it can be an expensive night out. Shows at the iconic **Moulin Rouge** have the expected formula of Doriss Girls, clad in feathers, sequins and rhinestones, dancing the cancan. At the **Lido**, it's the Bluebell Girls who are centre stage, accompanied by special laser effects, while at the **Paradis Latin**, designed by Gustave Eiffel, the dancers are joined by trapeze artists and a ventriloquist. **Crazy Horse**, meanwhile, advertises itself as an exponent of "the art of nudity", though it is more tasteful than the idea of topless dance routines suggests. To escape the domain of wealthy tourists, try the gloriously kitsch cross-dressing at **Chez Michou** or the even camper **Chez Madame Arthur**. For contact details, *see p225.*

Café de la Danse *eclectic sounds* `18 E2`
5 passage Louis-Philippe, 11ème • 01 47 00 57 59
>> www.chez.com/cafedeladanse

Despite its name, this intimate venue hosts everything
from folk-rock and world music to a cappella, as well
as modern dance. Overlooking the auditorium (which
holds about 450 people) is a small balcony with a
bar – the best vantage point from which to enjoy
bands that are normally found playing bigger venues.

Cirque d'Hiver Bouglione *circus* `11 D4`
110 rue Amelot, 11ème • 01 47 00 12 25
>> www.cirquedhiver.com Performances Oct–late Feb/early Mar

Built in 1852, this spectacular, polygonal circus ring witnessed the birth
of the trapeze when Jules Léotard appeared here almost 150 years ago.
Each winter, the Bouglione family devise a new, enthralling show that
features trapeze artists, clowns, magicians, contortionists and animal
acts from around the world. And every year (Jan–Feb), the venue hosts
an international festival featuring the circus stars of tomorrow.

Cartoucherie de Vincennes *radical theatre*
Route du Champ de Manœuvre, Bois de Vincennes, 12ème
Ⓜ Château de Vincennes with free shuttle bus

This complex of five small theatres and three workshops was converted from a disused munitions factory
in the 1970s. The site is off the beaten track and best
reached by taxi, but it's worth the trek as the theatres'
repertoires are prolific and stimulating.

Founded after the riots of 1968, the **Théâtre du Soleil**
was the first to establish itself here and, under the
direction of Arian Mnouchkine, is still turning out political epics. Philippe Adrien's energetic troupe stages a
mix of the avant-garde and the classical at the **Théâtre
de la Têmpète,** while Julie Brochen at the **Théâtre de
l'Aquarium** programmes imaginative productions of
Chekhov and Tolstoy alongside music-accompanied
poetry and Japanese *butô* dance. The **Théâtre du
Chaudron** favours young companies, often with women
directors, while the **Théâtre de l'Epée de Bois** is known
for its progressive take on contemporary works.

Performance

Bataclan *historic venue*
50 boulevard Voltaire, 11ème
01 47 00 55 22

This former vaudeville theatre may have lost its original Chinese pagoda façade, but the sumptuous interior still provides an enticing setting for the varied concerts of indie, trip-hop, French *chanson* and world music. The charming auditorium has a fantastic vibe, but the acoustics can be less than perfect.

La Flèche d'Or *rock on a railway theme*
102 rue de Bagnolet, 20ème • 01 43 72 04 23
›› www.flechedor.com • Ⓜ Alexandre Dumas/Maraîchers

Converted from an abandoned train station, the atmospheric Flèche d'Or puts on daily concerts – sometimes for free – of ska, reggae, pop and rock. Decorated with railway bric-a-brac, the large space has a bit of an underground feel and attracts an exciting mix of artists, creative types and students.

Le Regard du Cygne *experimental dance*
210 rue de Belleville, 20ème • 01 43 58 55 93
›› redcygne.free.fr • Ⓜ Télégraphe

This small and intimate dance space has been hugely influential in promoting new forms of artistic expression. The bare-bones studio is famed for its occasional Spectacles Sauvages, when artists showcase work in progress during lively ten-minute slots. Classical- and contemporary-music concerts are also held here.

La Guinguette Pirate *concerts afloat*
Quai Francois-Mauriac, 13ème • 01 43 49 68 68
›› www.guinguettepirate.com

This three-masted Chinese junk on the Seine hosts an extremely varied programme of music for party-loving audiences of up to 200. Feel the narrow boat rock to hip-hop and indie concerts or sway gently to jazz and world music. Film screenings and improvized theatre shows also make it aboard on occasions.

Théâtre de la Cité International

21 boulevard Jourdan, 14ème • 01 43 13 50 50
RER Cité Universitaire
>> www.theatredelacite.ciup.fr Box office open 2–7 Mon–Sat

This three-stage theatre is known for its creative and energetic shows. The Grand Théatre puts on modern plays, dance and circus acts; the Galerie's movable seating lends itself to cutting-edge theatre; and the tiny Reserre hosts readings and small productions.

MK2 Bibliothèque *cinema complex* `22 F3`

128–62 avenue de France, 13ème • 08 92 69 69 96
>> www.mk2.com/bibliotheque/seat.html

Paris's artiest cinema chain conceived its latest outpost under the slogan "a whole life [centred] around cinema". Located next to the Bibliothèque Nationale *(see p111)*, the stylish mega-complex has 14 screens, four eateries and two shops. Two-person lovers' seats on every row are an extra draw for couples.

Spectator Sports

Most sports events are within easy reach of the city. One of the big four tennis grand-slam events, the two-week French Open, is held at **Roland Garros** at the end of May. Apply for tickets two months before the tournament; guided tours and the museum are available year round. November brings the men back for the Tennis Masters Series at the **Palais Omnisport de Paris-Bercy** (POPB), while the leading women return in March for the Open Gaz de France (at the **Stade Pierre de Coubertin**).

Although most of France's leading footballers have been lured abroad, passionate crowds still cheer on Paris St-Germain at the 50,000-capacity **Parc des Princes**. International games and Cup finals, however, are hosted at the magnificent **Stade de France**. Major athletics meetings are also held here, as well as home games of the popular Six Nations rugby tournament (tickets for which can be hard to come by). The highly successful Stade Français rugby club plays at **Stade Jean-Bouin**.

For racecourses, head to the edges of Paris's two woods. **Paris-Vincennes** favours trotting (harness racing), while **Longchamp** is reserved for flat racing, including Europe's richest race, the Prix de l'Arc de Triomphe in October. Showjumping tops the bill at POPB in March, with the Jumping International de Paris. In fact, over the year, POPB hosts everything from windsurfing and motocross to international gymnastics, basketball and ice-skating.

Tickets for most sports fixtures can be purchased at major ticket agencies *(see p118)*, as well as through department stores **La Samaritaine** and **Les Galeries Lafayette** *(see p220)*. It is wise to book in advance for most events and avoid *revendeurs* (ticket touts). For all contact details, *see p226*.

bars & clubs

The City of Lights comes into its own after dark, when the bobos (bourgeois bohemians), beautiful people, intellectuals and other Parisian tribes set forth on their separate drinking trails. Pick your crowd, and explore the myriad bars, clubs and cafés scattered around the city – you're bound to find the cocktail and the company of your choice.

COCKTAILS	DESIGNER DRINKS	TRADITIONAL BARS
Hemingway Ritz Hotel, 15 place Vendôme, 1er The daddy of Paris's cocktail bars, and a super-sophisticated place to sip a superb dry Martini or the signature concoction, a Ritz 75. *(See p133)*	**AZ Bar** 62 rue Mazarine, 6ème Expect a lovely setting, amazing floral displays, beautiful people and expertly mixed drinks – all in true Conran style. *(See p142)*	**Le Café Noir** 65 rue Montmartre, 2ème The furnishings might be traditional, but Le Café Noir is a trendy spot, full of bright young things making themselves at home. *(See p135)*
Harry's 5 rue Danou, 2ème Birthplace of the Bloody Mary and the haunt of in-the-know cocktail aficionados. Be warned: they never stint on measures here. *(See p136)*	**Hotel Costes** 239 rue St-Honoré, 1er Designed by Jacques Garcia in 1997 and still resolutely hip. It's worth trying to get a table at the bar of the Hotel Costes. *(See p132)*	**Au Petit Fer à Cheval** 30 rue Vieille du Temple, 4ème The old-fashioned decor here was so well-loved that it was totally recreated after a recent fire. The zinc bar is the star of the show. *(See p138)*
Le Crocodile 6 rue Royer Collard, 5ème Eccentric and fun, Le Crocodile is a place to come if you love cocktails but hate the slick surroundings that often accompany them. *(See p141)*	**Le Bar du Plaza** Plaza Athenée, 25 ave Montaigne, 8ème A real see-and-be-seen destination bar: you'll find sleek design, potent cocktails and the rich-and-famous out on the town. *(See p145)*	**Bar des Théâtres** 6 avenue Montaigne, 8ème An old-fashioned bar-restaurant, with an unusually mixed clientele for such an up-market address. *(See p145)*
China Club 50 rue Charenton, 12ème One of the Bastille's most suave and sophisticated bars, with low lighting, huge sofas, a well-dressed crowd and serious cocktails. *(See p148)*	>> *The bars at any of the palace hotels (see p177) are a good option if you're looking for drinks that have a certain chichi style.* 	
Fu Bar 5 rue St-Sulpice, 6ème The Fu Bar is all about flavoured Martinis (try the apple, or the sweeter lychee), served with style and a smile. *(See p141)*		**Le Sancerre** 35 rue des Abbesses, 18ème For a slice of old Montmartre and its most exciting café crowd, Le Sancerre cannot be beaten. Great beer and bonhomie. *(See p148)*

MICROBRASSERIES

Frog & Princess
9 rue Princesse, 6ème
One of the four Parisian Frog pubs, the Princess is probably the most fun. It offers a choice of four or five different home brews. *(See p132)*

La Fabrique
56 rue de Faubourg St-Antoine, 11ème
Home brew and hipsters often don't mix, but beer fans love La Fabrique's hoppy brew while designer kids lap up the atmosphere. *(See p148)*

>> *When you order* un demi *don't expect to get half-a-litre of beer; the glass actually contains just half that amount of amber nectar.*

O'Neil
20 rue de Cannettes, 6ème
One of the quieter pubs in the area, O'Neil pulls in both French and international drinkers attracted by the beer brewed on the spot. *(See p132)*

>> *In Paris, microbrasseries, which brew their own beers, are few and far between and tend to be popular with English-speaking expats and Anglophones.*

AFTER HOURS

Le Connetable
55 rue des Archives, 3ème
A quintessentially French bar that is fantastic fun after 1am and shows that Parisians certainly do know how to let their hair down. *(See p137)*

Le Bar
27 rue Condé, 6ème
Whether you come to chat up or chill out, this is a stylish choice for rounding off the night. *(See p135)*

Mathi's
3 rue Ponthieu, 8ème
Very hip and hard to get into, Mathi's only starts to get exciting around 2am. Come before midnight if you want to try and get a table. *(See p145)*

WONDERFUL WINE

Juveniles
47 rue de Richelieu, 1er
British-owned and internationally known, this bar has an impressive New World list, and it also sells wine to take home. *(See p133)*

La Belle Hortense
31 rue Vieille du Temple, 4ème
Bookshop, bar and off-licence too, this place is ideal for intellectuals who appreciate their wine. Only French wines are on offer. *(See p139)*

Le Baron Rouge
1 rue Theophile Roussel, 12ème
Attracting a rambunctious crowd and brimming with exceptionally good red wine, Le Baron Rouge is a Paris institution. *(See p151)*

Le Clown Bar
114 rue Amelot, 11ème
Despite the clown memorabilia, not everything is taken lightly here. Certainly not the wine list, which is full of well-priced choices. *(See p149)*

Chai 33
33 court St-Emilion, 12ème
The largest and trendiest of the city's *bistrots à vins* has wine-based cocktails and a superb wine list. *(See p150)*

Bars & Clubs

Le Fumoir *chic and sleek all-rounder* `10 F5`
6 rue de L'Amiral de Coligny, 1er • 01 42 92 00 24
Open to 2am daily

With its beautiful, long mahogany bar, well-stocked library and trendy terrace across from the Louvre, Le Fumoir is equally perfect for pre-dinner drinks, late-night cocktails, a little light refreshment after some art appreciation or a quiet afternoon with a pot of tea and one of the books borrowed from the groaning shelves.

Le Cab *posh party place* `10 F4`
2 place du Palais Royal, 1er • 01 58 62 56 25
» **www.cabaret.fr** Open to 3am Mon & Tue, to 6am Wed–Sat

Very plush and upscale, Cab (formerly Cabaret) has been open for three years, but there's no such thing as growing old gracefully for a club like this. A make-over in 2003 – all leather wall coverings, squishy banquettes and smooth lines – has kept the beautiful people flocking here to pout, preen and party. **Adm**

Hotel Costes *sexy bar* `9 D3`
239 rue St-Honoré, 1er • 01 42 44 50 00
» www.hotelcostes.com Open to 1am daily

The bar here is a rare creature: a hot spot that has kept its cool, despite the fact that it's been serving drinks to the style set since 1996. The plush Napoleon II bordello decor continues to provide a lush, sensual backdrop for *le beau monde*, and the intimate nooks and crannies are still likely to hide a celebrity or two.

Brit Pubs

Parisians in search of a pint, anglophiles yearning for a bit of South Kensington-on-Seine and expats pining for a local all gravitate towards one of the city's pubs. Beer aficionados will love the home-brew at **O'Neils**, the **Frog & Princess** and **Freedom**. Trad pub decor and rowdy drinking can be found at **The Cricketer**, while a slightly more sedate crowd heads for the ale at the **Bombardier**. Pool players and gig lovers hang at the **Cruiscin Lan**, while other Irish *pubeen* fans swear by **Corcoran's** for great *craic*, or **Coolin** for Celtic cool. Whisky lovers drink at the **Auld Alliance** while Paris's other Scottish pub, **The Highlander,** is perfect for party animals: at weekends the bar and dance floor are open late and always packed. For further details, *see pp211, 212 & 217.*

Le Coeur Fou *lovely local* `10 G3`
55 rue Montmartre, 2ème • no phone
Open to 2am daily

Small but beautiful, Le Coeur Fou is always packed with friendly thirtysomethings who hit this place straight from their graphic design studios/art galleries/Internet start-ups for several rounds of apéritifs. You'll find modern art on the walls, a busy bar, smiley staff and an irrepressibly sociable vibe.

Juveniles *fine wine bar* `10 F3`
47 rue de Richelieu, 1er • 01 42 97 46 49
Open to midnight Mon–Sat

Here, you'll have to pick your way past the haphazardly stacked crates of great wine – especially the New World selection – to reach the bar. The staff (who know their wine but won't patronize you if you don't) and the loyal hard-drinking hacks from nearby newspaper offices make this a top place to savour a bottle or two.

Hemingway Bar *Ritzy experience* `9 D3`
Ritz Hotel, 15 place Vendôme, 1er • 01 43 16 30 30
>> www.ritzparis.com Open to 2am Mon–Sat

The first thing you need to know about the Hemingway Bar is how to find it. This gem of a drinking hole is expertly concealed (no signs) within the Ritz Hotel, but the trek past the reception to the back of the building – taking a right after the overstuffed sofas and roaring fire, and continuing along the carpeted corridor – is most definitely worth it.

The Hemingway is a tiny nook of dark-wood panelling, low-lighting, black-and-white photos of Papa himself, fascinating clientele and superb cocktails. The place abounds with stories, the most famous being the tale of Hemingway "liberating" the bar at the end of WWII. Legend has it that the Old Man deemed the bar at the Ritz *the* place to enjoy the first round of "free" drinks after the Allies arrived. A high accolade indeed, given that Hemingway drank in earnest and patronized almost every bar around at the time. For further tales of glamour, glitz and alcohol, ask head barman Colin Field, who was voted the world's best bartender for several consecutive years and is certainly Paris's most charming host. Colin's mouthwatering cocktail list is impressively extensive and includes the delicious Ritz Champagne (a wonderful mixture of apples and fizz), the Ritz 75 (a heady mix of gin, champagne and citrus fruits) and the stunning Raspberry Martini (fresh raspberries macerated in premium vodka).

This clubby den is probably the only place in Paris where you can listen to scratchy piano music played on a wind-up gramophone, watch the bartender sabre a bottle of vintage champagne, sip stunning drinks – which arrive with a flourish for the gentlemen and a flower for the ladies – and slip into a timeless reverie. The captains of industry, trust-fund babes, Lotharios and cocktail aficionados mingling at the bar aren't perturbed by the prices, and even more ordinary folk on tight budgets tend to think it's worth the splurge for a little slice of bar heaven.

Bars & Clubs

Kong *manga dream*

1 rue du Pont Neuf, 1er • 01 40 39 09 00
>> www.kong.fr Open to 2am daily

10 G5

Philippe Starck's Asian-inspired project, Kong, sits atop Kenzo's flagship store and offers a riot of designer-kitsch to shoppers and bar-hoppers alike. Kong's interior is a chaotic jumble of neon lights, acid colours, Zen-grey pebble rugs, Tokyo street scenes playing on big screens, life-size images of geishas, rocking chairs, Hello Kitty and manga merchandise, and Pokemon-motif cushions. And that's all before you've headed to the top floor – as everyone does – for the views over the Seine from the bar's wrap-around windows. The upper level's toilets are also worth a look, bedecked with glitter balls and beaded curtains, and guarded by giant images of sumo children.

This is definitely not the place to be if minimalism is your mantra. If, however, you like bright lights in your big city then the clutter and chaos of Kong is sure to tick all the boxes. The clientele is just as colourful as the backdrop: party puppies and fashionistas clamour for space at the bar, while trust-funders chill out in the rocking chairs. Cocktails are served in glasses of intense hues by surprisingly friendly aspiring models and wannabe actresses, and sipped to an eclectic soundtrack. This is played on an innovative music system that allows diners to vote for their favourite tunes from a menu of ten categories, including Sugar Pop and Glam Chic. A very reason-ably priced happy hour (6–8pm daily) means that this place gets going before most of the city's other fashionable drinking destinations. It's definitely best to get there early if you want to get one of the sleek, silver Starck-designed stools in a prime spot at the bar. Another way to guarantee a seat is to book a table for dinner. But beware: as in most see-and-be-seen destinations, the food is pricey, average and really not the point.

Le Next *friendly local DJ bar* `10 H3`
17 rue Tiquetonne, 2ème • 01 42 36 18 93
Open to 4am Mon–Fri, to 5am Sat

This often-rowdy joint, with its slightly schizophrenic design scheme (a nondescript bar at the front, leopard print and red velvet out back), attracts a big-drinking crowd. As its name suggests, Le Next is a perfect stop on a bar crawl, but it also cuts it as a destination drinking haunt or pre-club rendezvous.

Somo *chic and sleek* `10 G2`
168 rue Montmartre, 2ème • 01 40 13 08 80
>> www.hip-bars.com Open to 2am Mon–Thu, to 4am Fri & Sat

Somo's laid-back vibe attracts both twentysomethings and financial types from the nearby stock exchange. They come in droves for the great cocktails – try the delicious champagne-based mixes or the lethal-but-lovely mojitos. Low-slung leather chairs, chill-out music and subdued lighting complete the picture.

Le Café Noir *bobo spot* `10 G3`
65 rue Montmartre, 2ème • 01 40 39 07 36
Open to 2am Mon–Sat

A retro-chic café, complete with winking neon signs, formica tables and boozy bonhomie. Le Café Noir is home from home to countless bourgeois bohemians (bobos), who come to get their creative juices flowing and discuss anything from tonight's hottest club to the trainers worn by the bloke behind the bar.

Le Rex *superstar DJs, dedicated clubbers* `10 G1`
5 boulevard Poissonnière, 2ème • 01 42 36 10 96
>> www.rexclub.com Open to 6am Wed–Sat

Big on famous names and atmosphere, but low on attitude, this place is all about the music. Be prepared to queue for weekend sessions from top DJs (French and international), but other nights are ultimately no-fuss, hardcore dancing sessions led by the next big thing. Brilliant house music and truly top techno. **Adm**

Le Bar *well-kept secret* `16 F3`
27 rue Condé, 6ème • 01 43 29 06 61
Open to 4am Mon–Sat

Le Bar is a late-night gem: the narrow back bar's dim lighting and leather benches are perfect for a spot of seduction, and the gravel floor is certainly unusual. As this is such an insider's address, people tend to mingle easily. The owners often serve up iced vodka shots when it's time to stagger out in the early hours.

>> *In clubs, buying a bottle and smiling sweetly is often the best way to get a table*

Harry's Bar *home of the hangover cure* `10 E2`
5 rue Daunou, 2ème • 01 42 61 71 14
» www.harrys-bar.fr Open to 3am daily

The American accents, the saloon-bar look and US and UK college crests lining the walls might give the impression that this venerable drinking institution is little more than an ersatz slice of home for expats pining for Uncle Sam or John Bull. Not so. Harry's is a temple for all who shun temperance, regardless of their nationality. The owner's claim that the first Bloody Mary was invented in the bar comes as no surprise: given the loyalty of its regulars, the amount of time they spend propping up the bar and their commitment to all things alcoholic, inventing a brilliant hangover cure must have been a logical step. Harry's isn't for the lily-livered or the faint of heart: the measures are vast and it's a riotous place where people table-hop with gay abandon. But once you've been, you'll always come back, if only for a mean Bloody Mary the morning after the night before.

Pulp *wild club nights* `10 G1`
25 boulevard Poissonnière, 2ème • 01 40 26 01 93
» www.pulp-paris.com Open to 6am Wed–Sat

Except for Saturday's Lesborama – one of Paris's best lesbian club nights – this spot also welcomes boys (both gay and straight). Goths, rock chicks, R&B divas and disco queens are all catered for with Pulp's varied events – the common denominator being a deep-seated desire to party. Check the web for details. **Adm**

Café Thoumieux *sleek vodka bar* `8 H5`
4 rue de la Comète, 7ème • 01 45 51 50 40
» www.thoumieux.com Open to 2am Mon–Sat

In the bar-deprived 7th arrondissement, this spot is a good bet for a quiet night spent sipping cocktails. The speciality is flavoured vodka, of which there's an impressive range behind the colourful tiled bar. The velvet banquettes and comfy stools are usually occupied by well-heeled expats and young professionals.

Seek out the old cafés of Paris with » www.eparis.dk.com

Andy Wahloo *trendy souk-chic* `11 A3`
69 rue des Gravilliers, 3ème • 01 42 71 20 38
Open to 2am daily

Created by the same team behind Sketch (London) and
404 (Paris), Andy Wahloo proves that small can be
beautiful. Empty drums of paint serve as stools for the
hipsters who cram in to share a hookah, knock back
the cocktails or sip mint tea. Giant posters and rows
of pop bottles round off the atmospheric clutter.

Boob's Bourg *for ladies* `11 A4`
26 rue de Montmorency, 3ème • 01 42 74 04 82
Open to 2am Tue–Sun

It's worth seeking out this stellar lesbian bar, which is
a little off the beaten drinking path. Lovely ladies, old
lushes and straight female friends are guaranteed
a warm welcome at Boob's Bourg. Two floors of
relaxed girls – gossiping, giggling and giving good bar
banter – make for an attitude-free haven of a hang-out.

Le Connetable *traditional haunt* `11 B4`
55 rue des Archives, 3ème • 01 42 77 41 40
Open to 4am Mon–Thu, to 6am Fri & Sat

Think of all the clichés of the French *bon viveur*: moustachioed and merry, belting out *chanson*, smiling
lasciviously, smoking furiously and getting slowly
soused over several bottles of dubious wine. Then
come and join him and his friends at Le Connetable,
a highly idiosyncratic spot that comes into its own
after midnight, when the volume level rises, the sing-
ing kicks off, the couple in the corner start to get frisky,
and the groups at the bar freely intermingle. The dusty
silk-flower arrangements, dog-hair-covered sofa and
rowdiness might not seem the greatest of draws. However, pretty young things and aged *rouées* play up a
storm on the out-of-tune piano, notions of great
philosophical importance are hotly contested over yet
another glass of red, and fast friendships are made.
One of the city's best nights out, and one that almost
always goes on until dawn.

Amnesia *popular gay bar* `17 B1`

42 rue Vieille du Temple, 4ème • 01 42 72 16 94

» www.amnesia-cafe.com Open to 1:45am daily

Chilled-out by day, Amnesia turns up the tempo after aperitif-time, when it morphs into a buzzy little bar that is a popular pre-club venue. A Marais institution and one of the local gay bars that welcomes straights, this place has a well-deserved reputation as a fun spot for drinks, discussion and delightful company.

L'Etoile Manquante *great café* `17 B1`

34 rue Vieille du Temple, 4ème • 01 42 72 48 34

Open to 2am daily

This laid-back café is equally good for afternoon *cafés*, pre-dinner drinks or late nightcaps. Modern lighting and art perk-up the trad café decor, and don't worry about the video installation in the toilets: the cameras may catch you preening in the mirror, but the images are only shown in the bathroom area.

Au Petit Fer à Cheval *venerable zinc bar* `17 B1`

30 rue Vieille du Temple, 4ème • 01 42 72 47 47

» www.cafeine.com Open to 2am daily

Adored by many, Au Petit Fer à Cheval sports a handsome horseshoe-shaped bar (often said to be Paris's finest) that is invariably jammed with people sipping good red wine. Elbow room is hard to find, though, and it's worth settling for one of the tables for some of the Marais's finest people-watching opportunities.

Chez Richard *relaxed chic* `17 B1`

37 rue Vieille du Temple, 4ème • 01 42 74 31 65

Open to 2am Tue–Sat

Elegant but relaxed, Chez Richard is a great place to go for quiet drinks or as a prelude to a big night out. Expect exposed stone, leather banquettes, seating for romantic tête-à-têtes, and long tables downstairs for groups of friends or people who like to strike up conversations with strangers.

La Belle Hortense *bookworms & barflies* 17 B1

31 rue Vieille du Temple, 4ème • 01 48 04 71 60
» www.cafeine.com Open to 2am daily

A quintessentially Parisian mix of alcohol and intellectualism can be found at La Belle Hortense, an unusual combination of bookshop and bar. Serious tomes line the shelves and the clientele is encouraged to leaf through the latest Mario Vargas Llosa and indulge in a bit of lit-crit with the clever barflies perched at the zinc bar. The back room is smoke-free and quieter, with art for sale on the walls, leather banquettes, and low tables clustered together to make debating the latest hot topics that little bit easier.

The strictly French wine list, though relatively short, is well chosen and very well priced, and most of the bottles can be bought to take home. Listen, and you might hear tall tales from the regulars – who often claim to have been drinking partners with most of the 20th-century's great authors – philosophical arguments, debates about critical theory, or Sorbonne professors scoffing at their colleague's latest book. However, despite the formidable IQs present, this place is devoid of pretension, and it's not unusual for people to suddenly start dancing the tango, or engage in other less-dignified pursuits. For lofty literary minds, posters around the bar advertise plenty of events and meetings. Try the monthly Proust reading group or attend a happening book launch. (Catherine Millet's hit sexual memoir *La Vie Sexuelle de Catherine M* debuted here.) Or leaf through the piles of flyers for other cultural events taking place in venues across the city.

Les Etages *designer grunge* `17 B1`
35 rue Vieille du Temple, 4ème • 01 42 78 72 00
Open to 2am daily

In this tall, shabby building, magnificent mojitos and a surreal dive-bar ambience awaits. Each floor of the bar – which looks more like a squat than the chic spot it is – has a different mood, though the hobo decor reigns throughout. The top floors are where the fun is, but room-swapping is the way to make new friends.

Le Cox *gay hot spot* `11 A5`
15 rue des Archives, 4ème • 01 42 72 08 00
Open to 2am daily

Almost as risqué as its name suggests, Le Cox is always full of beautifully turned-out boys. The interior – remodelled every three months to keep things looking fresh – provides a fitting backdrop. There's plenty of eye-candy and eye contact at this gay mecca, so be sure to wear your best labels and be ready to sparkle.

The Lizard Lounge *buzzing bar* `17 B1`
18 rue Bourg Tibourg, 4ème • 01 42 72 81 34
>> www.hip-bars.com Open to 2am daily

A huge papier-mâché lizard mounted on the wall dominates this bar full of eager young professionals and hipsters getting drunk. Excellent cocktails, scrumptious Sunday brunches, occasional concerts and open-mic jam sessions in the cellar bar are the draw for a loud, friendly crowd.

Le Trésor *trendy Marais spot* `17 B1`
7 rue Trésor, 4ème • 01 42 71 35 17
Open to 1:30am daily

This perennial favourite is always packed with loyal pre-club crowds, kicking off their evening in style – whatever the day of the week. The bar is quite spacious, but it's best to arrive early as it can be difficult to get a table after 9pm. Don't miss the "rockstar" toilets with live goldfish swimming in the tanks.

Caveau des Oubliettes *weird & wacky* `16 H3`
52 rue Galande, 5ème • 01 46 34 23 09
Open to 2am Mon–Thu, to 5am Fri & Sat

Any place that lays real turf on the floor in the summer, proudly sports a huge guillotine near the bar, and organizes superb jazz jam sessions on Tuesdays in the cellar basement has got to be worth a visit. La Caveau des Oubliettes is utterly barmy, incredibly friendly and thoroughly good fun.

Le Pantalon *bargain drinks* `16 G4`
7 rue Royer Collard, 5ème • no phone
Open to 2am Mon–Sat

Due to the cheapness of the beer and wine, this bar pulls in an unlikely mix of Sorbonne students and pensioners. The bar staff are ebullient and friendly, the decor is bizarre (disco lights and palm trees in the loos) and there's always a rack of hard-boiled eggs on the counter, should you fancy a bar snack.

Le Crocodile *anti-chic cocktail bar* `16 G4`
6 rue Royer Collard, 5ème • 01 43 54 32 37
Open to 5am Mon–Sat

Yes, you do have to hammer on the closed shutters to get in, but, once there, expect a warm welcome and a phenomenal drinks list. This tiny bar offers over 200 cocktails, so don't be fazed if you are given paper and pen and a request to provide the drink's number along with its name when ordering.

Fu Bar *small but perfectly formed* `16 F3`
5 rue St-Sulpice, 6ème • 01 40 51 82 00
Open to 2am daily

Though the original owner, Sean, has moved on, regulars of this bar should not panic and newcomers should still get excited: the cocktails remain potent and the atmosphere outstanding. The miniscule downstairs bar is often packed and rowdy, so head to the upstairs seating area if you want a quiet chat.

Le Bar du Marché *popular zinc bar* `16 F2`
75 rue de Seine, 6ème • 01 43 26 55 15
Open to 2am daily

Le Bar du Marché is one of the prime people-watching spots in St-Germain. Great views of chic Parisians bustling past and a brilliant buzz – it's lively and full of laughter inside the bar, day or night – make this a great place to while away an afternoon or make pre-dinner drinks last a very long time.

Le Bar Dix *faded charm* `16 F3`
10 rue de L'Odeon, 6ème • 01 43 26 66 83
Open to 2am daily

Bags of charm and jugs of sangria are the big draws here. Le Bar Dix is all peeling black-and-white posters, nicotine-stained walls, thick Gauloise smoke, ripped velvet banquettes, and a boisterous crowd of all ages getting noisily merry on the house special. The sangria seems innocent, but beware – it packs a mighty punch.

AZ Bar *destination drinking* `16 F2`
62 rue Mazarine, 6ème • 01 53 10 19 99
≫ www.alcazar.fr Open to 2am daily

Situated above his Alcazar restaurant, Terence Conran's bar is a swanky, super-fun affair. A long bar, low banquettes, comfy chairs, candles and flattering lighting provide the perfect backdrop for the pretty PRs, young MDs and moneyed *demoiselles* who call the bar home from home. Depending on the night, the music ranges from funk to house via lounge and electro. The drinks, though, are always the same – expertly mixed, smilingly presented and a little on the expensive side. A perfect view into the "private" dining room is great for the curious, and check out the fabulous transvestite cigarette "girl", who tempts even non-smokers to buy an overpriced packet. The central pillars are just the spot to lean for those in search of stiletto-relief or trying to strike a foxy pose.

Café de la Mairie *St-Germain institution* `16 E3`
8 place St-Sulpice, 6ème • 01 43 26 67 82
Open to midnight daily

One of the 6th arrondissement's "correct addresses", this chichi café is consequently popular with wealthy Parisians. Occupying a prime spot opposite St-Sulpice, the terrace is often full of ladies who lunch, gentlemen of leisure and well-heeled art students sipping champagne and watching the world go by.

L'Urgence *pre-club theme bar* `16 F3`
45 rue Monsieur Le Prince, 6ème • 01 43 26 45 69
>> www.urgencebar.com Open 9pm–4am Tue–Sat

Hypochondriacs and medical students alike flock to this popular, if odd, venue that is decked out with medical equipment ranging from syringes and X-rays to biology text-book images of genitalia. Continuing with the theme, the bar is staffed by men in white coats who concoct drinks from a list that includes choices such as "Face Lift", "Suppository" and "Electro-Shock Therapy" – all of which, naturally, are served up in test tubes.

Don Carlos *Spanish hedonism* `16 F2`
66 rue Mazarine, 6ème • 01 43 54 53 17
Open to 5am Mon–Sat

On most nights at Don Carlos, guitarists alternately serenade beautiful girls and encourage the table-dancing crowd to indulge in rousing sing-alongs. Expect tequila shots, potent sangria, friendly staff and walls bearing photos of screen-greats who've drunk here (from Brigitte Bardot to Kevin Spacey).

WAGG *cool, classy club* `16 F2`
62 rue Mazarine, 6ème • 01 55 42 22 00
Open to 5am Thu–Sat

Legend has it that this club's former incarnation, the Whisky A Go-Go, was the last stop on Jim Morrison's final big night out. The party animals who flock here today always dress to impress the terrifying *physiognomiste* (style-bouncer), so follow suit. The UK-import 70s-groove Carwash is a must on Friday nights. **Adm**

Bars & Clubs

Nirvana Lounge *pricey posing* `8 H2`
3 avenue Matignon, 8ème • 01 53 89 18 91
Open to 5am daily

All curvy neon, pricey drinks and hard-to-get tables, the Nirvana Lounge is a must for poseurs and voyeurs. Claude Challe is behind the music, while Jonathan Amar dreamed up the decor, which is a mix of space-age motifs and Eastern promise and provides a perfect backdrop for the lithe and lovely crowd.

Toi *local chill-out joint* `8 H2`
27 rue Colisée, 8ème • 01 42 56 56 58
>> www.restaurant-toi.com Open to 2am Mon-Sat

Pink-and-orange neon, curvaceous chairs, lava lamps and a looming Buddha set the scene at Toi – popular with the BCBG (*bon chic bon genre*) set. The taped birdsong may help soothe fevered brows after one too many Tea Tois, house specials that combine iced tea, vodka, grenadine and peach liqueur to deadly effect.

La Suite *sleek, sexy, elite* `8 F2`
40 avenue George V, 8ème • 01 53 57 49 49
Open to 2am Mon–Wed, to 6am Thu–Sat

This is the latest project from the Guettas, the people who made club Les Bains into an international code for cool. It's impressively hard to get into (be sure to look moneyed to stand a chance), but once inside, pose on a low leather stool, marvel at the pristine white decor and keep an eye out for big-name celebs.

Four Seasons George V *hotel bar* `8 F2`
31 avenue George V, 8ème • 01 49 52 70 00
>> www.fourseasons.com Open to 1am Mon–Thu, to 2am Fri–Sat

It's worth pulling out all the financial and sartorial stops to soak up the atmosphere at this swanky spot. When martinis in individual shakers are poured with a flourish at your table; when fine chocolates and cakes accompany sweet choices, and nuts in silver salvers the sour ones, the world seems a much better place.

Bar des Théâtres *unusual mix* 8 G3
6 avenue Montaigne, 8ème • 01 47 23 34 63
Open all day to 2am daily

Popular with PRs from fashion houses, boys who work on the Bateaux Mouches, actors and audiences from the Théâtre du Champs Elysées *(see p121)* and anyone else who hangs out in Paris's Golden Triangle. A good spot for coffee or a café lunch, this is an attitude-free, rambunctious zinc bar and a rare find for the area.

Mathi's *insider address* 8 H2
3 rue Ponthieu, 8ème • 01 53 76 01 62
Open to 2am Sun–Thu, to 5am Fri & Sat

Tucked away in a nondescript hotel, Mathi's morphs into a hedonistic haven after midnight. This petite bar fills up with super-glamorous folk flirting over the buzz of rather dire 80s music and under the eagle eye of the scary leopard-print-clad hostess. Hard to get into, but most definitely worth a try.

Le Bar du Plaza *look-at-me bar* 8 G3
Plaza Athenée, 25 avenue Montaigne, 8ème • 01 53 67 66 65
≫ www.plaza-athenee-paris.com Open to 2am daily

Fashionistas, advertising executives and assorted beautiful people flock here to see and be seen. The interior offers high-set chairs and tables to perch at for maximum visibility, recessed seating to hide from prying eyes and flattering lighting to bring out everyone's best side. Serious cocktails at serious prices.

Le Queen *famous clubbers' favourite* 8 F1
102 avenue des Champs Elysées, 8ème • 01 53 89 08 90
Open to 6am daily

A real legend, Le Queen still entices glamorous gays and hip heteros past the notoriously difficult-to-access velvet rope. Disco divas love Monday's Disco Inferno, and fans of superstar DJs are bowled over by the sets of those who play here. Exhibitionists take note: women should dress scantily, men should dress tight. **Adm**

La Gare *posh, plush cocktail spot*
19 chaussée de la Muette, 16ème • 01 42 15 15 31
Ⓜ La Muette Open to 1:30am daily

Housed in a former train station, this is the epicentre of the smart and moneyed 16th-arrondissement set. The bar is a large circular room full of red velvet, gilt and glitz; the restaurant has food that is better and more reasonably priced than in similar joints. A good choice for an all-inclusive night out in this part of Paris.

La Fourmi *all-day hot spot* `4 F3`
74 rue des Martyrs, 18ème • 01 42 64 70 35
Open to 2am Sun–Thu, to 4am Fri & Sat

A lively spot on the edge of Abbesses, La Fourmi is worth travelling across town for. As busy by day as by night, it's the favourite of an arts-and-media crew, who while away the hours under a huge chandelier made from wine bottles to a backdrop of loud techno music. A fantastic source of flyers for the best clubs.

De la Ville *faded grandeur* `10 H2`
34 boulevard de la Bonne Nouvelle, 10ème • 01 48 24 48 09
Open to 2:30am daily

A former brothel, De la Ville has elaborate cornicing, a grand staircase, a massive mural, one toilet that does not lock and a resident flock of pigeons (the roof's a bit dodgy). Bohos come for the squat feel and clubbers move in when DJs perform warm-up sets (Thu–Sat) before hot nights at the Rex and Vogue, down the road.

Le Progres *quintessential bobo bar* `4 F2`
1 rue Yvonne le Tac, 18ème • no phone
Open to 2am daily

It's all about atmosphere at Le Progres – little more than a small space stuffed with a few trestle tables, an electric heater and some uncomfortable chairs. Oh, and an über-cool art-house crowd. Having said that, it's a very friendly bar where people flit from table to table flirting and chatting over a *demi* or three.

Xtremes *extremely good fun*   `9 D1`
10 rue Caumartin, 9ème • 01 44 94 05 61
>> www.xtremes.fr Open to 2am Mon–Sat, to midnight Sun

A sports bar with a twist, Xtremes has plasma screens that noiselessly run a series of insane extreme sports – it makes for mesmerizing viewing, whether you're a lifelong fan of ice-jumping *et al* or not. Popular with a funky, upbeat professional crowd quietly winding down after a hard day being bright young things.

La Patache *artily distressed*   `11 C1`
60 rue de Lancry, 10ème • no phone
Open to 2am daily

Just one small step away from being the wrong side of seedy, La Patache is a big hit with dishevelled creative types and their hangers-on. Pull up a rickety chair and don't be surprised if your neighbour starts sharing his haiku, bottle of rough red or theories on the meaning of life.

Project 101 *alternative underground club*   `4 E4`
44 rue de la Rochefoucauld, 9ème • no phone
>> www.project-101.com Open until late Fri–Sun

An alternative to expensive, exclusive, soulless *soirées*, Project 101 is a collective of artists and DJs that hosts intimate, friendly gatherings for like-minded people. Video projections, an honesty bar (pay 10€, then help yourself), knock-out sets by up-and-coming DJs and a totally different top time. **Adm**

Chez Prune *dishevelled chic*   `11 C1`
36 rue Beaurepaire, 10ème • 01 42 41 30 47
Open to 2am daily

Ever-packed Chez Prune is still the hottest spot on the Canal St-Martin. Dress vintage, drink retro (Suze is the current top tipple), ruffle your tousled hair and loudly discuss your current favourite art-house film, underground exhibition and esoteric designer – or just listen to those doing the same around you.

Bars & Clubs

Le Sancerre *boisterous, fun bar* `4 E2`
35 rue des Abbesses, 18ème • 01 42 58 08 20
Open to 2am Sun–Thu, to 4am Fri & Sat

The pick of Montmartre's bistros, full of charm and
character. Lovers, clubbers, transvestites and visitors
all squeeze in for a rowdy time, nodding along to
one of the frequent Sunday-night jazz concerts or
shouting over loud techno, all the while getting through
carafe after carafe of whatever is on special that day.

China Club *seductive cocktail joint* `18 E3`
50 rue Charenton, 12ème • 01 43 43 82 02
≫ www.chinaclub.cc Open to 2am daily

A very sexy take on a colonial-era gentleman's club,
with giant ceiling fans, deep Chesterfields, excellent
cocktails (the martinis are superb) and a low buzz of
civilized conversation pervading the ground floor.
Upstairs, the *fumoir* offers a more romantic setting,
while in the jazz cellar there's live music on weekends.

La Fabrique *cool, pre-club bar* `18 E2`
53 rue du Faubourg St-Antoine, 11ème • 01 43 14 32 32
Open to 5am Mon–Sat

La Fabrique's weird and wonderful combination of
micro-brasserie, eatery and pre-club haunt hosting hot
DJs is so successful that they've exported the concept
and opened up in Tokyo. It's easy to see why, too: if
you're looking for a quick drink, a good feed or a
thumping set by an up-and-coming DJ, you can find it
here. It's always worth checking listings, as special
events (usually on weekends) abound – La Fabrique
even lured Pulp frontman Jarvis Cocker to do a set on
the decks once. The music programme varies but is
generally focused on up-to-the-minute electro, except
for Sunday afternoons, when slinky jazz eases
brunchers' hangovers. Don't miss their home-brewed
beer (though real-ale enthusiasts need not apply),
while the large selection of bottled beers from around
the globe should fill any gaps for hard-core hops fans.
There's a happy hour daily from 6 to 8pm.

Pop In something for everyone 11 D4
105 rue Amelot, 11ème • 01 48 05 56 11
Open to 2am Tue–Sun

A rather odd mix of grungy local, student haunt and fashionista central, the Pop In is, truly, all things to all people. The weeknight indie concerts give way to DJs and dancing at weekends, with music that ranges from electroclash to sugar pop. Christian Dior once threw a huge party here – it's more chic than it looks.

Le Lèche-Vin quirky-but-cool bar 17 E1
13 rue Duval, 11ème • 01 43 55 98 91
Open to 2am daily

Ultra-kitsch, Le Lèche-Vin is stuffed full of iconography and Virgin Mary-related religious paraphernalia. It's more than disconcerting, but given that this place is also a shrine to the vine, don't feel too guilty about knocking back the cheap drinks in the company of the Bastille hipsters who hang out here.

Le Clown Bar themed wine bar 11 D4
114 rue Amelot, 11ème • 01 43 55 87 35
Open to 1am daily

All manner of clown-related clutter and big-top bits and bobs can be found here. If you find Pierrot & Co unsettling, calm your nerves with several glasses of excellent wine, picked from an interesting and varied list. Don't be afraid to ask for guidance – the staff are happy to discuss the various vintages in depth.

Café Charbon living legend 12 F3
109 rue Oberkampf, 11ème • 01 43 57 55 13
Open to 2am Sun–Thu, to 4am Fri & Sat

The original Oberkampf HQ, Charbon is still going strong. The huge mirrors, beautiful antique lighting and Belle Epoque feel keep a loyal crowd coming back for more. Get there early for the chance of a table or space at the bar, or go very late to enter the backroom club (with eclectic music roster), Le Nouveau Casino.

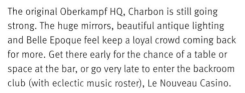

Bars & Clubs

Le Zero Zero *dippy-hippy bar* `11 D5`
89 rue Amelot, 11ème • 01 49 23 51 00
Open to 2am daily

A tiny but intriguing bar that is always busy with an intensely loyal boho-chic clientele. Everyone drinks hard and chats happily: you might arrive on your own, but by the bottom of the first glass, you'll have a posse of new best friends. Don't miss the minuscule alcove out back: the fairy lights are sure to work some magic.

Wax *ace club-bar* `18 E1`
15 rue Daval, 11ème • 01 40 21 16 16
Open to 2am Tue–Thu, to 5am Fri & Sat

All psychedelic swirls, bright colours, hard house and strong cocktails, Wax sounds migraine-inducing, but it is in fact a top spot for a night out. It works equally well as a pre-club joint to get you in the groove or as a one-stop shop where you can hit the bar first and the dance floor later.

Favela Chic *Brazilian party* `11 D2`
18 rue du Faubourg du Temple, 11ème • 01 40 21 38 14
>> www.favelachic.com Open to 2am Tue–Sat

Don't turn up late: the queues here might be a drag, but missing a dancing spot on one of the refectory tables that are leapt upon at the first chance is close to tragedy. Fuelled by cracking *caipirinhas* and crowd-pleasing music (from funk to reggae and R&B), this place is hot, exhibitionistic and really good fun.

Chai 33 *hip and happening* `22 H3`
33 cour St-Emilion, 12ème • 01 53 44 01 01
>> www.chai33.com Open to 2am daily

Bercy's only decent drinking spot, Chai (pronounced "*kay*") 33 is a vast converted wine warehouse run by the people behind Parisian legends Barfly and the Buddha Bar. Expect an industrial look, low lights, hard-core dance music, deck chairs to kick back in and rather special wine-based cocktails.

Barrio Latino *Latin quarter* `18 E2`

46 rue du Faubourg St-Antoine, 12ème • 01 55 78 84 75
Open to 2am Sun–Fri, to 3:30am Sat

A vast, slick, opulent affair, with lots of wrought iron, red velvet, expanses of coloured glass and hoards of designer-clad beautiful people, the Barrio Latino is a must for those keen to see and be seen Latino-style. Don't bother trying to reach the top floor – only those with a special elevator key can ascend to the gods.

Le Baron Rouge *zinc wine bar* `18 F3`

1 rue Theophile Roussel, 12ème • 01 43 43 14 32
Open to 10pm Mon–Sat, 10am–3pm Sun

Just around the corner from the marché d'Aligre, this is a jolly, traditional *bistrot à vins* that is always full of contented oenophiles slurping and swilling – but never spitting – their way through the impressive wine list. Ask the bar staff for recommendations – their blackboard full of goodies changes regularly and includes a large choice of wine by the glass. On Sundays, oysters are available in season; atmosphere in abundance is on tap all year round.

Limelight *exclusive clubbing destination* `22 F4`

162 avenue de France, 13ème • 01 56 61 44 04
Open to 2am Wed–Sun

Located inside the futuristic MK2 Bibliothèque cinema complex, the Limelight is a super-cool club with lofty ceilings, minimalist style and a terrace that can take 300 people. The management understands a hard-to-get-into allure and opens for one-off parties year-round and more regularly during the summer. **Adm**

Batofar *a clubbing beacon* `22 F2`

Opposite 11 quai François Mauriac, 13ème • 01 56 29 10 00
≫ www.batofar.net Open to midnight Mon, to 6am Tue–Sat

This scarlet ex-lightship has become a Paris landmark and clubbers' institution. Big-name DJs and local unknowns, plus an unpretentious, up-for-it crowd, make it one of Paris's best nightspots. A great chill-out deck and a fantastic summertime Sunday after-party on the *quai* round off the picture. **Adm**

Whatever the vintage, it is not considered chic to drink wine at a posh bar; spirits are more acceptable

streetlife

Paris has sights aplenty, but the real spectacle is on the street, whether it's in the chic 7th arrondissment or the gritty 20th. Year round, the city's markets overflow with shoppers searching for choice seasonal produce, retro clothing and bric-a-brac bargains. And in fine weather, restaurant terraces fill with sun-seekers and people-watchers, and café life spills out onto the pavements.

Streetlife

Beaubourg and the Quartier Montorgueil *hipster hang-out* `10 H4`

With its pedestrianized streets, quirky shops, good-value restaurants and eclectic bars and clubs, the area stretching west from the Centre Pompidou to the place des Victoires is one of the city's best districts for some retail therapy and just hanging out. Before 10 or 11am, try rue Montorgueil, an atmospheric shopping street that also has a variety of cafés – try **Les Petits Carreaux** (the most traditional) or **Santi** (the trendiest). From mid-morning, the area around the Pompidou swings into action: drinks on the terrace at the **Café Beaubourg**, opposite its namesake, are a Parisian institution, and ideal before or after taking in a show.

To the west is Les Halles, a hideous underground mall that's best avoided (especially on Saturdays, when it's a magnet for bored suburban youths). Instead, rue Etienne Marcel and rue Tiquetonne (running parallel and full of cute little shops) are much more attractive propositions for shoppers. Hightlights are offbeat women's boutique **Barbara Bui** *(see p65)*; trendy second-hand store **Killiwatch** *(see p65)*; **Le Shop**, a funky warehouse full of designer concessions; and **NotsoBig**, which sells all kinds of items for cool kids. Further west, everyone who's anyone heads to the indefinably chic **L'Eclaireur** *(see p63)*, while around the place des Victoires, the scene becomes noticeably more up-market, with plenty of top designers.

The area's night-time scene is buzzing too: try trendy **Le Café** or **Etienne Marcel** or **Wine and Bubbles** *(see p211 for all)* for fabulous fizz and the best wines. Other top drinking spots are **Le Next** *(see p135)* and **Le Café Noir** *(see p135)*, while clubs include one of Paris's best jazz spots, **Le Duc des Lombards** *(see p118)*, and, on rue Bourg l'Abbeye, the once legendary **Les Bains**, whose slip in status means that mere mortals can now get through the door. For late-night nibbles, **Au Pied du Cochon** *(see p24)* and **La Tour Montlhèry** *(see p25)* both keep serving through the early hours of the morning after the long night before.

To find more sights, eating places and shops in Paris's *quartiers* check ▶▶ **www.eparis.dk.com**

Le Marais *falafal, fashion and fun*   `17 B1`

Historically the city's Jewish ghetto and an area where market gardens were once cultivated, Le Marais (the marsh) is today one of Paris's most vibrant *quartiers*. Thronged by day and by night, it's a cosmopolitan mix; one where gay bars, kosher restaurants, boutiques, museums and antiques shops comfortably co-exist in beautiful buildings that have stood here for centuries.

The Marais is especially busy on Sunday afternoons, when most shops along rue des Francs Bourgeois defy the law by opening their doors. Among the most popular boutiques are **Abou d'Abi Bazar** *(see p68)*, source of affordable bobo (bohemian bourgeois) clothing; the unfailingly fashionable **Camper** for shoes; **Autour du Monde**, stocking stylish yet casual clothes; and the hip home accessories store **La Chaise Longue** *(see p68)*. Heading north, on the way to the Musée National Picasso *(see p96)* is rue Elzévir, recently colonized by stylish African restaurants and shops selling clothing and arty imported objects for the home. Further north, the up-and-coming rue Charlot is home to galleries and trendy restaurants, such as **R'Aliment** *(see p28)*.

The real heart of the Marais, though, is the ancient, narrow rue des Rosiers, where falafal shops such as **L'As du Fallafal** *(see p29)* vie to out-crunch each other, and chic designer boutiques lure in wealthy trendspotters. Around the corner, rue Vieille du Temple has a high concentration of cool cafés and restaurants, including **Les Petits Marseillais, Au Petit Fer à Cheval** and **Les Etages** *(see p28)*. This particular stretch is also a hub for the gay scene.

Down towards Bastille, the perfectly symmetrical 17th-century place des Vosges was once home to Victor Hugo and is now the playground of beautifully attired French toddlers, as well as unusually talented buskers. Locals gather here on weekends to picnic, watch the little ones frolic and generally take in the scene. Just to the south, the busy rue St-Antoine is where the locals do their food shopping in the traditional shops and supermarkets, while rue St-Paul hosts a notable collection of antiques shops and one of the city's best bakeries, **Boulangerie Malineau**, which sells an exceptional baguette.

Streetlife

St-Germain *conspicuous consumption* `16 E2`

Much of St-Germain's literary soul has been lost as
scores of designer boutiques have supplanted book-
shops, but the terraces of **Café de Flore** and **Les Deux
Magots,** on the boulevard St-Germain, remain haunts of
the area's intelligentsia and artists. But the new shops
aren't all about fashion: rue Bonaparte has some serious antiques stores, while rue de Buci and neighbouring rue de Seine are both lined with gourmet food
retailers. The real must for local foodies, however, is
Pierre Hermé at No. 72 rue Bonaparte, the beauty of
whose cakes rivals that of the YSL creations opposite.

In summer, there is no better place to people-watch
than the terrace of **Café de la Mairie** *(see p143).* In
fact, as far as bars go, this part of town is spoilt for
choice, especially along nearby rue des Canettes, aka
rue de la soif (the street of thirst). Heading towards the
river, rue St-Benoît, the jazz hub of Paris in the 1950s
and 60s, still has a couple of good jazz clubs and a
great Japanese noodle restaurant, **Yen** *(see p34).*

Rue Cler *edible elegance* `14 G1`

The sedate 7th arrondissement seems suddenly sexy
when you discover this lively street market (open
8am–1pm & 4–7pm Tue–Sat, 8am–1pm Sun) on one
of the few streets in Paris that hasn't been taken over
by chain shops. Extra draws are patisserie **Lenôtre**
and **Davoli,** a temple to porcine delights. The **Café du
Marché,** is where the locals soak up the scene all
year round thanks to its heated terrace.

Champ de Mars and Trocadéro `14 E1`

For all the formality of its design, the verdant Champ
de Mars – a former parade ground – is a laid-back
place to watch the world go by in summer, and a
prime spot from which to appreciate the engineering
marvel that is the Tour Eiffel. Over the bridge, at
Trocadéro, exhibition-goers mill around the beautiful
Palais de Chaillot *(see p104),* people cool down in the
fountains and skateboarders show off their moves.

Les Champs-Elysées *broad walk* `8 F1`

It may seem clichéd, but "Les Champs" is still a place to head for, especially on a Sunday, when its shops – mostly flagship stores – are open (unusual for Paris). Wandering up the avenue from place de la Concorde is a popular pastime, not to be missed when the Mairie (city hall) is staging one of its regular cultural events (recent extravaganzas have included TGV trains parked on the pavement and avant-garde art exhibitions).

At night, the lights along the avenue are spectacular, and there are several stores that are open late *(see p18–19)*, as well as some large multiscreen cinemas. Don't overlook the avenue's car showrooms: **Toyota** at No. 79 and **Renault** at No. 53, both of which feature in-store bars and restaurants and are trendy destinations for a unique and slightly bizarre combination of cars, cocktails and cuisine. The latest talking point, however, is the revamped **Publicis Drugstore** *(see p83)*, which contains a handful of shops and a very cool restaurant overseen by chef Alain Ducasse.

Boulevard des Batignolles *market* `3 B3`

Below the Sacré Coeur and seedy place de Clichy, the tree-lined boulevard des Batignolles plays host every Saturday to the city's best organic market, where many of the stallholders sell their own produce (as opposed to food bought from wholesale markets). Producers hawk everything – from perfectly ripe cheeses, to giant goose eggs and vegetables galore – to the area's increasingly trendy population.

Canal St-Martin *bohemian rhapsody* `5 C5`

A hub for Parisian hipsters, this area looks and feels like nowhere else in the city. A stroll along the leafy quai de Jemmapes or quai de Valmy, on either side of the tranquil canal, is a popular weekend pursuit. There are plenty of stops to choose from, including the café **Chez Prune** *(see p147)*, the comedy and music venue **Hotel du Nord** *(see p123)*, and trendy boutiques such as **Stella Cadente** *(see p87)* and **Coin Canal** *(see p89)*.

⟫ *Boat trips up the Canal St-Martin are a good way to soak up the local vibe* (see p106)   `157`

Streetlife

Abbesses *having a high old time* `4 F2`

The heart of Montmartre is one of the city's loveliest districts in which to while away some time. Expect winding cobbled streets, dilapidated old windmills, charm by the bucket-load and interesting company – the local Montmartrois include lots of bohemian types and artists. While many of the shops, such as the funky **Spree** concept store *(see p89)* and **Patricia Louisor** *(see p88)*, are worth crossing town for during the day, don't leave too soon, as it's in the evening that things really start to kick off here.

As well as outstanding restaurants – **La Famille** *(see p48)*, **La Mascotte** *(see p49)* and **Café Burq** *(see p46)* are all here – the 18th arrondissment has numerous atmospheric bars, such as **La Fourmi** *(see p146)* and **Le Sancerre** *(see p148)*. Other diversions come in the shape of eccentric, camp cabaret **Chez Michou** *(see p225)*, full of lip-synching, cross-dressing divas, and art-house cinema **Studio 28** *(see p123)*, with its beer garden that makes for an enchanting pre-film drink.

La Goutte d'Or *kaleidoscope of cultures* `5 A2`

This is perhaps the most multicultural and edgy area in central Paris. La Goutte mainly vibrates to an African beat, but other cultures are also in evidence. Head to rue de Laghouat for a taste of Algeria, rue Jean François Lépine to absorb Chinese culture and rue Gardes for young international fashion designers. For all its colour and vibrancy, this part of Paris is plagued by crime, so keep your wallet close and avoid visiting at night.

Puces de St-Ouen *mother of all flea markets*

Ⓜ Porte de Clignancourt
≫ www.les-puces.com Open 9:30–6 Sat–Mon

Also known as Les Puces de Clignancourt, this is the city's largest flea market where amid the piles of junk, bargains and beautiful pieces also lurk. There are 12 market areas, so if you know what you're looking for, head to the specific section: Serpette and Biron are top for antiques, while Malik has great vintage clothing.

Boulevard de Belleville *cultural X-roads* `12 F2`

This broad, leafy boulevard is home to one of the city's cheapest and liveliest markets (7:30–2:30 Tue & Fri) and to thriving Chinese, Jewish and Arab communities, each with its own shops and restaurants. Two of the best places to soak up the multicultural buzz are the excellent Jewish-Tunisian restaurant **Benisti** *(see p49)* and the **New Nioullaville** *(see p220)*, known for its outstanding dim sum.

Rue de la Butte-aux-Cailles *old Paris* `20 H5`

Attracting students from the nearby **Cité Universitaire** *(see p113)* with its cheap food and boho bars (try **Le Temps des Cerises** at No. 18 or **Chez Paul** at No. 22, a classy bistro), this street offers a slice of village life among the tower blocks of the *13ème*. Another draw is the 1920s-built outdoor pool at the **Piscine Butte-aux-Cailles** *(see p13)*. But this area really comes into its own at night, when cheap drinks draw the crowds.

Les Puces de Vanves *hagglers' heaven*
Avenue Georges Lafenestre and avenue Marc Sangrier, 14ème
Ⓜ **Porte de Vanves** Open 7:30–6 Sat & Sun

Vanves regulars swear that this is the best place for hidden treasures. It is smaller and friendlier than the other *puces* (flea markets), with around 350 stalls selling everything from chipped china to beautiful antique furniture, as well as retro jewellery and stacks of collectible magazines and books. Haggling is expected.

Rue Oberkampf *grungy good times* `12 F3`

Despite the fact that the area around and including rue Oberkampf has been comprehensively gentrified over the past five years, it still retains a multicultural feel and an urban vibe. But these days its residents are more likely to be cash-happy creatives than struggling immigrants or salt-of-the-earth types. This part of town is essentially a night-time destination and it's packed with bars and restaurants that are all either dive-like or designer-distressed to varying degrees. The oldest are still the best: **Café Charbon** *(see p149)* and **Mecano Bar** at No. 99 continue to pull in the crowds, just as **La Cithea** at No. 112 is still a popular club choice.

Running parallel, rue Jean-Pierre Timbaud is a little more down to earth, so expect good, cheap and unpretentious food at **Astier** *(see p49)*, people drawing on the paper tablecloths (crayons are provided) at the **Café Cannibale** at No. 93, and songs, readings, concerts and free couscous (weekends only) at the warm and welcoming **Café Bleu** at No. 83.

159

havens

Leafy parks and gardens provide essential breathing space in Paris, both literally and metaphorically, but there are other soothing diversions. When the city's hurly-burly gets too much and only a life-enhancing massage will do, there are plenty of spas to choose from. Or there are tranquil cafés high on atmosphere and low on attitude, and chapels and churches for quiet contemplation.

Havens

Place Dauphine *historical square* `16 G1`

Built in 1607, this delightfully shady spot on the Ile de
la Cité is a real slice of old Paris. Its three sides echo
the pointed tip of the island and were once lined with
32 identical 17th-century houses. Today only two of
the original buildings remain – they're the ones
facing the statue of Henry IV atop his trusty steed.
Linger over lunch in one of the local bistros, or just
find a bench and take in the picturesque scene.

Square du Vert-Galant *green peace* `16 F1`

This leafy square, perched on the point of the Ile de
la Cité, offers welcome respite from the hubbub of
the surrounding streets. In summer, sun-seekers
bypass the green benches and herbaceous borders
and head for the cobblestoned quays below to work
on their tans, have a waterside picnic or just enjoy
the views: Seine straight ahead, Louvre to the right
and the Institut de France's pretty cupola on the left.

Palais Royal *majestic oasis* `10 F3`

Place du Palais Royal, 1er
>> www.palais-royal.org Gardens open dawn to dusk daily

The elegant arcades and quiet garden enclave of the
17th-century Palais Royal have long been popular for
contemplation or a promenade, with luxury shops and
restaurants as added draws. Before the Revolution,
prostitutes and dissidents gathered in cafés in the
arcades to plot the downfall of the old regime, and
the Palais was a favoured haunt of gamblers. Today,
the most illicit fun you're likely to have is devouring
an extra dessert at the Restaurant du Palais Royal
(see p24) or splashing out in one of the swish
boutiques located in the building's *galeries*.

The garden is a serene oasis in the city's heart,
with striking tree-lined alleyways that harbour rows
of benches. Modern art fans will appreciate Pol
Bury's steel-ball sculptures and Daniel Buren's once-
controversial black-and-white striped columns, which
echo the regularity of the architecture behind.

To find the most luxurious personal makeovers in Paris, check >> www.eparis.dk.com

Nickel *male order* `11 B5`
48 rue des Francs Bourgeois, 3ème • 01 42 77 41 10
» www.nickel.fr Open 9:30–7 Mon–Sat (to 9 on Thu)

Philippe Dumont opened Nickel in 1996 so that boys wouldn't have to rub just-waxed shoulders with the girls when they were in need of a top-to-toe spruce-up. Nickel specializes in old-fashioned wet shaves, as well as treatments such as manicures and facials. There's also a range of Nickel beauty products for men.

32 Montorgueil *beauty boost* `10 H3`
32 rue Montorgueil, 1er • 01 55 80 71 40
Open 9–7:30 Mon–Sat (to 9 Wed & Thu)

The tiny stream running through this spa whispers "relax" – something that's instantly achievable with a solar plexus massage followed by a fruit-and-flowers exfoliation, or an acacia honey wrap and a soothing foot rub. And, for a lavish fee, hairdresser to the stars John Nollet will clip your locks into elegant submission.

St-Julien-le-Pauvre *12th-century church* `16 H2`
Rue St-Julien-le-Pauvre, 5ème • 01 43 54 52 16
Open 10–7:30 daily

One of the oldest churches in Paris, St-Julien has been a place of refuge for hundreds of years. These days, it's weary tourists and workers, rather than worshippers, who find sanctuary under its barrel-vaulted ceilings and in its Gothic apses. Outside there's a calm little park with shaded benches.

L'Imprévu *laid-back living* `10 H5`
9 rue Quincampoix, 4ème • 01 42 78 23 50
Open noon–2am Mon–Sat, 1pm–2am Sun

Pull up an old barber's chair or plump for a comfy leopard-print couch and kick back with a cocktail (or creamy coffee) after an afternoon of art appreciation in the nearby Centre Pompidou *(see p99)*. The lighting is low-key, the vibe relaxed and the mellow jazz soundtrack easy on the ears.

La Grande Mosquée *exotic baths* `17 A5`

39 rue Geoffroy St-Hilaire, 5ème • 01 43 31 18 14

>> **www.mosque-de-paris.org** Baths open 2–9 Fri, 10–9 Sat–Wed (women only: Mon, Wed, Fri & Sat; men only: Tue & Sun); café open 9am–11pm; restaurant open lunch & dinner daily; tours 9–noon & 2–6 Sat–Thu

Built in the 1920s, the Paris mosque – with its immaculate white walls and intricately carved wood-work – was inspired by the famous Alhambra in Spain and the Boulnania Mosque in Morocco. It's an environ-ment where tranquillity reigns, from the grand patio and sunken garden through to the tiled minaret and the prayer room, all of which (except the latter) can be visited on a guided tour. The *hammam* (Turkish baths) and the tearoom, however, are the main draws here. And if your idea of relaxation is being steamed, scrubbed and massaged to within an inch of your life, then this is definitely the place for you. After a session in the searing sauna, followed by a *gommage* (body scrub) and then a spirited and oily massage, you can stretch out on a cushion in the lush purple-and-gold rotunda and sip some sweet mint tea as Arabic music and hushed voices float around you – a scene straight out of Ingres's *Le Bain Turc*.

In winter, the *hammam*'s the thing, but in summer, sipping tea in the shade of the fig tree on the blue-tiled terrace of the Café Maure can be equally appealing. Alternatively, drop on to one of the richly coloured banquettes inside, under the amazing coffered ceiling, and watch waiters dart about with trays of mint tea and honey-drizzled cakes, or tureens of couscous destined for the restaurant. It's another world.

City Parks and Gardens

The **Jardin du Luxembourg** (Map 16 E4) is one of the city's most beloved parks. Offering everything from fountains to *boules* pitches and chairs aplenty, it's basically a backyard for all those without one. If you want something more formal, head for the quintessential French garden, the **Jardin des Tuileries** (Map 9 D4), laid out in the 17th century by royal gardener Le Nôtre, with a sweeping central avenue bordered by geometric flower beds and topiary. **Parc Monceau** (Map 2 H4) is worlds apart with its fanciful Roman temple, Egyptian pyramid, Japanese pagoda and Dutch windmill – as well as lawns and islands of flowers. But if flowers are your pleasure, the rose garden of the **Parc de Bagatelle** *(see p217)*, with some 1300 varieties, is truly heaven.

Jardins des Plantes *floral fancy* `17 B5`

Entrances on rue Buffon, rue Cuvier, rue Geoffroy St-Hilaire, place Valhubert, 5ème Open summer 8–5:30, winter 8–5:30

Escape dreary, wintry Paris inside steamy tropical glasshouses alive with lush cacti, ferns and orchids. In May, cherry trees add a burst of colour between the sweeping shaded avenues. And, for a dose of nature deep in the city, visit the wild *parc écologique*, which is frequented by more than 75 species of birds.

Mariage Frères *historic tearoom* `16 F1`

13 rue des Grands Augustins, 6ème • 01 40 51 82 50
≫ www.mariage-freres.fr Open noon–7 Mon–Fri, 3–7 Sat & Sun

The Mariage family have been trading tea for 150 years and this tranquil tearoom is the perfect place to discover their wares. Hardwood floors, high-backed chairs, silver tea services, white-coated waiters and 500 kinds of tea imbue this 17th-century building with a distinct aroma of the old East Indies.

Toupary Restaurant *bird's-eye view* `10 F5`

La Samaritaine, 2 quai du Louvre, 1er • 01 40 41 29 29
≫ www.toupary.com Open 11:45–3, 3:30–6 & 7:30–11 Mon–Sat

When you can shop no more, drag your aching feet up to the fifth floor of the Samaritaine department store. Here, a restorative cup of almond-and-orange tea, a hefty slice of apple tart and stunning panoramic views – from Notre Dame to the Eiffel Tower and beyond – awaits. The 10th-floor terrace is open in fine weather.

Hôtel des Invalides *war and peace* `15 A1`

Esplanade des Invalides, 7ème • 01 44 42 54 52
Open summer 10–6 daily; winter 10–5 daily

Built by Louis XIV to house his wounded soldiers (part of it remains a hospital today), the Hôtel des Invalides contains the grandiose tomb of Napoleon I and a massive army museum. Less well known are the restful gardens, with their perfectly trimmed triangular trees, and flowerbeds overlooking a tinkling fountain.

Chapelle Expiatoire *fit for a king* 9 C1
729 rue Pasquier, 8ème • 01 42 65 35 80
Open 1–5pm Thu–Sat

Louis XVI and Marie-Antoinette (as well as other vic-
tims of the guillotine) were originally buried on this
spot, which prompted Louis XVIII to build a chapel in
1815 in their memory. Rest on a bench under 100-year-
old trees or peruse the huge stone tombs of the Swiss
Guards who died defending the luckless Louis XVI.

Four Seasons George V *sleek spa* 8 F2
31 avenue George V, 8ème • 01 49 52 70 00
>> www.fourseasons.com Open 6:30am–10pm daily

The spa of this five-star hotel oozes style, from the
Jacuzzi and pool with trompe-l'oeil frescoes, to the
relaxation lounge with linen-covered day beds, soft
music and fresh fruit for the taking. Opt for a his-and-
hers hot-stone massage, a tequila-based *punta mita*
massage or a cosseting aromatherapy facial.

Parc des Buttes Chaumont *wild park* 6 G4
Entrances on rue Manin and rue Boltzaris, 19ème
Open 7:30am–9pm (in summer to 11pm)

Cliffs and gushing waterfalls give this former rubbish
tip and quarry an untamed alpine look. But it's all
man-made, from the lake and cave complete with
stalactites, to the Temple of Sybil, from which you can
survey urban Paris – including the distinctive outline
of the Sacré Coeur in the distance.

Cinq Mondes *world-class pampering* 9 D1
6 square de l'Opéra Louis Jouvet, 9ème • 01 42 66 00 60
Open noon–8 Mon–Sat (to 10 Thu)

Each of Cinq Mondes' nine face and body treatments
begins with a dreamy head-and-shoulder rub. Then the
world tour begins: Ayurvedic massage with warm oil;
a *hammam* treatment complete with black soap, vigor-
ous scrub down and massage; or a soak in a Japanese
petal-strewn *o-furo* bath, perfumed with essential oils.

La Promenade Plantée *linear park* `18 G5`
Entrances include ave Daumesnil, ave Ledru Rollin and rue Edouard-Lartet, 12ème
Open 8–6 Mon–Fri, 9–6 Sat & Sun (in summer to 9pm)

This green strip running 4.5km (3 miles) atop an old railway viaduct starts off at urbanized Bastille and ends at the verdant Bois de Vincennes, to the east of the city. Planted with roses, lavender, shrubs and herbs, the promenade appeals to joggers, strollers and the curious, as its elevated position makes it easy to gaze down at the streets below or into the apartments and offices that line the route.

Cimetière du Montparnasse *tombs* `19 C2`
3 boulevard Edgar Quinet, 14ème • 01 44 10 86 50
Open 9–5:30 daily (but times can vary)

Reflect on Paris's artistic and literary past, immortalized here. Among the graves are those of Baudelaire, Sartre and companion Simone de Beauvoir, and French crooner Serge Gainsbourg, whose grave is always covered with fans' tributes. Brancusi's superb sculpture *Kiss* commemorates the double suicide of two friends.

Parc André Citroën *themed gardens* `13 A5`
Entrances include quai André Citroën & rue St-Charles, 15ème
Open from dawn Mon–Fri, 9am Sat & Sun; closing times vary according to the time of year and day of the week

Laid out on the site of the old Citroën car factory, this 21st-century French garden is a long way from the formal, keep-off-the-grass parks dotted around the city. Based on four themes – architecture, artifice, movement and nature – the park is characterized by clean lines and lots of glass, in the shape of two huge glasshouse pavilions. There's a vast lawn, a black garden and a white garden, five coloured gardens designed to represent the five senses, and a moving garden (full of grasses blowing in the breeze). Water plays a central role, with canals, waterfalls and the dancing fountain – a square that shoots jets of water into the air at random heights. It's a magnet for giggling children cooling off in summer. Added attractions include leafy labyrinths for quiet contemplation and a tethered hot-air balloon for fabulous views over the city *(see p16)*.

hotels

Ranging from posh palaces to bohemian bedrooms, hotels in Paris come in all styles and cater to all budgets. Charming chintz explosions are no longer the norm in decor – minimalism can be enjoyed in some of the city's burgeoning boutique hotels. Finding a single bed in the city can be a challenge, though, so be prepared for hefty single supplements – or bring a friend.

DESIGN STATEMENTS

Hotel Bourg Tibourg
19 rue Bourg Tibourg, 4ème
With its far-from-minimal, eclectic design, this hotel is a huge hit with in-the-know design fans in search of some luxury. *(See p173)*

Hilton Paris Arc de Triomphe
51–7 rue des Courcelles, 8ème
The design of this hotel is inspired by 1930s ocean liners and is guaranteed to transport guests back to an era of luxury and elegance. *(See p179)*

Pershing Hall
49 rue Pierre-Charon, 8ème
The latest Parisian hotel from interiors guru Andrée Putman is an ultra-chic spot for design junkies with deep pockets. *(See p178)*

>> *Booking your hotel room online will often get you a better rate than reserving over the phone.*

Villa d'Estrées
17 rue Git-le-Couer, 6ème
The Villa d'Estrées is one of Paris's best boutique hotels. Extremely discreet and chic, it is known for its opulent furnishings. *(See p174)*

CHEAP CHIC

Hotel Mayet
3 rue Mayet, 6ème
Bright and breezy, the upbeat Hotel Mayet is full of primary colours and funky furniture. High on style and low on price. *(See p176)*

>> *At weekends, it is often possible to get cheaper deals in the more expensive hotels that are popular with business travellers during the week.*

Hotel Eldorado
18 rue des Dames, 17ème
A popular choice with guests who like flea-market chic and individually decorated rooms. *(See p179)*

ROOMS WITH A VIEW

Hotel du Panthéon
19 place du Panthéon, 5ème
Rooms at the front of this refined hotel overlook the stunning Panthéon church. *(See p175)*

Novotel Tour Eiffel
61 quai de Grenelle, 15ème
The high-rise Novotel is not the most attractive building in Paris, but every room boasts impressive views over the city. *(See p181)*

Hotel du Quai Voltaire
19 quai Voltaire, 7ème
You'll pay a premium, but the street-facing rooms here have gorgeous panoramas of the Louvre and the River Seine. *(See p176)*

Royal Fromentin
11 rue Fromentin, 9ème
Rooms here offer spectacular views of Montmartre, which are also beautifully framed by Art-Deco windows in the central stairwell. *(See p180)*

WEIRD & WONDERFUL	ROMANTIC HIDEAWAYS	ARTISTIC STYLE
Hotel du St-Merry 78 rue de la Verrerie, 4ème Gothic furnishings (including a confessional box in the reception) and a chequered history lend the St-Merry a little quirky kudos. *(See p173)*	**Pavillion de la Reine** 28 place des Vosges, 4ème An oasis of calm situated on a romantic square. The beams and beautiful beds create a perfect haven for lovers. *(See p172)*	**Artus** 34 rue de Buci, 6ème Rising and established artists were commissioned to paint the doors here, and a graffiti guru was let loose on the staircases. *(See p175)*
L'Hotel 13 rue des Beaux Arts, 6ème Rooms to match the wildest fantasies are found in this hotel. One of them recreates Oscar Wilde's last resting place. *(See p175)*	**Hotel du Vigny** 9–11 rue Balzac, 8ème Discreet staff, magnificent rooms and a prevailing sense of elegance set the tone here. *(See p177)*	**Hotel Square** 3 rue des Boulainvilliers, 16ème Inside this hotel – itself a work of modern art – is a gallery with some interesting work by renowned French artists. *(See p179)*
		>> *This might be the land of Gitanes and Gauloises, but it's not uncommon for moderate and expensive hotels to have non-smoking rooms, or even floors.*
Hotel du Septième Art 20 rue St-Paul, 4ème Stuffed with movie memorabilia, this is an offbeat choice for film fans. It also has a terrific location near the Marais. *(See p173)*	**Hotel du Lys** 23 rue Serpente, 6ème A hideaway for couples looking for a special stay, the Hotel du Lys has charm in abundance. *(See p174)*	**Hotel A** 4 rue d'Artois, 8ème One-off works of art grace the doors, bedrooms and lobby area of the Hotel A, and art books line the shelves of its library. *(See p177)*

Hotel Tonic *pleasant retreat* `10 G5`

12 rue du Roule, 1er • 01 42 33 00 71
>> www.tonichotel.com

The central location and elegant rooms are the big draws here. Some of the intimate bedrooms reveal ancient stone walls (the building dates from the 17th century) and all come complete with heavy red brocade bedspreads and simple wooden headboards. Superior rooms have Jacuzzis to soothe aching bones. **Moderate**

Hotel Roubaix *homely spot* `10 H3`

6 rue Greneta, 3ème
01 42 72 89 91

Traditional decor, a rickety lift and delightfully courteous, old-school owners contribute to the Roubaix's charm. The rooms are a little faded and down at heel, but extremely clean. And the wonderful welcome from the staff – who greet both first-timers and regulars alike as if they were old family friends – more than makes up for the odd creaky bed-spring. **Cheap**

Pavillon de la Reine *17th-century treat* `17 D1`

28 place des Vosges, 4ème • 01 40 29 19 19
>> www.pavillon-de-la-reine.com

Arguably the most romantic hotel in Paris, this place will transform even the most hard-bitten cynic. The prime location is just the start; add a divine courtyard, rooms with beams and giant beds, friendly staff and a gorgeous sitting room complete with an honesty bar, and you may never want to leave. **Expensive**

Booking Agencies

The official tourist office website (www.paris-touristoffice.com) is a useful site for finding and booking a hotel on the web, though you do not need to pay online. If you arrive in Paris without a hotel, try branches of the Office du Tourisme *(see p231)* at the Gare de Lyon and the Gare du Nord. A small commission is usually charged.

Hotel Tiquetonne *budget beds* `10 H4`

6 rue Tiquetonne, 2ème
01 42 36 94 58

It might be around the corner from the unsalubrious – though colourful – rue St-Denis, but this is a great find in the city's buzzy Montorgueil *quartier*. The hotel is located on a cobbled street full of trendy shops and quirky bars, and its airy rooms are simple, functional and bigger than most in this bracket. **Cheap**

Hotel St-Merry *memorable nights* `17 A1`
78 rue de la Verrerie, 4ème
01 42 78 14 15

Here, a boho vibe and quirky gothic feel set the scene.
Formerly part of the neighbouring church and at one
point a bordello, the St-Merry has cosy rooms, one of
which features a flying buttress above the bed. Only
the suite has a TV, so guests staying in other rooms
have to amuse themselves. **Moderate**

Hotel du Septième Art *on a film theme* `17 C2`
20 rue St-Paul, 4ème
01 44 54 85 00

Film fans favour this hotel that pays homage to
cinema, the seventh art. The bedrooms (the quietest
ones face the courtyard), stairwells and bar, full of old
movie posters and kitsch Hollywood memorabilia, are
a little dusty. However, the art-house atmosphere and
convenient location are real pluses. **Cheap**

Hotel Bourg Tibourg *eclectic style* `17 B1`
19 rue Bourg Tibourg, 4ème
01 42 78 47 39

The little-known Bourg Tibourg is popular with design
buffs looking for some lower-price chic. Part of the
Costes group, the hotel is just as stylish, but more
affordable than its more famous siblings.

Designed by flash furnishings guru Jacques Garcia
(the man behind the decor throughout the Costes
empire), the interior here is a sexy mish-mash of
periods and styles. The lobby is a riot of neo-gothic,
offbeat Orientalism and old-school French, and the
rooms range from stark stripes to nautical blue via
luxuriant red. The dark-wood panelling, fabric-covered
walls, velvet overload and explosion of gilt, however,
feature in every room, as do the bathrooms clad with
black marble. The light-filled interior garden is ideal
for escaping the visual overload, and the boutiques
and bars of the Marais are a stone's throw away for
other designer distractions. **Moderate**

Hotels

Hotel du Degrés de Notre Dame *perennial favourite* 16 H3
10 rue des Grands Degrès, 5ème
01 55 42 88 88

With its beams and wood panelling, helpful staff, wonderful location set back from the Seine and great value for money, this hotel is justly popular. Be sure to try dinner on the terrace or in the candle-filled dining room, and book your room well in advance. **Moderate**

Hotel Esméralda *shabby charm* 16 H2
4 rue St-Julien-le-Pauvre, 5ème
01 43 54 19 20

Set on a pretty square across the river from Notre Dame, this charming hotel is a perfect base for indulging in some Left Bank pursuits. The 17th-century building contains 19 slightly run-down – yet romantic – rooms, complete with antique furnishings and uneven floors. Book ahead (no credit cards accepted). **Cheap**

Villa D'Estrées *chic boutique hotel* 16 G2
17 rue Git-le-Couer, 6ème • 01 55 42 71 11
>> www.paris-hotel-latin-quarter.com

Such a closely guarded secret that it's deliberately ex-directory, the Villa D'Estrées is definitely worth knowing about. With ten beautiful rooms, conceived by Yann Descamp (protégé of über-designer Jacques Garcia), the hotel is all warm tones and Empire-style furniture. Perfect for a hush-hush weekend. **Moderate**

Hotel du Lys *romantic bargain* 16 G2
23 rue Serpente, 6ème
01 43 26 97 57

The Hotel du Lys is a timeless, typically French hotel, all winding staircases, scrubbed floorboards, tapestries and fading floral arrangements. The rooms are simply furnished and some tend towards the tiny, but if you're looking for a no-fuss place to hole up with your beloved, it is ideal. **Cheap**

L'Hotel *indulgent fantasies* `16 E1`
13 rue des Beaux Arts, 6ème • 01 44 41 99 00
» www.l-hotel.com

Oscar Wilde spent his last days here, famously claiming that he was dying beyond his means. There's no need to take it quite that far, but a night here is worth the expense. L'Hotel is a temple to opulence, with 20 rooms – individually decorated by the ubiquitous Jaques Garcia – leading off the circular lightwell. Part the heavy drapes at the door of the Léopard Room to reveal a riot of purple taffeta, velvet, gilt and leopard print. There's also a red marble bathroom with a sunken tub. The Roi de Naples Room features a huge bed, a fireplace and impressive chandeliers while the St Petersburg is an imperial dream of jade, mirrors and marble. In the basement, the perpetual-wave pool, mosaic steam room and circular chill-out lounge provide a heaven for hedonists. However, shy Sybarites will be pleased to discover that this spa area can only be reserved for private sessions. **Expensive**

Artus *chic on the cheap* `16 E2`
34 rue de Buci, 6ème • 01 43 29 07 20
» www.artushotel.com

Superbly located, the Artus has friendly, relaxed staff, a young and hip clientele and decent prices. The arty touch alluded to in the hotel's name? Check out the bedroom doors, each painted by an up-and-coming artist. If you can, splash out on the duplex room with a truly striking, sumptuous bathroom. **Moderate**

Hotel du Panthéon *elegant living* `16 G4`
19 place du Panthéon, 5ème • 01 43 54 32 95
» www.hoteldupantheon.com

It's always wise to book ahead for the Hotel du Panthéon; its prime location and attentive staff have won it a legion of fans. Booking also increases the chance of getting one of the few rooms with spectacular Panthéon views. All rooms have château-style furnishings, including some four-poster beds. **Moderate**

» *Not all cheap hotels accept credit cards. Call to check whether they do, and if so which ones*

Hotel Mayet *funky design* `15 B4`
3 rue Mayet, 6ème
01 47 83 21 35

A rare departure from the chintzy interiors usually found in cheaper Parisian hotels, the Mayet's rooms are a breath of fresh air, especially those on the fifth floor, which have their own balconies. Expect fuss-free furniture, primary colours and clean lines, and guests who expect a little style for their euros. **Cheap**

Hotel des St-Pères *St-Germain star* `15 D2`
65 rue des St-Pères, 6ème
01 45 44 50 00

The St-Pères is a kind of up-market boarding house for the bookish. Its rooms – elegant, individually deco-rated and opening onto an interior courtyard – and bar are popular with publishers and authors from nearby publishing houses. Romantics and art-lovers will adore the painted bathroom ceiling in Room 100. **Moderate**

Hotel Lenox *updated Art Deco* `15 D1`
9 rue de l'Université, 7ème • 01 42 96 10 95
» www.lenoxsaintgermain.com

Follow in the footsteps of James Joyce, Ezra Pound and T S Eliot by checking into the Lenox. The Art Deco bar and lobby offer a stylish backdrop for cocktails; the exterior glass lift provides an adrenaline kick for those staying on the top floors; and the comfortable rooms are a perfect cocoon from the outside world. **Moderate**

Hotel du Quai Voltaire *room with a view* `9 D5`
19 quai Voltaire, 7ème • 01 42 61 50 91
» www.quaivoltaire.fr

Staying here is really all about location. The rooms can be a little small and the sparse furnishing tends towards the shabby, so make sure you book a top-floor, river-facing room. These are a little larger than most, have less traffic noise and, of course, the most spectacular views. **Moderate**

Hotel Malar *characterful cheapie* `8 G5`
29 rue Malar, 7ème • 01 45 51 38 46
>> www.hotelmalar.com

Tucked away in this chic part of town, near the Tour Eiffel, the Malar is a real gem. The reception area is all wood beams and long-stemmed roses, the interior courtyard a delightful place to breakfast, and the rooms are simple yet spotlessly clean. The charming staff offer a genuinely warm welcome. **Cheap**

Hotel A *urban cool* `8 H1`
4 rue d'Artois, 8ème • 01 42 56 99 99
>> www.hotel-le-a.com

The A looks like something out of *Wallpaper** magazine and is a magnet for fashion and media folk. The all-white bedrooms boast sleek stone bathrooms and original artworks: those on the sixth floor are flooded with light via skylights. Down in the lobby, recline on a chaise longue with a long drink from the bar. **Expensive**

Hotel de Vigny *insider address* `8 F1`
9–11 rue Balzac, 8ème • 01 42 99 80 80
>> www.relaischateaux.com

A palatial, prestigious hotel, the de Vigny is a well-kept secret among discerning visitors. It's the only Relais et Chateaux hotel in Paris, and offers chic and elegant rooms. A roaring fire in the mahogany-panelled lounge, an Art Deco-style bar with vintage champagne on ice, and discreet staff complete the picture. **Expensive**

The *Grandes Dames*

Paris's palace hotels are temples to the art of high living, and while gilt, marble, crystal, velvet and shocking room rates are universal to them all, each has its own specialities. **Le Ritz** is perhaps the most (in)famous, and its health club is one of the world's most beautiful. **Le Crillon** is the city's poshest hotel; the quiet, sun-trap courtyard is a well-kept secret for summer drinks. The **Four Seasons George V** boasts an army of staff for each guest and a trendy spa *(see p166)*. **Le Meurice** is a little hipper than its rivals, hosting glittering private parties and offering an amazing personal-shopping service, while **La Plaza Athenée** is surrounded by the city's top designer boutiques and has a fabulous bar *(see p145)*. For further details, *see p227*.

Hotels

Pershing Hall *happening scene* 8 G2

49 rue Pierre-Charron, 8ème • 01 58 36 58 00
>> www.pershinghall.com

Even if you do not usually opt for up-market accommodation, Pershing Hall, the city's hippest hotel, is really worth the splurge. An unremarkable façade with a small sign conceals a super-sleek haven created by design maven Andrée Putman. The lobby sets the off-beat, modish tone, with fashion photographs, a bizarre tree-trunk sculpture "growing" from a pool in the centre of the room and staff who look as if they're filling in on their day off from the catwalk. A cascade of beaded curtains leads to the interior courtyard restaurant where *le beau monde* drink in the amazing vista along with their Bollinger; the entire back wall of the courtyard is covered with a stunning vertical garden. And in summer, the glass roof retracts so that guests can top up their (real) St-Tropez tans.

The rooms are as minimal and chic as one would expect from Putman, featuring white bed linen, ash furniture, aubergine taffeta drapes and blue-stained parquet. Interesting extras include suites with sliding panels that allow the bathroom to become part of the bedroom (some rooms only have showers), state-of-the-art plasma TV/DVDs and a free mini-bar complete with trendy mini-bottles of Pop champagne. Take advantage of the freebies before heading to Pershing Lounge, the upper-level bar/club where the subdued neon lighting, see-and-be-seen balcony area and dove-grey leather sofas all contribute to make this spot a favourite with Paris's party people. One of the capital's hottest places to do drinks, the Lounge has a different DJ every night of the week, occasional funky-jazz concerts, upscale ladies' nights complete with speed-dating sessions and tarot-card readings, and an ever hip-and-happy vibe. **Expensive**

Hilton Paris Arc de Triomphe `2 G4`
51–7 rue des Courcelles, 8ème • 01 58 36 17 17
>> www.hilton.com

Hilton's latest Paris hotel harks back to an era of elegance and sophistication. Star designer Jacques Garcia has decked out the vast 512-room hotel in classic 1930s style: the sweeping wrought-iron staircase illuminated by an amazing chandelier is *the* place to make a grand entrance, while the courtyard garden and Purple bar are great chill-out spots. Period-style furnishings dot the hallways and the rooms are full of ebony, green imitation shark-skin wall coverings, cream leather seating and luxurious bedding.

There's even an Executive floor; the rooms aren't much better, but the swanky VIP lounge with a fully stocked free bar and foie gras nibbles, plus the private check-in and complimentary breakfast, makes it worth the extra euros. Guests who like to be pampered should head to the spa; in addition to treatments, there's a Turkish bath and sauna area. **Expensive**

Hotel Square *tastefully trendy* `13 A2`
3 rue des Boulainvilliers, 16ème • 01 44 14 91 90
>> www.hotelsquare.com

Housed in a curving granite building, this is an ideal choice for lovers of all things minimal and modern. Twenty-two tasteful rooms feature sleek furnishings, impressive hi-fi systems and stacks of arty magazines. The first-floor gallery often hosts temporary exhibitions, book launches and private parties. **Expensive**

Hotel Eldorado *hip and happening* `3 C2`
18 rue des Dames, 17ème
01 45 22 35 21

The Eldorado's attractive rooms are bright and airy, and its patio is ideal for lunching and lounging. The triples and quads are great value, but be sure to book ahead, especially during fashion weeks (Mar and Oct), when this place fills with models who aren't yet super enough to stay at a palace hotel *(see p177)*. **Cheap**

 Rates in more expensive hotels can vary wildly from season to season

Royal Fromentin *good-value good times* `4 E3`
11 rue Fromentin, 9ème • 01 48 74 85 93
➤➤ www.hotelroyalfromentin.com

It was a swinging 1930s cabaret spot, and entertaining is still part of this hotel's soul: it is often the hotel of choice for bands playing at the nearby concert halls. The lobby bar's decor recalls the good old days, while some of the agreeable rooms have amazing views which will inspire anyone to get lyrical. **Cheap**

Hotel Terrass *lovely location* `4 E2`
12–14 rue Joseph de Maistre, 18ème • 01 44 92 34 14
➤➤ www.terrass-hotel.com

The Terrass offers a peaceful night's sleep in down-to-earth Montmartre. The decor is immaculate, if a little bland, but the welcome is warm and the trendy location hard to beat. In summer, the roof-top restaurant barbecue is very romantic and quite an "in" destination with fashionable folk. **Moderate**

Hotel Langlois *atmospheric charm* `3 D5`
63 rue St-Lazare, 9ème
01 48 74 78 24

Formerly the Hotel des Croises, this place's name changed after it was featured as the Hotel Langlois in the 2002 movie *The Truth about Charlie*. The pristine Art Nouveau building hides a rickety lift that takes guests to rooms stuffed with antiques and charm, some of which boast stunning views. **Cheap**

Aparthotels

If you're after a private pad, aparthotels are the way to go. The most luxurious is the **Carré d'Or** complex off the Champs-Elysées, popular with A-listers from the worlds of film, fashion and serious wealth. Less stratospheric, but still impressive, are the **Citadines** buildings dotted around the city (the best is in St-Germain), which are generally favoured by those whose company is picking up the tab. At the **Hotel Résidence Henri IV**, the atmosphere is much more intimate, with its five apartments located off a beautiful square in the 5ème. The studios run by **Hotel du Degrès du Notre Dame** also offer a Left Bank address, but a more vibrant one. Independent lets (of at least one week) can also be found via **France Apartments**. For further details, *see p226.*

Hotel des Arts *picture perfect* `4 E2`
5 rue Tholoze, 18ème
01 46 06 30 52

The Hotel des Arts' location – up a steep little street, opposite one of the city's best art-house cinemas and just down from an old windmill – is quintessential Montmartre. The hotel itself doesn't disappoint either, with friendly staff and comfortable, floral bedrooms, some of which have cityscape views. **Cheap**

Hotel Utrillo *Montmartre scene* `4 E2`
7 rue Aristide Bruant, 18ème
01 42 58 13 44

The simple, spare rooms at the Utrillo are well kept, and the sloping ceilings of the garret rooms lend a romantic feel to this bargain sleep. In contrast, the breakfast room is much more bright and distinctly cheery. Don't forget to take advantage of the in-hotel sauna (at a small extra charge). **Cheap**

Hotel Beaumarchais *bargain chic* `11 D4`
3 rue Oberkampf, 11ème • 01 53 36 86 86
>> www.hotelbeaumarchais.com

One of the first places in Paris to do reasonably priced, modern designer flair, the Beaumarchais has a loyal following. Expect bedrooms in primary colours, comfy beds and funky nick-nacks. A rue Oberkampf location means that all manner of trendy shops, bars and restaurants are just a short stroll away. **Cheap**

Novotel Tour Eiffel *luxury chain* `13 B3`
61 quai de Grenelle, 15ème • 01 40 58 20 00
>> www.novotel.com

The Novotel has swathes of marble, a chic bar, two noteworthy restaurants and panoramic views. Rooms are stylish, and the small indoor pool (with retractable roof) is a terrific plus. Depending on the season, prices can be expensive, but the web often has last-minute deals year-round. **Moderate**

Paris Street Finder

Inner Paris is relatively compact and is delineated by the boulevard Périphérique. Within this ringroad, the city is divided into 20 numbered postal districts or arrondissements, which spiral outwards from the 1st arrondissement located on the Right Bank. The main map below shows the division of the Street Finder, along with postcodes, and the smaller one shows the extent of Greater Paris.

Almost every listing in this guide features a (boxed) page and grid reference to the maps in this section. The few entries that fall outside the area of these maps give transport details instead.

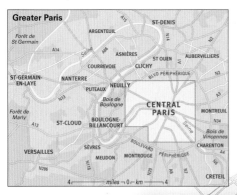

Key to Street Finder

- ▦ Sight/public building
- Ⓜ Metro station
- ⓇⒺⓇ RER station
- 🚆 Railway station
- 🚢 River boat pier
- 🚌 Main bus stop
- ⓘ Tourist information office
- ✚ Hospital with casualty unit
- Ⓟ Police station
- 🛈 Church
- ✡ Synagogue
- ⊗ Post office
- Ⓟ Car park
- ═ Railway line
- ▬ Pedestrian street
- ▭ Motorway

Scale of maps 1–22

0 metres	250
0 yards	250

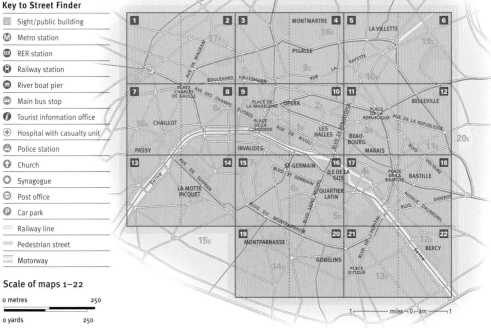

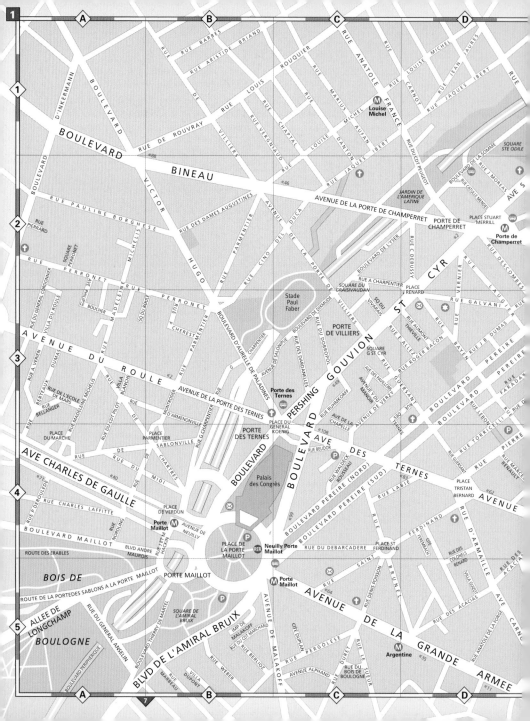

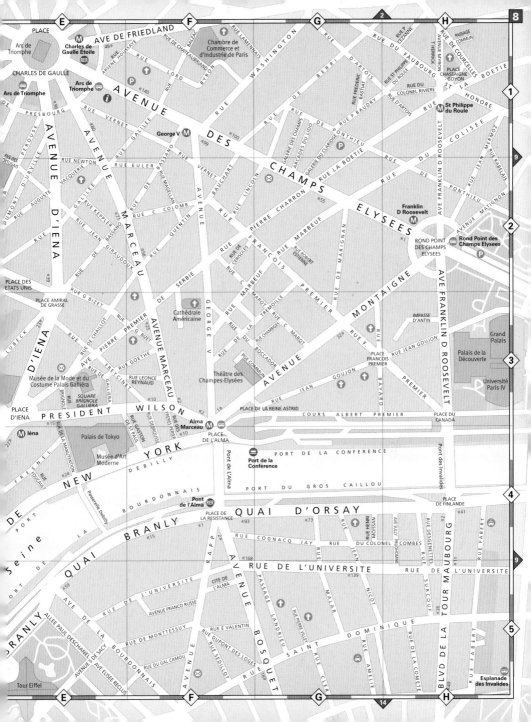

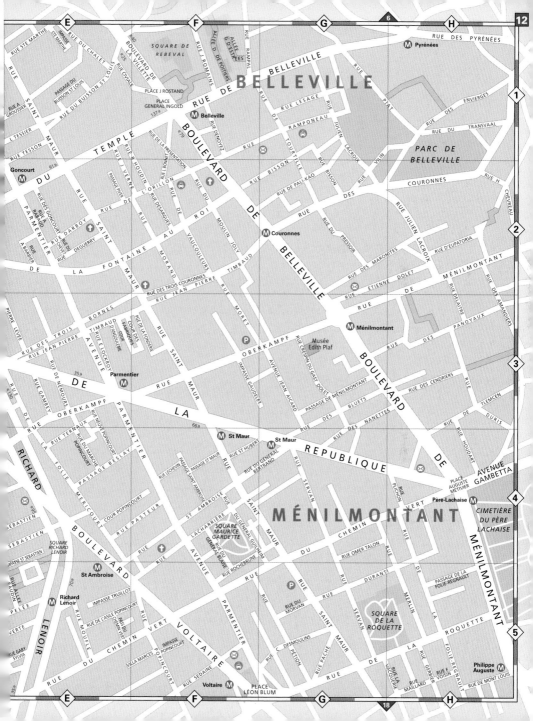

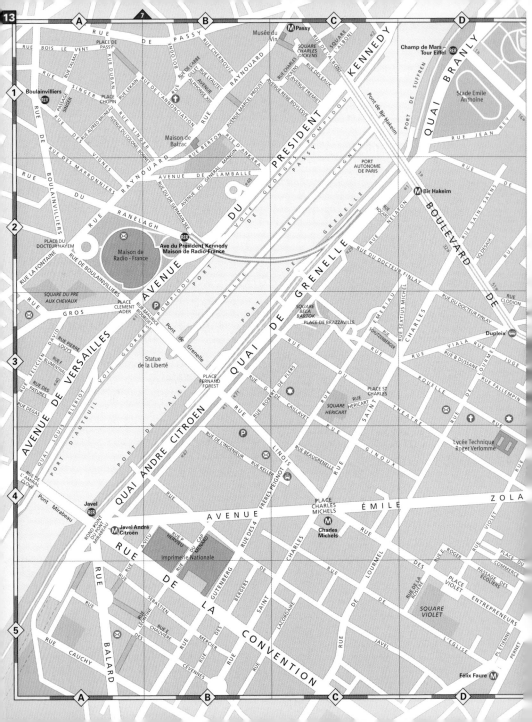

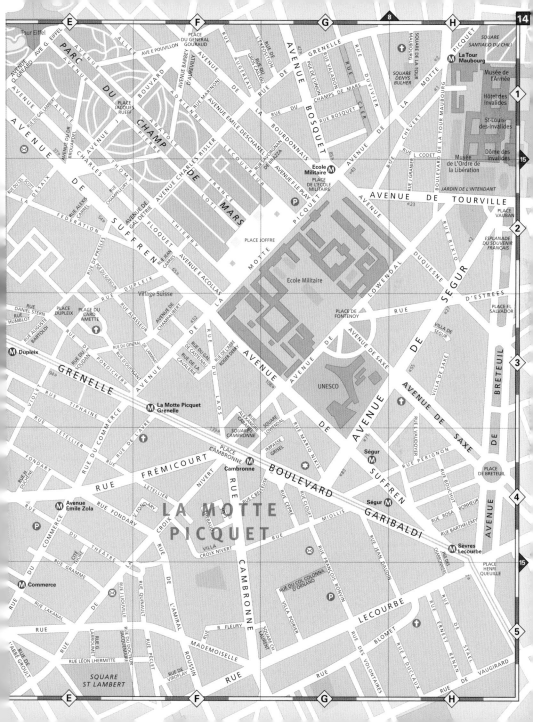

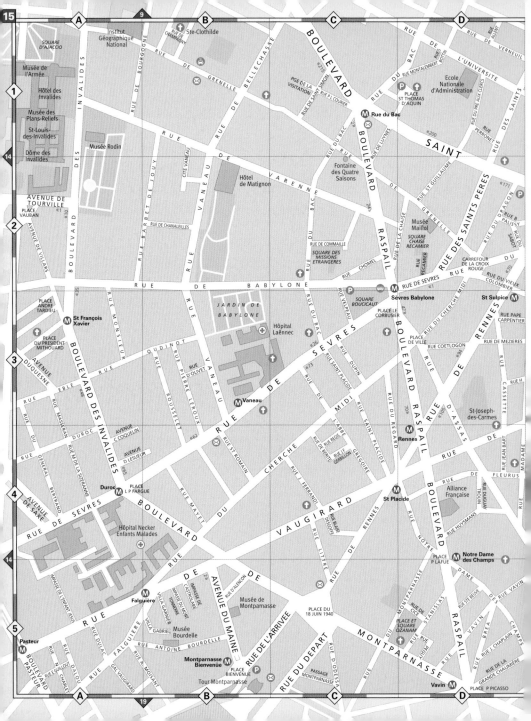

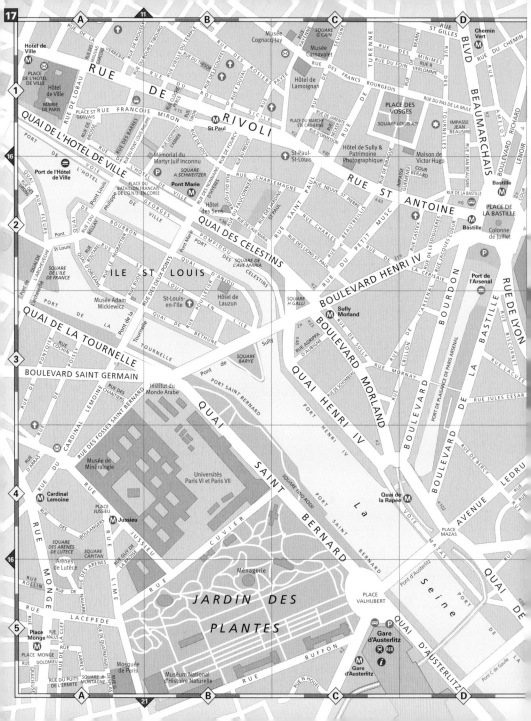

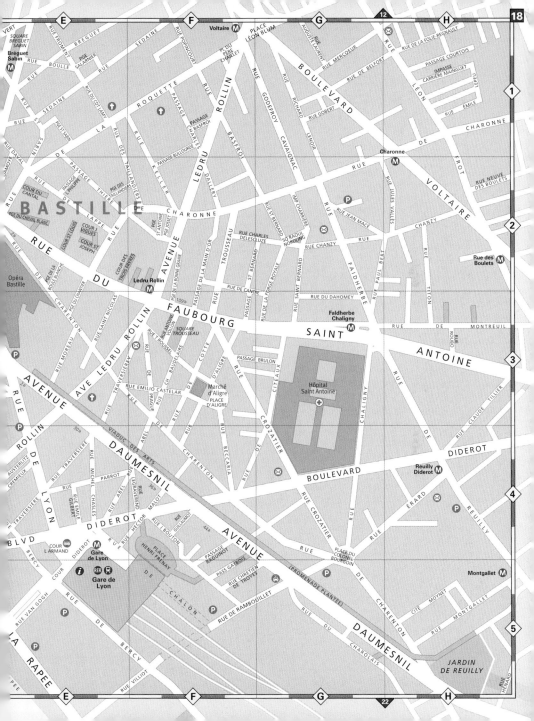

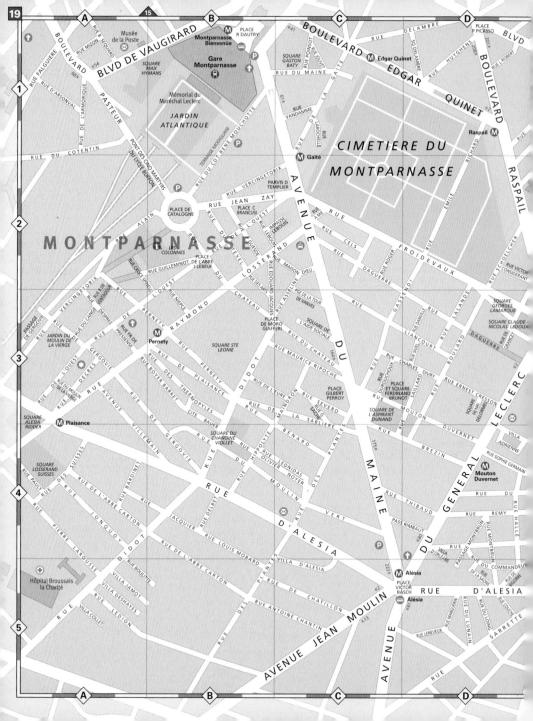

Centre

Restaurants

1st arrondissement

Angelina *(see p220)*

A Priori Thé *(see p220)*

L'Ardoise (p24)   €€
28 rue du Mont Thabor
(Map 9 C3)
Bistro

Au Pied de Cochon (p24)   €€
6 rue Coquillière
(Map 10 G4)
Bistro

Aux Lyonnais (p25)   €€
32 rue St-Marc (Map 10 F2)
Bistro

Chez Vong (p25)   €€
10 rue de la Grande Truanderie
(Map 10 H4)
Chinese

L'Espadon (p24)   €€€
Hôtel Ritz, 15 place Vendôme
(Map 9 D2)
Haute cuisine

Higuma (p26)   €
32bis rue Ste-Anne (Map 10 E2)
01 47 03 38 59
Japanese

Laï Laï Ken (p26)   €
7 rue Ste-Anne (Map 10 E2)
Japanese

Le Meurice (p25)   €€€
Hotel Meurice, 228 rue de
Rivoli (Map 9 D3)
Haute cuisine

Restaurant du Palais Royal €€
(p24)
110 galérie Valois
(Map 10 F3)
Modern French

Toupary Restaurant (p165)
La Samaritaine, 2 quai du
Louvre (Map 10 F5)
French restaurant

La Tour de Montlhéry (p25) €€
5 rue des Prouvaires
(Map 10 G4)
Bistro

2nd arrondissement

Café Moderne (p25)   €€
40 rue Notre-Dame-des-
Victoires (Map 10 G2)
Modern French

Chez Georges (p26)   €€
1 rue du Mail (Map 10 G3)
Bistro

Le Grand Colbert *(see p218)*

L'Iode (p26)   €€
48 rue d'Argout (Map 10 G3)
Fish & Seafood

3rd arrondissement

L'Ambassade d'Auvergne   €€
(p27)
22 rue du Grenier St-Lazare
(Map 11 A4)
Regional

Anahi (p27)   €€
49 rue Volta (Map 11 B3)
Latin American

Les Enfants Rouges (p27) €€
9 rue de Beauce (Map 11 C4)
Wine bar

Le Pamphlet (p28)   €€
38 rue Debelleyme (Map 11 C4)
Bistro

Le Petit Dakar (p26)   €
6 rue Elzévir (Map 11 C5)
African

Les Petits Marseillais (p28) €€
72 rue Vieille du Temple
(Map 11 B5)
Bistro

Le Potager du Marais (p28) €
22 rue Rambuteau (Map 11 A5)
Vegetarian

R'Aliment (p28)   €€
57 rue Charlot (Map 11 C4)
Modern French

4th arrondissement

L'Ambroisie (p29)   €€€
9 place des Vosges
(Map 17 C1)
Haute cuisine

L'As du Fallafal (p29, p38) €€
34 rue des Rosiers (Map 17 B1)
Middle Eastern

Brasserie de l'Ile St-Louis
(see p218)

Café de la Poste (p30)   €
13 rue Castex
(Map 17 D2)
French

L'Enoteca (p30)   €€
25 rue Charles V
(Map 17 C2)
Italian

Georget (p30)   €€
64 rue Vieille du Temple
(Map 11 B5)
Bistro

Mon Vieil Ami (p31)   €€
69 rue St-Louis-en-l'Ile
(Map 17 A2)
Modern French

L'Osteria (p31)   €€
10 rue de Sévigné (Map 17 C1)
Italian

Le Vieux Bistro (p30)   €€
14 rue du Cloître Notre Dame
(Map 16 H2)
Bistro

5th arrondissement

Anahuacalli (p31)   €€
30 rue des Bernardins
(Map 16 H3)
Mexican

Le Balzar *(see p219)*

Le Cosi (p32)   €€
9 rue Cujas
(Map 16 G4)
Regional

Les Délices d'Aphrodite   €€
(p32)4 rue de Candolle
(Map 20 H1)
Greek

Fogon St-Julien (p32)   €€
10 rue St-Julien-le-Pauvre
(Map 16 H2)
Spanish

Le Pré Verre (p33)   €€
8 rue Thénard (Map 16 G3)
Bistro

Le Reminet (p32)   €€
3 rue des Grands-Degrés
(Map 16 H3)
Bistro

Restaurant Marty (p33)   €€
20 avenue des Gobelins
(Map 21 A2)
Brasserie

La Tour d'Argent (p33)   €€€
15–17 quai de la Tournelle
(Map 17 A3)
Haute cuisine

6th arrondissement

Abazu (p34)   €€
3 rue André-Mazet (Map 16 F2)
Japanese

Allard (p34)   €€
41 rue St-André-des-Arts
(Map 16 F2)
Bistro

L'Epi Dupin (p34)   €€
11 rue Dupin (Map 15 C3)
Bistro

La Maison de la Chine
(see p220)

Le Salon d'Hélène (p35) €€€
4 rue d'Assas (Map 15 D3)
Regional

La Table d'Aude (p35)   €€
8 rue de Vaugirard
(Map 16 F3)
Regional

Le Timbre (p35)   €€
3 rue Ste-Beuve (Map 15 D5)
Bistro

Yen (p34)   €€
22 rue St-Benoît (Map 16 E2)
Japanese

7th arrondissement

L'Ami Jean (p36)   €€
27 rue Malar (Map 8 G5)
Regional

L'Arpège (p36)   €€€
84 rue de Varenne (Map 15 A1)
Haute cuisine

L'Atelier de   €€€
Joël Robuchon (p37)
5 rue de Montalembert
(Map 15 D1)
Modern French

Au Bon Accueil (p38)   €€
14 rue de Montessuy (Map 8 F5)
Bistro

Bellota-Bellota (p36)   €€
18 rue Jean-Nicot (Map 8 G5)
Spanish

Café Constant (p38)   €€
139 rue St-Dominique
(Map 8 F5)
Bistro

Shops

1st arrondissement

L'Artisan Parfumeur (p62)
2 rue Amiral de Coligny
(Map 10 F5)
Perfumes

by Terry (p60)
21 galérie Véro-Dodat
(Map 10 F4)
Beauty

Christian Louboutin (p60)
19 rue Jean-Jacques Rousseau
(Map 10 F4)
Shoes

Colette *(see p220)*

L'Eclaireur (p63)
10 rue Hérold (Map 10 G3)
Fashion

Etam *(see p221)*

Fifi Chachnil (p60)
231 rue St-Honoré (Map 9 D3)
Lingerie

Flavie Furst (p64)
16 rue de la Soudière
(Map 10 E3)
Accessories

Helmut Lang (p61)
219 rue St-Honoré (Map 10 E4)
Fashion

John Galliano *(see p221)*

Lavinia (p64)
3–5 blvd de la Madeleine
(Map 9 D2)
Food & drink

Madelios (p61)
23 blvd de la Madeleine
(Map 9 C2)
Fashion

Maria Luisa (p62)
2 rue Cambon (Map 9 C3)
Fashion

Martin Margiela (p62)
25bis rue de Montpensier
(Map 10 F3)
Fashion

Pierre Hardy (p61)
156 galérie de Valois (Map 10 F4)
Shoes

Salons du Palais Royal (p62)
25 rue de Valois (Map 10 F3)
Perfume

Ventilo (p63)
13–15 blvd de la Madeleine
(Map 9 C2)
Fashion

Yves Rocher *(see p220)*

2nd arrondissement

Barbara Bui (p65)
23 rue Etienne Marcel
(Map 10 H4)
Fashion

Erik & Lydie (p65)
7 passage du Grand Cerf
(Map 10 H3)
Accessories

Et Vous Stock *(see p221)*

Killiwatch (p65)
64 rue Tiquetonne (Map 10 G3)
Second-hand & vintage

Odette & Zoe (p63)
4 rue des Petits Champs
(Map 10 F3)
Accessories

Papageno *(see p222)*

3rd arrondissement

AB33 (p69)
33 rue Charlot (Map 11 C4)
Fashion

Abou d'Abi Bazar (p68)
10 rue des Francs Bourgeois
(Map 17 C1)
Fashion

Atelier Narakas (p66)
79 rue du Temple (Map 11 B4)
Fashion

La Chaise Longue (p68)
20 rue des Francs Bourgeois
(Map 17 C1)
Interiors

Food (p67)
58 rue Charlot (Map 11 C4)
Food & drink

Galerie Simone (p68)
124 rue Vieille du Temple
(Map 11 C4)
Concept store

Goumanyat & Son Royaume
(p66)
3 rue Charles François Dupuis
(Map 11 C3)
Food & drink

Karine Dupont (p67)
22 rue Poitou (Map 11 C4)
Accessories

Robert Le Héros (p65)
13 rue de Saintonge
(Map 11 C4)
Interiors

Shoe Bizz (p66)
48 rue Beaubourg (Map 11 A5)
Shoes

4th arrondissement

A L'Olivier (p74)
23 rue de Rivoli (Map 17 B1)
Food & drink

Antik Batik (p67)
18 rue de Turenne (Map 17 C1)
Fashion

A-poc (p70)
47 rue des Francs Bourgeois
(Map 11 B5)
Fashion

Azzedine Alaïa (p70)
7 rue de Moussy (Map 17 A1)
Fashion

Bô (p74)
8 rue St-Merri (Map 11 A5)
Interiors

Brontibay (p70)
6 rue de Sévigné (Map 17 C1)
Accessories

Calligrane (p71)
4–6 rue du Pont Louis-Philippe
(Map 17 A2)
Stationery

Comptoir des Cotonniers (p70)
33 rue des Francs Bourgeois
(Map 11 B5)
Fashion

Hervé Gambs (p71)
9bis rue des Blancs Manteaux
(Map 11 B5)
Interiors

Hervé Van der Straeten (p74)
11 rue Ferdinand Duval
(Map 17 B1)
Accessories

Martin Grant (p72)
44 rue Vieille du Temple
(Map 11 B5)
Fashion

Sentou (p73)
18 & 24 rue du Pont Louis-
Philippe (Map 17 B1)
29 rue François Miron
(Map 17 B1)
Interiors

Yukiko (p71)
97 rue Vieille du Temple
(Map 11 C4)
Second-hand & vintage

5th arrondissement

Diptyque (p74)
34 boulevard St-Germain
(Map 17 A3)
Interiors

Paris Jazz Corner *(see p223)*

6th arrondissement

Agnès b (p76)
6 & 12 rue du Vieux Colombier
(Map 15 D2)
Fashion

APC (p76)
3 & 4 rue Fleurus (Map 15 D4)
Fashion

APC Solde *(see p221)*

Christian Tortu (p79)
6 carrefour de l'Odéon
(Map 16 F2)
Interiors

Dépôt-Vente de Buci *(see p221)*

Free Lance (p76)
30 rue du Four (Map 15 D2)
Shoes

Jamin Puech (p78)
43 rue Madame
(Map 16 E3)
Accessories

Centre

Shops *continued...*

Lagerfeld Gallery (p77)
40 rue de Seine (Map 16 E1)
Fashion

Loft Design by (p78)
56 rue de Rennes (Map 16 E2)
Fashion

La Maison du Chocolat (p75)
19 rue de Sèvres (Map 15 C3)
Food & drink

Marie Mercié (p78)
23 rue St-Sulpice (Map 16 E3)
Accessories

Les 3 Marches de Catherine B (p76)
1 & 3 rue Guisarde (Map 16 E2)
Second-hand & vintage

Onward (p78)
147 blvd St-Germain (Map 16 E2)
Fashion

Paul & Joe (p77)
40 rue du Four (Map 16 E2)
Fashion

Sabbia Rosa (p75)
73 rue des Sts-Pères (Map 15 D2)
Lingerie

Shadé (p79)
63 rue des Sts-Pères
(Map 15 D2)
Fashion

Tara Jamon (p75)
18 rue du Four (Map 16 E2)
Fashion

Vanessa Bruno (p77)
25 rue St-Sulpice (Map 16 E3)
Fashion

Vannina Vesperini (p75)
63 rue des Sts-Pères
(Map 15 D2)
Lingerie

Woman (p77)
4 rue de Grenelle (Map 15 D2)
Lingerie

7th arrondissement

Le Bon Marché *(see p220)*

Carine Gilson (p80)
36 rue de Varenne (Map 15 C2)
Lingerie

Catherine Arigoni (p82)
14 rue Beaune (Map 15 D1)
Second-hand & vintage

Deyrolle (p79)
46 rue du Bac (Map 15 C1)
Interiors

Editions de Parfums Frédéric Malle (p80)
37 rue de Grenelle (Map 15 C2)
Perfumes

La Grande Epicerie (p80)
Le Bon Marché, 22 rue des Sèvres (Map 15 C3)
Food & drink

Iris (p80)
28 rue de Grenelle (Map 15 D2)
Shoes

Iunx (p83)
48–50 rue de l'Université
(Map 15 D1)
Perfumes

Jean-Baptiste Rautureau (p82)
24 rue de Grenelle (Map 15 D2)
Shoes

Lucien Pellat-Finet (p81)
1 rue Montalembert
(Map 15 D1)
Fashion

Martine Sitbon (p81)
13 rue Grenelle (Map 15 D2)
Fashion

Paul Smith (p81)
22 & 24 blvd Raspail
(Map 15 D3)
Fashion

Rue Cler (p156) (Map 14 G1)
Markets

Thomas Boog (p82)
52 rue de Bourgogne
(Map 15 A1)
Interiors

Art & Architecture

1st arrondissement

Chez Robert Electron Libre (p94)
59 rue de Rivoli (Map 10 G5)
Exhibition space

La Conciergerie *(see p224)*

Eglise St-Eustache (p97)
Rue du Jour (Map 10 G4)
Church

Jeu de Paume (p95)
1 pl de la Concorde (Map 9 C3)
Exhibition space

Musée du Louvre *(see p224)*

Musée de la Publicité (p96)
107 rue de Rivoli (Map 10 E4)
Museum

Ste-Chapelle (p94)
4 blvd du Palais (Map 16 G1)
Church

Tour St-Jacques (p94)
(Map 16 H1)
Historic building

2nd arrondissement

Bibliothèque Nationale de France – Richelieu (p95)
58 rue de Richelieu (Map 10 F3)
Exhibition space

3rd arrondissement

Musée d'Art et d'Histoire du Judaïsme (p96)
71 rue du Temple (Map 11 A5)
Museum

Musée Carnavalet (p95)
23 rue de Sevigné (Map 17 C1)
Museum

Musée National Picasso (p96)
5 rue de Thorigny
(Map 11 C5)
Museum

4th arrondissement

Atelier Brancusi (p97)
Pl Centre Pompidou (Map 11 A5)
Exhibition space

Centre Pompidou *(see p224)*

Maison Européene de la Photographie (p98)
5–7 rue de Fourcy
(Map 17 B1)
Exhibition space

Musée Cognacq-Jay (p97)
8 rue Elzévi (Map 17 C1)
Museum

Notre Dame (p110)
Place du Parvis-Notre-Dame
(Map 16 H2) 01 42 34 56 10
Church

Patrimoine Photographique (p97)
62 rue St-Antoine (Map 17 C2)
Exhibition space

5th arrondissement

Abbaye du Val-de-Grâce (p99)
227bis rue St-Jacques
(Map 20 F1)
Museum

Arènes de Lutèce (p99)
Entrances on 49 rue Monge & 7 rue de Navarre (Map 17 A5)
Historic building

Institut du Monde Arabe (p98)
1 rue des Fossés St-Bernard
(Map 17 B3)
Exhibition space

Musée de l'Assistance Publique (p99)
47 quai de la Tournelle
(Map 17 A3)
Museum

Musée National du Moyen Age (p98)
6 pl Paul-Painlevé
(Map 16 G3)
Museum

St-Julien-le-Pauvre (p163)
Rue St-Julien-le-Pauvre
(Map 16 H2)
Church

La Sorbonne (p99)
47 rue des Ecoles (Map 16 G3)
Historic building

6th arrondissement

Eglise St-Sulpice (p100)
Place St-Sulpice (Map 16 E3)
Church

Musée du Luxembourg (p100)
19 rue de Vaugirard
(Map 16 E3)
Exhibition space

Musée National Eugène Delacroix (p100)
6 rue de Furstenberg
(Map 16 E2)
Museum

7th arrondissement

Assemblée Nationale (p110)
126 rue de l'Université
(Map 9 A4) 01 40 63 60 00
Historic building

**Musée Maillol – Fondation
Dina Vierny** (p101)
59–61 rue de Grenelle
(Map 15 D2)
Museum

Musée d'Orsay *(see p225)*

Musée Rodin (p111)
77 rue de Varenne (Map 15 A1)
Museum

Tour Eiffel *(see p224)*

Performance

1st arrondissement

Comédie Française (p119)
2 rue de Richelieu (Map 10 H4)
Theatre

Duc des Lombards (p118)
42 rue des Lombards
(Map 10 H5)
Live music

Forum des Images (p118)
Forum des Halles (Map 10 G4)
Cinema

Théâtre du Châtelet (p119)
1 place du Châtelet (Map 16 H1)
Multi-function venue

2nd arrondissement

Le Grand Rex (p119)
1 blvd Poissonnière
(Map 10 H2)
Cinema

4th arrondissement

Café de la Gare (p119)
41 rue du Temple (Map 11 A5)
Comedy

Le Point Virgule (p118)
7 rue St-Croix de la Bretonnerie
(Map 17 B1)
Comedy

Théâtre de la Ville (p121)
2 place du Châtelet
(Map 16 H1)
Multi-function venue

5th arrondissement

Action Ecoles *(see p225)*

Le Champo *(see p225)*

Grand Action *(see p225)*

Images d'Ailleurs *(see p225)*

Paradis Latin *(see p225)*

Quartier Latin *(see p225)*

Reflet Medicis *(see p225)*

Studio Galande *(see p225)*

6th arrondissement

Action Christine Odeon
(see p225)

Lucernaire (p121)
53 rue Notre-Dame-des-
Champs (Map 15 D5)
Multi-function venue

Racine Odeon *(see p225)*

St-André-des-Arts *(see p225)*

7th arrondissement

La Pagode (p118)
57bis rue de Babylone
(Map 15 A2)
Cinema

Bars & Clubs

1st arrondissement

Cab (p132)
2 pl du Palais Royal
(Map 10 F4)
Club

The Cruiscin Lan (p132)
8 rue des Halles
(Map 10 H5)
01 45 08 99 15
Pub

Le Fumoir (p132)
6 rue de L'Amiral de Coligny
(Map 10 F5)
Bar

Hemingway Bar (p133)
Ritz Hotel,
15 place Vendome
(Map 9 D3)
Bar

Hotel Costes (p132)
239 rue St Honoré (Map 9 D3)
Bar

Juveniles (p133)
47 rue de Richelieu (Map 10 F3)
Bar

Kong (p134)
1 rue du Pont Neuf (Map 10 G5)
Bar

Wine & Bubbles (p154)
3 rue Française (Map 10 H4)
01 44 76 99 84
Bar

2nd arrondissement

Le Café (p154)
62 rue Tiquetonne (Map 10 G3)
01 40 39 08 00
Bar

Le Café Noir (p135)
65 rue Montmartre (Map 10 G3)
Bar

Le Coeur Fou (p133)
55 rue Montmartre (Map 10 G3)
Bar

Etienne Marcel (p154)
34 rue Etienne Marcel
(Map 10 G3) 01 45 08 01 03
Bar

Harry's Bar (p136)
5 rue Daunou (Map 10 E2)
Bar

Le Next (p135)
17 rue Tiquetonne (Map 10 H3)
Bar

Pulp (p136)
25 blvd Poissonnière (Map 10 G1)
Club

Le Rex (p135)
5 blvd Poissonière (Map 10 G1)
Club

Somo (p135)
168 rue Montmartre
(Map 10 G2)
Bar

3rd arrondissement

Andy Wahloo (p137)
69 rue des Gravilliers
(Map 11 A3)
Bar

Boob's Bourg (p137)
26 rue de Montmorency
(Map 11 A4)
Bar

Le Connetable (p137)
55 rue des Archives (Map 11 B4)
Bar

4th arrondissement

Amnesia (p138)
42 rue Vieille du Temple
(Map 17 B1)
Bar

The Auld Alliance (p132)
80 rue François Miron
(Map 17 B1)
Pub

Au Petit Fer à Cheval (p138)
30 rue Vieille du Temple
(Map 17 B1)
Bar

La Belle Hortense (p139)
31 rue Vieille du Temple
(Map 17 B1)
Bar

Chez Richard (p138)
37 rue Vieille du Temple
(Map 17 B1)
Bar

Le Cox (p140)
15 rue des Archives
(Map 11 A5)
Bar

Les Etages (p140)
35 rue Vieille du Temple
(Map 17 B1)
Bar

L'Etoile Manquante (p138)
34 rue Vieille du Temple
(Map 17 B1)
Bar

Lizard Lounge (p140)
18 rue Bourg Tibourg
(Map 17 B1)
Bar

Le Trésor (p140)
7 rue Trésor (Map 17 B1)
Bar

5th arrondissement

The Bombardier (p132)
2 pl Panthéon (Map 16 G4)
Pub

Savy (p41) €€
23 rue Bayard (Map 8 G3)
Bistro

16th arrondissement

L'Astrance (p42) €€€
4 rue Beethoven (Map 7 C5)
Modern French

Le Cristal Room (p40) €€€
La Maison Baccarat, 11 place
des Etats-Unis (Map 8 E2)
Modern French

La Grande Armée (p43) €€
3 avenue de la Grande Armée
(Map 7 E1)
Brasserie

Jamin (p43) €€€
32 rue de Longchamp
(Map 7 D3)
Haute cuisine

Le Petit Rétro (p43) €€
5 rue Mesnil (Map 7 C2)
Bistro

17th arrondissement

Le Bistrot d'à Côte Flaubert
(p44) €€
10 rue Gustave-Flaubert
(Map 2 F3)
Bistro

L'Entredgeu (p43) €€
83 rue Laugier
(Map 1 D2)
Bistro

La Table de Lucullus (p44) €€€
129 rue Legendre (Map 3 C1)
Fish & seafood

Shops

8th arrondissement

André *(see p223)*

Balenciaga *(see p221)*

Bottega Veneta *(see p220)*

Chanel *(see p221)*

Charles Jourdan (p84)
86 avenue des Champs-
Elysées (Map 8 G1)
Shoes

Chloé *(see p221)*

Christian Lacroix *(see p221)*

Dior *(see p221)*

Dolce & Gabbana *(see p221)*

Emmanuel Ungaro *(see p221)*

Erès (p84)
2 rue Tronchet
(Map 9 C1)
Lingerie

fnac *(see p222)*

Galerie Noémie (p84)
92 ave des Champs-Elysées
(Map 8 F1)
Beauty

Givenchy *(see p223)*

Gucci *(see p220)*

Jean-Paul Gaultier *(see p221)*

Lanvin *(see p221)*

Louis Vuitton *(see p220)*

Marni *(see p221)*

La Parfumerie Générale (p85)
6 rue Robert-Estienne
(Map 8 G2)
Beauty

Prada *(see p222)*

Publicis Drugstore (p83)
133 ave des Champs-Elysées
(Map 8 F1)
Music & book

Renaud Pellegrino (p83)
14 rue du Faubourg-St-Honoré
(Map 9 B2)
Accessories

Résonances (p85)
3 blvd Malesherbes
(Map 9 C2)
Interiors

Roger Vivier (p86)
29 rue du Faubourg-St-Honoré
(Map 9 B2)
Shoes

Stephane Kélian (p86)
5 rue du Faubourg-St-Honoré
(Map 9 C2)
Shoes

Valentino *(see p222)*

Virgin Megastore
(see p223)

Zadig & Voltaire (de luxe) (p84)
18–20 rue François Premier
(Map 8 G3)
Fashion

16th arrondissement

Réciproque *(see p222)*

Art & Architecture

8th arrondissement

Chapelle Expiatoire (p166)
729 rue Pasquier (Map 9 C1)
Church

Eglise de la Madeleine (p102)
Pl de la Madeleine (Map 9 C2)
Church

Eglise St-Augustin (p102)
46 blvd Malesherbes
(Map 3 B5)
Church

Grand Palais (p103)
Ave Winston-Churchill (Map 9 A3)
01 44 13 17 17
Exhibition space

Musée Jacquemart-André (p102)
158 blvd Haussmann (Map 2 H5)
Museum

Palais de la Découverte (p103)
Avenue Franklin D Roosevelt
(Map 8 H3)
01 56 43 20 21
www.palais-decouverte.fr
Museum

Petit Palais (p103)
Avenue Winston Churchill
(Map 9 A3)
01 42 65 12 73
Exhibtion space

16th arrondissement

Cimetière de Passy (p109)
(Map 7 C4)
Cemetery

Fondation Le Corbusier (p105)
Villa la Roche, 10 sq du Dr
Blanche (Métro Jasmin)
Museum

Musée d'Art Moderne de la
Ville de Paris (MAMVP; p104)
11 avenue du Président Wilson
(Map 8 E3)
Museum

Musée Galliéra (p102)
10 avenue Pierre 1er de Serbie
(Map 8 E3)
Museum

Musée Guimet (p105)
6 place d'Iéna (Map 8 E3)
Museum

Musée Marmottan-Monet
(p105)
2 rue Louis Boilly
(Métro Ranelagh)
Museum

Palais de Chaillot (p104)
17 place du Trocadéro
(Map 7 C4)
Museum

Palais de Tokyo (p104)
13 avenue du Président Wilson
(Map 8 E3)
Exhibition space

Western Suburbs

Chateau de St-Germain (p106)
Place Charles de Gaulle
(RER St-Germain-en-Laye)
Museum

Musée Départemental Maurice
Denis "Le Prieuré" (p106)
2bis rue Maurice Denis
(RER St-Germain-en-Laye)
Museum

Performance

8th arrondissement

Crazy Horse *(see p225)*

Lido *(see p225)*

Théâtre des Champs-Elysées
(p121)
15 ave Montaigne
(Map 8 G3)
Multi-function venue

16th arrondissement

Hippodrome de Longchamp
(see p226)

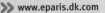

Coin Canal (p88)
1 rue de Marseille (Map 11 C1)
Interiors

E2 (p87)
15 rue Martel (Map 11 A1)
Vintage

Ginger Lyly (p87)
33 rue Beaurepaire (Map 11 C2)
Fashion

Stella Cadente (p87)
93 quai de Valmy (Map 11 C1)
Fashion

Viveka Bergström (p88)
23 rue de la Grange-aux-Belles
(Map 5 D5)
Accessories

18th arrondissement

En Avant La Zizique *(see p222)*

Lili Perpink (p88)
22 rue la Vieuville (Map 4 F2)
Fashion

Patricia Louisor (p88)
16 rue Houdon
(Map 4 F3)
Fashion

Spree (p89)
16 rue la Vieuville (Map 4 F2)
Concept store

Northern Suburbs

Puces de St-Ouen (see p158)
(Métro Porte de Clignancourt)
Market

Art & Architecture

9th arrondissement

Musée Gustave Moreau (p109)
14 rue de la Rochefoucauld
(Map 4 E4)
Museum

10th arrondissement

Gare du Nord (p110)
(Map 5 A4)
Historic building

**Porte St-Denis & Porte-St
Martin** (p109) (Map 11 A2)
Historic building

18th arrondissement

Café des Deux Moulins (p107)
15 rue Lepic (Map 4 E2)
01 42 54 90 50
Historic building

Cimetière de Montmartre
(p109) (Map 3 D1)
Cemetery

Moulin de la Galette (p107)
75 rue Lepic (Map 4 E1)
Historic building

Moulin de Radet (p107)
83 rue Lepic (Map 4 F1)
Historic building

Musée de l'Erotisme (p106)
72 blvd de Clichy (Map 4 E3)
Museum

Musée de Montmartre (p107)
12 rue Cortot (Map 4 F1)
01 46 06 61 11
Museum

Sacré Cœur (p107)
35 rue du Chevalier de la Barre
(Map 4 G2) 01 53 41 89 00
Church

19th arrondissement

**Cité des Sciences et de
l'Industrie** (p108)
Parc de la Villette, 30 ave
Corentin Cariou
(Métro Porte de Pantin)
Museum

Musée de la Musique (p108)
Cité de la Musique,
221 avenue Jean Jaurès
(Métro Porte de Pantin)
Museum

Northern Suberbs

Basilique St-Denis (p108)
1 rue de la Légion d'Honneur
(Métro Basilique de St-Denis)
Church

**Musée d'Art et d'Histoire de
St-Denis** (p109)
22bis rue Gabriel Péri
(Métro St-Denis Porte de Paris)
Museum

Stade de France (p198, 127)
rue Francis de Pressensé
(Métro St-Denis Porte de Paris)
Modern architecture

Performance

9th arrondissement

Opéra Garnier *(see p224)*

10th arrondissement

Bouffes du Nord (p122)
37bis boulevard de la Chapelle
(Map 5 B2)
Multi-function venue

Hotel du Nord (p123)
102 quai de Jemmapes
(Map 11 C1)
Comedy

New Morning (p122)
7–9 rue des Petites-Ecuries
(Map 11 A1)
Live music

18th arrondissement

Bal du Moulin Rouge *(see p225)*

Chez Madame Arthur *(see p225)*

Chez Michou *(see p225)*

Elysée Montmartre (p123)
72 blvd Rochechouart (Map 4 G3)
Live music

Studio 28 (p123)
10 rue Tholozé (Map 4 E2)
Cinema

19th arrondissement

Cinéma en Plein Air (p124)
Parc de la Villette
(Métro Porte de Pontin)
Cinema

Cité de la Musique (p123)
221 avenue Jean Jaurès
(Métro Porte de Pantin)
Live music

Le Zénith (p124)
211 avenue Jean Jaurès
(Métro Porte de Pantin)
Multi-function venue

Northern Suberbs

Centre National de la Danse
(p124)
1 rue Victor Hugo
(Métro Hoche, RER Pantin)
Dance

Stade de France (p198, p127)
rue Francis de Pressensé
(Métro St-Denis Porte de Paris)
Sport

Bars & Clubs

9th arrondissement

Project 101 (p147)
44 rue de la Rochefoucauld
(Map 4 E4)
Club

Xtremes (p147)
10 rue Caumartin (Map 9 D1)
Bar

10th arrondissement

Chez Prune (147)
36 rue Beaurepaire (Map 11 C1)
Bar

De la Ville (p146)
34 boulevard de la Bonne
Nouvelle (Map 10 H2)
Bar/Club

La Patache (p147)
60 rue de Lancry
(Map 11 C1)
Bar

18th arrondissement

La Fourmi (p146)
74 rue des Martyrs (Map 4 F3)
Bar

Le Progrès (p146)
1 rue Yvonne le Tac
(Map 4 F2)
Bar

La Sancerre (p148)
35 rue des Abbesses (Map 4 E2)
Bar

Havens: Parks,
Squares & Gardens

19th arrondissement

Parc des Buttes-Chaumont
(p166) (Map 6 G4)

Havens: Spas &
Treatments

9th arrondissement

Cinq Mondes (p166)
6 sq de l'Opéra Louis Jouvet
(Map 9 D1)

Bars & Clubs

11th arrondissement

Café Charbon (p149)
109 rue Oberkampf (Map 12 F3)
Bar/Club

Le Clown Bar (p149)
114 rue Amelot (Map 11 D4)
Bar

La Fabrique (p148)
53 rue du Faubourg St-Antoine
(Map 18 E2)
Bar

Favela Chic (p150)
18 rue du Faubourg du Temple
(Map 11 D2)
Club

Le Lèche-Vin (p149)
13 rue Duval (Map 17 E1)
Bar

Pop In (p149)
105 rue Amelot (Map 11 D4)
Club

Wax (p150)
15 rue Daval (Map 18 E1)
Bar/Club

Le Zero Zero (p150)
89 rue Amelot (Map 11 D5)
Bar

12th arrondissement

Le Baron Rouge (p151)
1 rue T Roussel (Map 18 F3)
Bar

Barrio Latino (p151)
46 rue du Faubourg St Antoine
(Map 18 E2)
Club

Chai 33 (p150)
33 cour St-Emilion (Map 22 H3)
Bar

China Club (p148)
50 rue Charenton (Map 18 E3)
Bar

Havens: Parks, Squares & Gardens

12th arrondissement

La Promenade Plantée (p167)
(Map 18 G5)

Hotels

11th arrondissement

Hotel Beaumarchais (p181)   €
3 rue Oberkampf
(Map 11 D4)

South

Restaurants

13th arrondissement

L'Avant Goût (p52)   €€
26 rue Bobillot (Map 21 A4)
Bistro

Les Cailloux (p53)   €€
58 rue des Cinq-Diamants
(Map 20 H5)
Italian

Tricotin (p53)   €
15 avenue de Choisy
(Métro Porte de Choisy)
Chinese

14th arrondissement

L'Assiette (p54)   €€€
181 rue du Château (Map 19 C3)
Bistro

Au Petit Marguery (p53)   €€
9 blvd de Port-Royal
(Map 20 H2)
Bistro

La Coupole (*see p218*)

Natacha (p53)   €€
17 bis rue Campagne-Première
(Map 19 E1)
Bistro

15th arrondissement

Chez Foong (p55)   €€
32 rue de Frémicourt (Map 14 F4)
Southeast Asian

**L'Os à Moëlle & La Cave
de l'Os à Moëlle** (p54)   €€
3 rue Vasco de Gama & 181 rue
Lourmel (Métro Lourmel)
Bistro

Le Père Claude (p54)   €€
51 avenue de la Motte-Piquet
(Map 14 F3)
Bistro

Le Suffren (p55)   €€
84 ave de Suffren (Map 14 F3)
Brasserie

Le Troquet (p55)   €€
21 rue François-Bonvin
(Map 14 G5)
Bistro

Shops

14th arrondissement

Afric' Music (*see p222*)

Cacharel (*see p221*)

Art & Architecture

13th arrondissement

**Bibliothèque Nationale de
France – François Mitterrand**
(p111)
11 quai François Mauriac
(Map 22 F3)
Exhibition space

Les Frigos (p112)
rue des Frigos (Map 22 F4)
Exhibition space

Louise Weiss, rue (p112)
(Map 21 D3)
Exhibition space

Manufacture des Gobelins
(p112)
42 ave des Gobelins
(Map 21 A3)
Museum

14th arrondissement

Catacombes (p113)
1 pl Denfert Rochereau
(Map 20 E3)
Historic building

Cimetière du Montparnasse
(p167)
3 blvd Edgar Quinet (Map 19 C2)
Cemetery

Cité Universitaire (p112)
Boulevard Jourdan
(Métro Cité Universitaire)
Modern architecture

**Fondation Cartier pour l'Art
Contemporain** (p113)
261 boulevard Raspail
(Map 19 D2)
Exhibition space

**Fondation Henri Cartier-
Bresson** (p113)
2 impasse Lebouis
(Map 19 B2)
Exhibition space

15th arrondissement

Mémorial du Maréchal Leclerc
(p113)
23 allée de la Deuxième
(Map 19 B1)
Museum

Performance

13th arrondissement

La Guinguette Pirate (p126)
Quai Francois-Mauriac
(Map 22 F3)
Live music

MK2 Bibliothèque (p127)
128–62 ave de France
(Map 22 F3)
Cinema

14th arrondissement

Théâtre de la Cité (p127)
21 boulevard Jourdan
(RER Cité Universitaire)
Theatre

Bars & Clubs

13th arrondissement

Batofar (p151)
Opposite 11 quai François
Mauriac (Map 22 F2)
Club

Limelight (p151)
162 ave de France
(Map 22 F4)
Bar

Havens: Parks, Squares & Gardens

15th arrondissement

Parc André Citroën (p167)
(Map 13 A5)

Hotels

15th arrondissement

Novotel Tour Eiffel (p181)   €€
61 quai de Grenelle
(Map 13 B3)

Restaurants

African

Benisti (p49) €
108 boulevard de Belleville
(Map 12 F1)
East/20th arrondissement

Chez Dom (p45) €€
34 rue de Sambre et Meuse
(Map 6 E5)
North/10th arrondissement

L'Homme Bleu (p50) €€
55bis rue Jean-Pierre Timbaud
(Map 12 E3)
East/11th arrondissement

Martel (p45) €€
3 rue Martel (Map 11 A1)
North/10th arrondissement

Le Petit Dakar (p26) €
6 rue Elzévir
(Map 11 C5)
Centre/3rd arrondissement

Le Souk (p51) €€
1 rue Keller (Map 18 F2)
East/11th arrondissement

Bistros

Allard (p34) €€
41 rue St-André-des-Arts
(Map 16 F2)
Centre/6th arrondissement

L'Angle du Faubourg (p39) €€
195 rue du Faubourg St-Honoré
(Map 2 G5)
West/8th arrondissement

L'Ardoise (p24) €€
28 rue du Mont Thabor
(Map 9 C3)
Centre/1st arrondissement

L'Assiette (p54) €€€
181 rue du Chateau
(Map 19 C3)
South/14th arrondissement

Astier (p49) €€
44 rue Jean-Pierre Timbaud
(Map 12 E3)
East/11th arrondissement

Au Bon Accueil (p38) €€
14 rue de Monttessuy
(Map 8 F5)
Centre/7th arrondissement

Au Petit Marguery (p53) €€
9 boulevard de Port-Royal
(Map 20 H2)
South/14th arrondissement

Au Pied de Cochon (p24) €€
6 rue Coquillière (Map 10 G4)
Centre/1st arrondissement

Aux Lyonnais (p25) €€
32 rue St-Marc (Map 10 F2)
Centre/2nd arrondissement

L'Avent Gout (p52) €€
26 rue Bobillot (Map 21 A4)
South/13th arrondissement

Le Bistrot d'à Côté Flaubert €€
(p44)
10 rue Gustave-Flaubert
(Map 2 F3)
West/17th arrondissement

Le Bistrot Paul Bert (p51) €€
18 rue Paul-Bert
(Métro Faidherbe-Chaligny)
East/11th arrondissement

Café Burq (p46) €€
6 rue Burq (Map 4 E2)
North/18th arrondissement

Café Constant (p38) €€
139 rue St-Dominique
(Map 8 F5)
Centre/7th arrondissement

Café Noir (p49) €€
15 rue St-Blaise
(Métro Porte de Bagnolet)
East/20th arrondissement

Casa Olympe (p44) €€
48 rue St-Georges (Map 4 F5)
North/9th arrondissement

Chez Georges (p26) €€
1 rue du Mail (Map 10 G3)
Centre/2nd arrondissement

Chez Toinette (p47) €€
20 rue Germain-Pilon
(Map 4 E2)
North/18th arrondissement

L'Entredgeu (p43) €€
83 rue Laugier (Map 1 D1)
West/17th arrondissement

L'Epi Dupin (p34) €€
11 rue Dupin
(Map 15 C3)
Centre/6th arrondissement

Georget (p30) €€
64 rue Vieille du Temple
(Map 11 B5)
Centre/4th arrondissement

La Mascotte (p49) €€
52 rue des Abbesses
(Map 4 E2)
North/18th arrondissement

Natasha (p53) €€
17bis rue Campagne-Première
(Map 19 E1)
South/14th arrondissement

L'Os à Moëlle (p54) €€
3 rue Vasco de Gama
(Métro Lourmel)
South/15th arrondissement

La Cave de l'Os à Moëlle €€
(p54)
181 rue Lourmel
(Métro Lourmel)
South/15th arrondissement

Le Pamphlet (p28) €€
38 rue Debelleyme (Map 11 C4)
Centre/3rd arrondissement

Le Père Claude (p54) €€
51 avenue de la Motte-Piquet
(Map 14 F3)
South/15th arrondissement

Le Petit Keller (p51) €
13bis rue Keller (Map 18 F1)
East/11th arrondissement

Le Petit Retro (p43) €€
5 rue Mesnil (Map 7 C2)
West/16th arrondissement

Les Petits Marseillais (p28) €€
72 rue Vieille du Temple
(Map 11 B5)
Centre/3rd arrondissement

Le Poulbot Gourmet (p54) €€
39 rue Lamark (Map 4 F1)
North/18th arrondissement

Le Pré Verre (p33) €€
8 rue Thénard (Map 16 G3)
Centre/5th arrondissement

Le Reminet (p32) €€
3 rue des Grands-Degrés
(Map 16 H3)
Centre/5th arrondissement

Savy (p41) €€
23 rue Bayard (Map 8 G3)
West/8th arrondissement

Le Square Trousseau (p52) €€
1 rue Antoine-Vollon
(Map 18 F3)
East/12th arrondissement

Le Timbre (p35) €€
3 rue Ste-Beuve (Map 15 D5)
Centre/6th arrondissement

La Tour de Montlhéry (p25) €€
5 rue des Prouvaires
(Map 10 G4)
Centre/1st arrondissement

Le Troquet (p55) €€
21 rue François-Bonvin
(Map 14 G5)
South/15th arrondissement

Velly (p45) €€
52 rue Lamartine (Map 4 F5)
North/9th arrondissement

Le Vieux Bistro (p30) €€
14 rue du Cloître Notre Dame
(Map 16 H2)
Centre/4th arrondissement

Brasseries

Le Balzar (p29) €€
49 rue des Ecoles (Map 16 G3)
01 43 54 13 67
Centre/5th arrondissement

Brasserie Flo (p29) €€
7 cour des Petites-Ecuries
(Map 11 A1) 01 47 70 13 59
North/10th arrondissement

Brasserie de l'Ile St-Louis (p29) €€
55 quai Bourbon (Map 17 A2)
01 43 54 02 59
Centre/4th arrondissement

La Coupole (p53) €€
102 blvd de Montparnasse
(Map 15 D5)
01 43 20 14 20
South/14th arrondissement

Garnier (p39) €€€
111 rue St-Lazare (Map 3 C5)
West/8th arrondissement

La Grande Armée (p43) €€
3 avenue de la Grande Armée
(Map 7 E1)
West/16th arrondissement

Le Grand Colbert (p29) €€
2–4 rue Vivienne (Map 10 F3)
01 42 86 87 88
Centre/2nd arrondissement

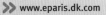

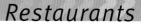

Julien (p29)   €€
16 rue du Faubourg St-Denis
(Map 11 A2)
01 47 70 12 06
North/10th arrondissement

Restaurant Marty (p33)   €€
20 avenue des Gobelins
(Map 21 A2)
Centre/5th arrondissement

Le Suffren (p55)   €€
84 avenue de Suffren
(Map 14 F3)
South/15th arrondissement

Terminus Nord (p46)   €€
23 rue de Dunkerque
(Map 5 A4)
North/10th arrondissement

Le Train Bleu (p51)   €€
Gare de Lyon, place Louis-
Armand (Map 18 E5)
East/12th arrondissement

British

Rose Bakery (p45)   €
46 rue des Martyrs (Map 4 F4)
North/9th arrondissement

Chinese

Chez Vong (p25)   €€
10 rue de la Grande Truanderie
(Map 10 H4)
Centre/1st arrondissement

Tricotin (p53)   €
15 avenue de Choisy
(Métro Porte de Choisy)
South/13th arrondissement

Fish & Seafood

L'Iode (p26)   €€
48 rue d'Argout (Map 10 G3)
Centre/2nd arrondissement

La Table de Lucullus (p44) €€€
129 rue Legendre
(Map 3 C1)
West/17th arrondissement

Food to Go

Be (p38)
73 boulevard de Courcelles
(Map 2 F4)
01 46 22 20 20
West/8th arrondissement

La Grande Epicerie (*see p210*)

Cojean (p38)
4 rue de Sèze
(Map9 C2)
01 40 06 08 80
North/9th arrondissement

French

Café de la Poste (p30)   €
13 rue Castex
(Map 17 D2)
Centre/4th arrondissement

Greek

Les Délices d'Aphrodite   €€
(p32)
4 rue de Candolle
(Map 20 H1)
Centre/5th arrondissement

Haute Cuisine

L'Ambroisie (p29)   €€€
9 place des Vosges
(Map 17 C1)
Centre/4th arrondissement

L'Arpège (p36)   €€€
84 rue de Varenne
(Map 15 A1)
Centre/7th arrondissement

L'Espadon (p24)   €€€
Hôtel Ritz, 15 place Vendôme
(Map 9 D2)
Centre/1st arrondissement

Jamin (p41)   €€€
32 rue de Longchamp
(Map 7 D3)
West/16th arrondissement

Lucas Carton (p41)   €€€
9 place de la Madeleine
(Map 9 C2)
West/8th arrondissement

Le Meurice (p25)   €€€
Hotel Meurice, 228 rue de
Rivoli (Map 9 D3)
Centre/1st arrondissement

La Tour d'Argent (p33)   €€€
15–17 quai de la Tournelle
(Map 17 A3)
Centre/5th arrondissement

Indian

Kastoori (p44)   €
4 place Gustave Toudouze
(Map 4 F4)
North/9th arrondissement

Italian

Le Bistrot Napolitain (p39) €€
18 avenue Franklin D Roosevelt
(Map 8 H1)
West/8th arrondissement

Les Cailloux (p53)   €€
58 rue des Cinq-Diamants
(Map 20 H5)
South/13th arrondissement

L'Enoteca (p30)   €€
25 rue Charles V (Map 17 C2)
Centre/4th arrondissement

L'Osteria (p31)   €€
10 rue de Sévigné (Map 17 C1)
Centre/4th arrondissement

Sardegna a Tavola (p52)   €€
1 rue de Cotte (Map 18 F3)
East/12th arrondissement

Japanese

Abazu (p34)   €€
3 rue André-Mazet
(Map 16 F2)
Centre/6th arrondissement

Higuma (p26)   €
32bis rue Ste-Anne
(Map 10 E2)
01 47 03 38 59
Centre/1st arrondissement

Laï Laï Ken (p26)   €€
7 rue Ste-Anne (Map 10 E2)
Centre/1st arrondissement

Yen (p34)   €€
22 rue St-Benoît (Map 16 E2)
Centre/6th arrondissement

Latin American

Anahi (p27)   €€
49 rue Volta (Map 11 B3)
Centre/3rd arrondissement

Mexican

Anahuacalli (p31)   €€
30 rue des Bernardins
(Map 16 H3)
Centre/5th arrondissement

Middle Eastern

L'As du Fallafal (p29, p38) €
34 rue des Rosiers
(Map 17 B1)
Centre/4th arrondissement

Modern French

L'Astrance (p42)   €€€
4 rue Beethoven (Map 7 C5)
West/16th arrondissement

L'Atelier de Joël Robuchon €€€
(p37)
5 rue de Montalembert
(Map 15 D1)
Centre/7th arrondissement

A Toutes Vapeurs (p41)   €
7 rue de l'Isly (Map 3 C5)
West/8th arrondissement

Café Moderne (p25)   €€
40 rue Notre-Dame-des-
Victoires (Map 10 G2)
Centre/2nd arrondissement

La Cave Gourmande (p47)   €€
10 rue de Général-Brunet
(Métro Botzaris)
North/19th arrondissement

Le Cristal Room (p40)   €€€
La Maison Baccarat, 11 place
des Etats-Unis (Map 8 E2)
West/16th arrondissement

La Famille (p48)   €€
41 rues des Trois-Frères
(Map 4 F2)
North/18th arrondissement

Flora (p39)   €€
36 avenue George V
(Map 8 F2)
West/8th arrondissement

Maison Blanche (p40)   €€€
15 avenue Montaigne
(Map 8 G3)
West/8th arrondissement

Market (p40)   €€€
15 avenue Matignon
(Map 9 A2)
West/8th arrondissement

Mon Vieil Ami (p31)   €€
69 rue St-Louis-en-l'Ile
(Map 17 A2)
Centre/4th arrondissement

R'Aliment (p28)   €€
57 rue Charlot (Map 11 C4)
Centre/3rd arrondissement

Restaurant du Palais Royal €€
(p24)
110 galérie Valois (Map 10 F3)
Centre/1st arrondissement

Printemps (p83)
64 boulevard Haussmann
01 42 82 57 87 (Map 9 D1)
North/9th arrondissement

Fashion

AB33 (p69)
33 rue Charlot (Map 11 C4)
Centre/3rd arrondissement

Abou d'Abi Bazar (p68)
10 rue des Francs Bourgeois
(Map 17 C1)
Centre/3rd arrondissement

Agnès b (p76)
6 (women's) & 12 (men's) rue
du Vieux Colombier (Map 15 D2)
Centre/6th arrondissement

Alter Mundi (p90)
41 rue du Chemin Vert
(Map 12 E5)
East/11th arrondissement

Anne Willi (see p91)
13 rue Keller (Map 18 F2)
01 48 06 74 06
East/11th arrondissement

Annexe des Créateurs (p67)
19 rue Godot de Mauroy
(Map 9 C2)
01 42 65 46 40
North/9th arrondissement

Antik Batik (p67)
18 rue de Turenne (Map 17 C1)
Centre/4th arrondissement

Antoine & Lili (p87)
95 quai de Valmy (Map 11 C1)
North/10th arrondissement

APC (p76)
3 & 4 rue Fleurus (Map 15 D4)
Centre/6th arrondissement

APC Solde (p67)
32 rue de Cassette
(Map 15 D4)
01 45 48 43 71
www.apc.fr
Centre/6th arrondissement

A-poc (p70)
47 rue des Francs Bourgeois
(Map 11 B5)
Centre/4th arrondissement

Atelier Narakas (p66)
79 rue du Temple (Map 11 B4)
Centre/3rd arrondissement

Azzedine Alaïa (p70)
7 rue de Moussy (Map 17 A1)
Centre/4th arrondissement

Balenciaga (p86)
10 avenue George V (Map 8 F3)
01 47 20 21 11
www.balenciaga.com
West/8th arrondissement

Barbara Bui (p65)
23 rue Etienne Marcel
(Map 10 H4)
Centre/2nd arrondissement

Cacharel (see p67)
114 rue d'Alésia
(Map 19 C4)
01 45 42 53 04
www.cacharel.com
South/14th arrondissement

Catherine Magnan (see p91)
39 rue Charonne
(Map 18 F2)
01 43 55 56 57
East/11th arrondissement

Chanel (p86)
42 ave Montaigne
(Map8 G3)
01 47 23 74 12
www.chanel.com
West/8th arrondissement

Chloé (p86)
54–56 rue du Faubourg-St-
Honoré
(Map 9 B2)
01 44 94 33 00, www.chloe.com
West/8th arrondissement

Christian Lacroix (p86)
73 rue du Faubourg-St-Honoré
(Map 9 B2)
01 42 68 79 04
www.christian-lacroix.com
West/8th arrondissement

Comptoir des Cotonniers (p70)
33 rue des Francs Bourgeois
(Map 11 B5)
Centre/4th arrondissement

Dépôt-Vente de Buci (p67)
4–6 rue Bourbon le Château
(Map 16 E2)
01 46 34 45 05
Centre/6th arrondissement

Dior (p86)
30 ave Montaigne (Map8 G3)
www.dior.com
West/8th arrondissement

Dolce & Gabbana (p86)
22 ave Montaigne (Map 8 G3)
01 42 25 68 78
www.dolcegabbana.com
West/8th arrondissement

L'Eclaireur (p63)
10 rue Hérold (Map 10 G3)
Centre/1st arrondissement

Emmanuel Ungaro (p86))
2 ave Montaigne (Map 8 F3) 01
53 57 00 00
www.emmanuelungaro.fr
West/8th arrondissement

Etam (p68)
67 rue de Rivoli (Map 17 A1)
01 44 76 73 73
www.etam.com
Centre/1st arrondissement

Et Vous Stock (p67)
17 rue de Turbigo (Map 10 H4)
01 40 13 04 12
Centre/2nd arrondissement

Gaëlle Barré (p91)
17 rue Keller (Map 18 F2)
01 43 14 63 02
East/11th arrondissement

Ginger Lyly (p87)
33 rue Beaurepaire
(Map 11 C2)
North/10th arrondissement

Guerrisol (p67)
17bis blvd de Rochechouart
(Map 4 H3)
01 45 26 13 12
North/9th arrondissement

Helmut Lang (p61)
219 rue St-Honoré (Map 10 E4)
Centre/1st arrondissement

Isabel Marant (p90)
16 rue de Charonne
(Map 18 E2)
East/11th arrondissement

Jean-Paul Gaultier (p86)
44 avenue George V (Map8 F2)
01 44 43 00 44
www.jeanpaulgaultier.com
West/8th arrondissement

John Galliano (p86)
384 rue St-Honoré
(Map9 C3)
01 55 35 40 40
www.johngalliano.com
Centre/1st arrondissement

Kookaï (p67, p68)
82 rue Réamur
(Map 11 A3)
01 45 08 93 69
www.kookai.fr
Centre/2nd arrondissement

Lagerfeld Gallery (p77)
40 rue de Seine
(Map 16 E1)
Centre/6th arrondissement

Lanvin (p86)
15 rue du Faubourg-St-Honoré
(Map19 B2)
01 44 71 33 33
www.lanvin.fr
West/8th arrondissement

Lili Perpink (p88)
22 rue Vieuville (Map 4 F2)
North/10th arrondissement

Loft Design by (p78)
56 rue de Rennes
(Map 16 E2)
Fashion
Centre/6th arrondissement

Lucien Pellat-Finet (p81)
1 rue Montalembert
(Map 15 D1)
Centre/7th arrondissement

Madelios (p61)
23 boulevard de la Madeleine
(Map 9 C2)
Centre/1st arrondissement

Maria Luisa (p62)
2 rue Cambon
(Map 9 C3)
Centre/1st arrondissement

Marni (p86)
57 ave Montaigne (Map 8 H2)
01 56 88 08 08
www.marni.com
West/8th arrondissement

Martine Sitbon (p81)
13 rue Grenelle
(Map 15 D2)
Centre/7th arrondissement

Martin Grant (p72)
44 rue Vieille du Temple
(Map 11 B5)
Centre/4th arrondissement

Martin Margiela (p62)
25bis rue de Montpensier
(Map 10 F3)
Centre/1st arrondissement

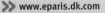

Paris Jazz Corner (p81)
5&7 rue de Navarre
(Map 17 A5)
01 43 36 78 92
www.parisjazzcorner.com
Centre/5th arrondissement

Publicis Drugstore (p83)
133 avenue des Champs-
Élysées (Map 8 F1)
West/8th arrondissement

Techno Import (p81)
16–18 rue Taillandiers
(Map 18 F2), 01 48 05 71 56
East/11th arrondissement

Virgin Megastore
52–60 ave des Champs-
Elysées (Map 8 G2)
01 49 53 50 00
www.virginmega.fr
West/8th arrondissement

Waves (p81)
36 rue Keller
(Map18 F1)
01 40 21 86 98
East/11th arrondissement

Perfumes

L'Artisan Parfumeur (p62)
2 rue Amiral de Coligny
(Map 10 F5)
Centre/1st arrondissement

Editions de Parfums Frédéric Malle (p80)
37 rue de Grenelle
(Map 15 C2)
Centre/7th arrondissement

Givenchy (p86)
3 avenue George V
(Map 8 F3)
08 25 82 55 90
www.givenchy.com
West/8th arrondissement

Iunx (p83)
48–50 rue de l'Université
(Map 15 D1)
Centre/7th arrondissement

La Parfumerie Générale (p85)
6 rue Robert-Estienne
(Map 8 G2)
West/8th arrondissement

Salons du Palais Royal (p62)
25 rue de Valois
(Map 10 F3)
Centre/1st arrondissement

Second-hand & Vintage

Catherine Arigoni (p82)
14 rue Beaune (Map 15 D1)
Centre/7th arrondissement

E2 (p87)
15 rue Martel (Map 11 A1)
North/10th arrondissement

Killiwatch (p65)
64 rue Tiquetonne (Map 10 G3)
Centre/2nd arrondissement

Les Nuits de Satin (p89)
9 rue Oberkampf (Map 11 D4)
East/11th arrondissement

Les 3 Marches de Catherine B (p76)
1 & 3 rue Guisarde (Map 16 E2)
Centre/6th arrondissement

Yukiko (p71)
97 rue Vieille du Temple (Map 11 C4)
Centre/4th arrondissement

Shoes

André
2 rue Isly (Map 3 C5)
01 44 69 32 63
www.andre.fr
West/8th arrondissement

Charles Jourdan (p84)
86 ave des Champs-Elysées
(Map 8 G1)
West/8th arrondissement

Christian Louboutin (p60)
19 rue Jean-Jacques Rousseau
(Map 10 F4)
Centre/1st arrondissement

Free Lance (p76)
30 rue du Four (Map 15 D2)
Centre/6th arrondissement

Iris (p80)
28 rue de Grenelle (Map 15 D2)
Centre/7th arrondissement

Jean-Baptiste Rautureau (p82)
24 rue de Grenelle
(Map 15 D2)
Centre/7th arrondissement

Pierre Hardy (p61)
156 galérie de Valois
(Map 10 F4)
Centre/1st arrondissement

Renaud Pellegrino (p83)
14 rue du Faubourg-St-Honoré
(Map 9 B2)
West/8th arrondissement

Roger Vivier (p86)
29 rue du Faubourg-St-Honoré
(Map 9 B2)
West/8th arrondissement

Shoe Bizz (p66)
48 rue Beaubourg (Map 11 A5)
Centre/3rd arrondissement

Stephane Kélian (p86)
5 rue du Faubourg-St-Honoré
(Map 9 C2)
West/8th arrondissement

Stationery

Calligrane (p71)
4–6 rue du Pont Louis-Philippe
(Map 17 A2)
Centre/4th arrondissement

Art & Architecture

Cemeteries

Cimitière du Montmartre
(p109; Map 3 D1)
North/18th arrondissement

Cimitière du Montparnasse
(p167; Map 19 C2)
South/14th arrondissement

Cimitière du Passy (p109;
Map 7 C2)
West/16th arrondissement

Cimitière du Père-Lachaise
(p109; Map 12 H4)
East/20th arrondissement

Churches

Basilique St-Denis (p108)
1 rue de la Légion d'Honneur
(Métro Basilique de St-Denis)
North/Northern suburbs

Chapelle Expiatoire (p166)
Rue Pasquier (Map 9 C1)
West/8th arrondissement

Eglise de la Madeleine (p102)
Pl de la Madeleine (Map 9 C2)
West/8th arrondissement

Eglise St-Eustache (p97)
Rue du Jour (Map 10 G4)
Centre/1st arrondissement

Eglise St-Augustin (p102)
46 blvd Malesherbes (Map 3 B5)
West/8th arrondissement

Eglise St-Sulpice (p100)
Place St-Sulpice (Map 16 E3)
Centre/6th arrondissement

Notre Dame (p110)
Place du Parvis-Notre-Dame
(Map 16 H2)
01 42 34 56 10
Centre/4th arrondissement

Sacré Coeur (p107)
35 rue du Chevalier de la Barre
(Map 4 G2)
01 53 41 89 00
North/18th arrondissement

St-Chapelle (p94)
4 blvd du Palais
(Map 16 G1)
Centre/1st arrondissement

St-Julien-le-Pauvre (p163)
Rue St-Julien-le-Pauvre
(Map 16 H2)
Centre/5th arrondissement

Exhibition Spaces

Atelier Brancusi (p97)
Pl Centre Pompidou (Map 11 A5)
Centre/4th arrondissement

Bibliothèque Nationale de France – François Mitterand (p111)
11 quai François Mauriac
(Map 22 F3)
South/13th arrondissement

Bibliothèque Nationale de France – Richelieu (p95)
58 rue de Richelieu
(Map 10 F3)
Centre/2nd arrondissement

Chez Robert Electron Libre (p94)
59 rue de Rivoli (Map 10 G5)
Centre/1st arrondissement

Fondation Cartier pour l'Art Contemporain (p113)
261 blvd Raspail
(Map 19 D2)
South/14th arrondissement

Index by Type

Art & Architecture

Exhibition Spaces
continued...

Fondation Henri Cartier-Bresson (p113)
2 impasse Lebouis
(Map 19 B2)
South/14th arrondissement

Les Frigos (p112)
rue des Frigos
(Map 22 F4)
South/13th arrondissement

Grand Palais (p103)
Avenue Winston-Churchill
(Map 9 A3)
01 44 13 17 17
West/8th arrondissement

Institut du Monde Arabe (p98)
1 rue des Fossés St-Bernard
(Map 17 B3)
Centre/5th arrondissement

Jeu de Paume (p95)
1 pl de la Concorde
(Map 9 C3)
Centre/1st arrondissement

Louise Weiss. rue (p112)
(Map 21 D3)
South/13th arrondissement

Maison Européene de la Photographie (p98)
5–7 rue de Fourcy
(Map 17 B1)
Centre/4th arrondissement

Musée du Luxembourg (p100)
19 rue de Vaugirard
(Map 16 E3)
Centre/6th arrondissement

Palais du Tokyo (p104)
13 avenue du Président Wilson
(Map 8 E3)
West/16th arrondissement

Patrimoine Photographique (p97)
62 rue St-Antoine (Map 17 C2)
Centre/4th arrondissement

Petit Palais (p103)
Avenue Winston Churchill
(Map 9 A3)   01 42 65 12 73
West/8th arrondissement

Historic Buildings

Arènes de Lutèce (p99)
Entrance on 49 rue Monge &
7 rue de Navarre
(Map 17 A5)
Centre/5th arrondissement

Assemblée Nationale (p110)
126 rue de l'Université
01 40 063 60 00
(Map 9 A4)
Centre/7th arrondissement

Catacombes (p113)
1 pl Denfert Rochereau
(Map 20 E3)
South/14th arrondissement

Chateau de St-Germain (p106)
Place Charles de Gaulle
(RER St-Germain-en-Laye)
West/Western Suburbs

La Conciergerie (p110)
1 quai de l'Horloge
(Map 16G1)
01 53 73 78 50
Centre/1st arrondissement

Gare du Nord (p110) (Map 5 A4)
North/10th arrondissement

Moulin de la Galette (p107)
75 rue Lepic
(Map 4 E1)
North/18th arrondissement

Moulin de Radet (p107)
83 rue Lepic
(Map 4 F1)
North/18th arrondissement

Opéra Garnier (p110, p122)
Place de l'Opéra
(Map 9 D1)
08 36 69 78 68
www.opera-de-paris.fr
North/9th arrondissement

La Sorbonne (p99)
47 rue des Ecoles
(Map 16 E3)
Centre/5th arrondissement

Tour Eiffel (p110)
Champs de Mars
01 44 11 23 11
www.tour-eiffel.com
Centre/7th arrondissement

Tour St-Jacques (p94)
Place du Châtelet
Centre/1st arrondissement

Modern Architecture

Cité Universitaire (p112)
Boulevard Jourdan
(Métro Cité Universitaire)
South/14th arrondissement

Ministère des Finances (p111)
(Map 22 F1)
East/12th arrondissement

Stade de France (p198, p127)
rue Francis de Pressensé
St-Denis (Métro St-Denis Porte
de Paris)
North/Northern suburbs

Museums

Abbaye du Val-de-Grâce (p99)
227bis rue St-Jacques
(Map 20 F1)
Centre/5th arrondissement

Centre Pompidou (p100)
Rue Beaubourg (Map 11 A5)
01 44 78 12 33
www.centrepompidou.fr
Centre/4th arrondissement

Cité des Sciences et de l'Industrie (p108)
Parc de la Villette, 30 ave
Corentin Cariou (Métro Porte
de Pantin)
North/19th arrondissement

Fondation Le Corbusier (p105)
Villa la Roche, 10 square du Dr
Blanche (Métro Jasmin)
West/16th arrondissement

Manufacture des Gobelins (p112)
42 avenue des Gobelins
(Map 21 A3)
South/13th arrondissement

Mémorial du Maréchal Leclerc (p113)
23 allée de la deuxième
(Map 19 B1)
South/15th arrondissement

Musée d'Art et d'Histoire du Judaïsme (p96)
71 rue du Temple (Map 11 A5)
Centre/3rd arrondissement

Musée d'Art et d'Histoire de St-Denis (p109)
22bis rue Gabriel Péri (Métro
St-Denis Porte de Paris)
North/Northern suburbs

Musée de l'Assistance Publique (p99)
47 quai de la Tournelle
(Map 17 A3)
Centre/5th arrondissement

Musée Carnavalet (p95)
23 rue de Sevigné (Map 17 C1)
Centre/3rd arrondissement

Musée du Cinéma (p111)
51 rue de Bercy (Map 22 G2)
East/12th arrondissement

Musée Cognacq-Jay (p97)
8 rue Elzévi (Map 11 C5)
Centre/4th arrondissement

Musée Départemental Maurice Denis "Le Prieuré" (p106)
2bis rue Maurice Denis
(RER St-Germain-en-Laye)
West/Western suburbs

Musée d'Erotisme (p106)
72 blvd de Clichy (Map 4 E3)
North/18th arrondissement

Musée Galliéra (p102)
10 avenue Pierre 1er de Serbie
(Map 8 E3)
West/16th arrondissement

Musée Guimet (p105)
6 place d'Iéna (Map 8 E3)
West/16th arrondissement

Musée Gustave Moreau (p109)
14 rue de la Rochefoucauld
(Map 4 E4)
North/9th arrondissement

Musée Jacquemart-André (p102)
158 blvd Haussmann
(Map 2 H5)
West/8th arrondissement

Musée du Louvre (p100)
Cour Napoléon (Map 10 E5)
01 40 20 53 17
www.louvre.fr
Centre/1st arrondissement

Musée Maillol – Fondation Dina Vierny (p101)
59–61 rue de Grenelle
(Map 15 D2)
Centre/7th arrondissement

Musée Marmottan-Monet (p105)
2 rue Louis Boilly
(Métro Ranelagh)
West/16th arrondissement

Musée de Montmartre (p107)
12 rue Cortot (Map 4 F1)
01 46 06 61 11
North/18th arrondissement

Musée de la Musique (p108)
Cité de la Musique,
221 ave Jean Jaurès
(Métro Porte de Pantin)
North/19th arrondissement

Musée National d'Art Moderne (MAMVP) (p104)
11 ave du Président Wilson
(Map 8 E3)
West/16th arrondissement

Musée National Eugène Delacroix (p100)
6 rue de Furstemberg
(Map 16 E2)
Centre/6th arrondissement

Musée National du Moyen Age (p98)
6 pl Paul-Painlevé (Map 16 G3)
Centre/5th arrondissement

Musée Nationale Picasso (p96)
5 rue de Thorigny (Map 11 C5)
Centre/3rd arrondissement

Musée d'Orsay (p100)
1 rue de la Légion d'Honneur
(Map 9 C5) 01 45 49 11 11
Centre/7th arrondissement

Musée de la Publicité (p96)
107 rue de Rivoli (Map 10 E4)
Centre/1st arrondissement

Musée Rodin (p111)
77 rue de Varenne (Map 15 A1)
Centre/7th arrondissement

Palais de Chaillot (p104)
17 pl du Trocadéro (Map 7 C4)
West/16th arrondissement

Palais de la Découverte (p103)
Avene Franklin D Roosevelt
(Map 8 H3) 01 56 43 20 21
www.palais-decouverte.fr
West/8th arrondissement

Performance

Cinema

Action Christine Odeon (p120)
4 rue Christine (Map 16 F2)
01 43 29 11 30
Centre/6th arrondissement

Action Ecoles (p120)
23 rue des Ecoles (Map 16 H3)
01 43 29 79 89
Centre/5th arrondissement

Le Champo (p120)
51 rue des Ecoles (Map16 H3)
01 43 54 51 60
www.lechampo.com
Centre/5th arrondissement

Cinéma en Plein Air (p124)
Parc de la Villette
(Métro Porte de Pontin)
North/19th arrondissement

Grand Action (p120)
5 rue des Ecoles
(Map 17 A4)
01 43 29 44 40
Centre/5th arrondissement

Le Grand Rex (p119)
1 blvd Poissonnière
(Map 10 H2)
Centre/2nd arrondissement

Forum des Images (p118)
Forum des Halles (Porte Eustache; Map 10 G4)
Centre/1st arrondissement

Images d'Ailleurs (p120)
21 rue de la Clef
(Map 21 A1)
01 45 87 18 09
Centre/5th arrondissement

MK2 Bibliothèque (p127)
128–62 avenue de France
(Map 22 F3)
South/13th arrondissement

La Pagode (p118)
57bis rue de Babylone
(Map 15 A2)
Centre/7th arrondissement

Quartier Latin (p120)
9 rue Champollion (Map 16 G3)
01 43 26 84 65
Centre/5th arrondissement

Racine Odeon (p120)
6 rue de l'Ecole de Médecine
(Map16 F3)
01 46 33 43 71
Centre/6th arrondissement

Reflet Medicis (p120)
3 rue Champollion (Map 16 G3)
01 43 54 42 34
Centre/5th arrondissement

St-André-des-Arts (p120)
30 rue St André des Arts
(Map 16 F2), 01 43 26 48 18
Centre/6th arrondissement

Studio Galande (p120)
42 rue Galande (Map 16 H3)
01 43 26 94 08
www.studiogalande.fr
Centre/5th arrondissement

Studio 28 (p123)
10 rue Tholozé (4 E2)
North/18th arrondissement

Circus & Cabaret

Bal du Moulin Rouge (p124)
82 blvd de Clichy (Map 4 E2)
01 53 09 82 82
www.moulinrouge.com
North/18th arrondissement

Chez Madame Arthur (p124)
75bis rue des Martyrs (Map 4 F3)
01 42 54 40 21
North/18th arrondissement

Chez Michou (p124)
80 rue des Martyrs
(Map 4 F3)
01 46 06 16 04
www.michou.com
North/18th arrondissement

Cirque d'Hiver Bouglione (p125)
110 rue Amelot (Map 11 D4)
East/11th arrondissement

Crazy Horse (p124)
12 avenue George V
(Map 8 F3)
01 47 23 97 90
www.lecrazyhorseparis.com
West/8th arrondissement

Lido (p124)
116bis avenue des Champs-Elysées (Map 8 F1)
01 40 76 56 10
www.lido.fr
West/8th arrondissement

Paradis Latin (p124)
28 rue du Cardinal Lemoine
(Map 17 A4)
01 43 25 28 28
www.paradis-latin.com
Centre/5th arrondissement

Comedy

Café de la Gare (p119)
41 rue du Temple
(Map 11 A5)
Centre/4th arrondissement

Hotel du Nord (p123)
102 quai de Jemmapes
(Map 11 C1)
North/10th arrondissement

Le Point Virgule (p118)
7 rue St-Croix de la Bretonnerie
(Map 17 B1)
Centre/4th arrondissement

Dance

Centre National de la Danse (p124)
1 rue Victor Hugo, Pantin
(Métro Hoche RER Pantin)
North/Northern Suburbs

Le Regard du Cygne (p126)
210 rue de Belleville
(Métro Télégraphe)
East/20th arrondissement

Live Music

Bataclan (P126)
50 blvd Voltaire
(Map 12 E4)
East/11th arrondissement

Cité de la Musique (p123)
221 avenue Jean Jaurès
(Métro Porte de Pantin)
North/19th arrondissement

Duc des Lombards (p118)
42 rue des Lombards
(Map 10 H5)
Centre/1st arrondissement

Elysée Montmartre (p123)
72 blvd Rochechouart
(Map 4 G3)
North/18th arrondissement

Le Flèche d'Or (p126)
102 rue de Bagnolet
(Métro Alexandre Dumas/Maraîchers)
East/20th arrondissement

Index by Type

Performance

Live Music *continued...*

La Guinguette Pirate (p126)
Quai Francois-Mauriac
(Map 22 F3)
South/13th arrondissement

Maison de la Radio France
(p122)
116 avenue Président Kennedy
(Map 13 B2)
West/16th arrondissement

New Morning (p122)
7–9 rue des Petites-Ecuries
(Map 11 A1)
North/10th arrondissement

Le Zénith (p124)
211 avenue Jean Jaurès
(Métro Porte de Pontin)
North/19th arrondissement

Multi-function venues

Bouffes du Nord (p122)
37bis boulevard de la Chapelle
(Map 5 B2)
North/10th arrondissement

Café de la Danse (p125)
5 psg Louis-Philippe (Map 18 E2)
East/11th arrondissement

Lucernaire (p121)
53 rue Notre-Dame-des-
Champs (Map 15 D5)
Centre/6th arrondissement

Opéra Garnier (p110, p122)
Place de l'Opéra (Map 9 D1)
08 36 69 78 68
www.opera-de-paris.fr
North/9th arrondissement

Théâtre des Champs-Elysées
(p121)
15 ave Montaigne
(Map 8 G3)
West/8th arrondissement

Théâtre du Châtelet
(p119)
1 pl du Châtelet
(Map 16 H1)
Centre/1st arrondissement

Théâtre de la Ville (p121)
2 pl du Châtelet
(Map 16 H1)
Centre/4th arrondissement

Opera

Opéra Bastille (p122)
2–6 place de la Bastille
(Map 18 E2)
01 44 73 13 99
www.opera-de-paris.fr
East/12th arrondissement

Sport

Hippodrome de Vincennes
(p127)
2 route de la Ferme
(RER Maisons-Alforts)
01 49 77 17 17
East/12th arrondissement

Hippodrome de Longchamp
(p127)
Routes des Tribunes, Bois de
Boulogne
(Métro Boulogne J Jaurès)
01 49 10 20 30
West/16th arrondissement

**Palais Ominsport de Paris-
Bercy (POPB)** (p127)
8 blvd de Bercy (Map 22 F1)
08 92 39 04 90
www.bercy.fr
East/12th arrondissement

Parc des Princes (p127)
24 rue du Commandant
Guilbaud (Métro Porte St-Cloud)
01 49 87 29 29
www.psg.fr
West/16th arrondissement

Stade de France (p127, p198)
rue Francis de Pressensé
(Métro St-Denis Porte de Paris)
North/Northern suburbs

Stade Jean-Bouin (p127)
26 avenue du Général-Sarrail
(Métro Porte de St-Cloud)
01 40 71 71 00
www.stade.com
West/16th arrondissement

Stade Pierre de Coubertin
(p127)
82 avenue Georges Lafont
(Métro Porte de St-Cloud)
01 45 27 79 12
West/16th arrondissement

Stade Roland Garros (p127)
2 avenue Gordon Bennett
(Métro Porte d'Auteuil)
www.fft.fr/rolandgarros/fr
West/16th arrondissement

Theatre

Cartoucherie de Vincennes
(p125)
Route du Champ de
Manœuvre, Bois de Vincennes
(Métro Château de Vincennes)

Comédie Française (p119)
2 rue de Richelieu
(Map 10 H4)
Centre/1st arrondissement

Théâtre de l'Aquarium
01 43 74 99 61
www.theatredelaquarium.com

Théâtre des Champs-Elysées
(p121)
15 avenue Montaigne (8 G3)
West/8th arrondissement

Théâtre du Chaudron
01 43 28 97 04

Théâtre de la Cité (p127)
21 boulevard Jourdan
(RER Cité Universitaire)
South/14th arrondissement

Théâtre de l'Epée de Bois
01 48 08 39 74
East/12th arrondissement

Théâtre du Soleil
01 43 74 24 08
www.theatre-du-soleil.fr

Théâtre de la Têmpete
01 43 28 36 36
www.la-tempete.fr

Hotels

Aparthotels

Citadines (p180)
08 25 00 35 05
www.citadines.com

France Apartments (p180)
97 ave des Champs-Elysées
(Map 8 F1)
01 56 89 31 00
www.france-appartements.com
West/8th arrondissement?

**Hotel du Degrès de Notre
Dame** (p174, p180)
10 rue des Grands Degrés
(Map 16 H3)
Centre/6th arrondissement

Hotel Résidence Henri IV (p180)
50 rue Bernadins (Map 16 H3)
01 44 41 31 81
www.residencehenri4.com
Centre/5th arrondissement

Residence Carré d'Or (p180)
46 ave George V (Map 8 F1)
01 40 70 05 05
West/8th arrondissement

Cheap

Hotel des Arts (p181)
5 rue Tholoze (Map 4 E2)
North/18th arrondissement

Hotel Beaumarchais (p181)
3 rue Oberkampf (Map 11 D4)
East/11th arrondissement

Hotel Eldorado (p179)
18 rue des Dames (Map 3 C2)
West/17th arrondissement

Hotel Esméralda (p174)
4 rue St-Julien-le-Pauvre
(Map 16 H2)
Centre/5th arrondissement

Hotel Langlois (p180)
63 rue St-Lazare (Map 3 D5)
North/9th arrondissement

Hotel du Lys (p174)
23 rue Serpente
(Map 16 G2)
Centre/6th arrondissement

Hotel Malar (p177)
29 rue Malar (Map 8 G5)
Centre/7th arrondissement

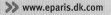

Hotel Mayet (p176)
3 rue Mayet (Map 15 B4)
Centre/6th arrondissement

Hotel Roubaix (p172)
6 rue Greneta (Map 10 H3)
Centre/3rd arrondissement

Hotel Tiquetonne (p172)
6 rue Tiquetonne
(Map 10 H4)
Centre/2nd arrondissement

Hotel Utrillo (p181)
7 rue Aristide Bruant
(Map 4 E2)
North/18th arrondissement

Royal Fromentin (p180)
11 rue Fromentin (Map 4 E3)
North/9th arrondissement

Moderate

Artus (p175)
34 rue de Buci (Map 16 E2)
Centre/6th arrondissement

Hotel Lenox (p176)
9 rue de l'Université
(Map 15 D1)
Centre/7th arrondissement

Hotel du Panthéon (p175)
19 pl du Panthéon
(Map 16 G4)
Centre/5th arrondissement

Hotel du Quai Voltaire
(p176)
19 quai Voltaire (Map 9 D5)
Centre/7th arrondissement

Hotel des St-Pères
(p176)
65 rue des St-Pères (Map 15 D2)
Centre/6th arrondissement

Hotel Terrass (p180)
12–14 rue Joseph de Maistre
(Map 4 E2)
North/18th arrondissement

Hotel Tonic (p172)
12 rue du Roule
(Map 10 G5)
Centre/1st arrondissement

Novotel Tour Eiffel (p181)
61 quai de Grenelle (Map 13 B3)
South/15th arrondissement

Villa D'Estrées (p174)
17 rue Git-le-Couer (Map 16 G2)
Centre/6th arrondissement

Expensive

Le Crillon (p177)
10 pl de la Concorde (Map 9 B3)
01 44 71 15 00
www.crillon.com
West/8th arrondissement

Hilton Paris Arc de Triomphe
(p179)
51–57 rue des Courcelles
(Map 2 G4)
West/8th arrondissement

L'Hotel (p175)
13 rue des Beaux Arts (Map 16 E1)
Centre/6th arrondissement

Hotel A (p177)
4 rue d'Artois (Map 8 H1)
West/8th arrondissement

Hotel Square (p179)
3 rue des Boulainvilliers
(Map 13 A2)
West/16th arrondissement

Le Meurice (p177)
228 rue de Rivoli (Map 9 D3)
01 44 58 10 10
www.meuricehotel.com
Centre/1st arrondissement

Pavillon de la Reine (p172)
28 pl des Vosges (Map 17 D1)
Centre/4th arrondissement

Pershing Hall (p178)
49 rue Pierre-Charron
(Map 8 G2)
West/8th arrondissement

La Plaza Athenée (p177)
25 ave Montaigne (Map 8 G3)
01 53 67 66 65
www.plaza-athenee-paris.com
West/8th arrondissement

Ritz Hotel (p177)
15 pl Vendôme (Map 9 D3)
01 43 16 30 30
www.ritzparis.com
Centre/1st arrondissement

Hotel de Vigny (p177)
9–11 rue Balzac (Map 8 F1)
West/8th arrondissement

Travel Information

Paris's public transport network (RATP) comprises the Métro, the RER (suburban train service), buses and trams, and is both efficient and reasonably priced. Taxis and the Batobus (water bus) service provide alternatives, but visitors often find that it is easier, quicker and more rewarding to explore the heart of Paris on foot. The following information covers the key aspects of getting around Paris; for further details, see www.eparis.co.uk.

Arrival

Paris has two airports: Roissy Charles de Gaulle is the largest and handles international flights; Orly serves national and European destinations.

Roissy Charles de Gaulle

The most popular public-transport link is RER B (via the Roissyrail bus), with a journey time of around 30 minutes into central Paris. Alternatively, Roissybus will drop you at Opéra, taking 50 minutes. Both services run approximately 6am–11:30pm. Air France also runs two bus services: to Porte Maillot and Etoile (5:45am–11pm) and to Gare de Lyon and Montparnasse (7am–9:30pm). For details of times and ticket prices, check the **ADP** website. **Bus de Nuit** bus services run through the night. For hassle-free transfers, you can book a shuttle bus (try **Paris Airports Service** or **Airport Connection**) direct to your hotel. The price depends on the number of passengers (usually about 16–25€ per person) but is cheaper than taking a taxi (around 50€). Limousine transfers are offered by companies such as **Airport Limousine Service** (around 100E).

Orly

To get into town by train, there are three options: catch the Orlyval shuttle train that connects with RER B, the Orlyrail bus for RER C, or the Jetbus to get on to the Métro. Alternatively, you can travel direct to Denfert-Rochereau on the Orlybus service, which takes around 30 minutes. Air France coaches take around 30 minutes to reach Montparnasse and Invalides. Check the **ADP** website for details. Taxi, shuttle bus and limousine services are also available from Orly – check the websites of **PariShuttle**, **Airport Connection** and **Airport Limousine Service** for more details.

By Train

Paris has six long-distance train stations, each serving a different region. All train stations are centrally located and have Métro stations, bus stops and taxi ranks nearby. High-speed services between the UK, Germany and Benelux are provided by **Eurostar** and **Thalys**; within France, the railway network is run by **SNCF**.

Getting Around

Central Paris is compact and easy to tackle on foot, but the excellent public transport system is a pleasure to use.

Public Transport

Paris's Métro system is one of the best in the world, and still improving – most recently with the addition of hi-tech driverless trains on the new line 14. The Métro runs from 5:30am to 1am, and is the quickest and most reliable way of getting across town. Short hops (especially those involving transfers) are not recommended, however, as they often take longer – and involve more legwork – than simply walking from A to B.

Buses are faster than the Métro over short distances, with the added bonus of being able to see where you're going, but it is at night-time that the bus network really comes into its own: Noctambuses (see the **RATP** website) are the only form of public transport in operation between 1 and 5am. These are very user-friendly and a must for night owls who don't want to take taxis – they operate outwards from the centre, leaving Châtelet hourly on the half hour and leaving their end stops hourly on the hour to travel back into town. Travel passes are valid, but single tickets *(see below)* are not. Fares start at 2.30€.

Single tickets, valid on all public transport, cost 1.30€ each, or 9.60€ for a *carnet* (book) of ten. A Métro trip uses one ticket – including transfers, as long as you don't leave the Métro system. (Inattentive travellers beware: it is not always possible to change direction without exiting the station.) Bus and tram journeys within central Paris also use one ticket each, but transfers are not permitted.

The Carte Mobilis (5€ for zones 1 and 2) allows you to travel on all bus, Métro, RER and tram lines all day; if you are staying longer than a few days,

Carte Orange (with photo ID) offers the same deal on a weekly (Mon–Sun only; 13.75€) or monthly (calendar month only; 46.05€) basis. The tourist option is the Paris Visite ticket – available for 1, 2, 3 or 5 days. As well as unlimited travel, this offers discounts on tours and some shops (such as Les Galeries Lafayette), but at 8.35€ for the 1-day version, you really do have to use the discounts to get your money's worth.

Tickets (but not passes) must be validated at the start of your journey – either in station turnstiles (Métro and RER) or as you board buses and trams. When travelling by bus, you should also show your ticket to the driver.

Taxis

The best way to get a taxi is to queue at one of the city's many taxi ranks. This is often quicker and cheaper than calling for a cab, and easier than hailing one on the street (they never stop near a rank). You'll find taxi ranks at railway stations and at bigger Métro stops, for a full list and more tips on Parisian taxis, see **www.paris-taxi.net**.

Driving

There is really little benefit to driving in Paris: the city is well known for its aggressive drivers and if you must take to the road, you will need nerves of steel and an up-to-date map of the city's labyrinthine one-way systems. Drivers from outside the EU should also carry an international licence. The city speed limit is 50 km/h (31 mph) – though many drivers ignore this – and parking spaces are as sparse as they are expensive.

Bicycles & Roller Blades

Bicycle hire is possible (try **Paris à Velo c'est Sympa**) and cycle maps are available from major Métro stations. Hiring roller blades is also an option *(see p18)*, but the streets of Paris are not the place for novices. Take care – drivers have scant respect for any other road users' rights or safety.

Tours

There are plenty of guided walks, bus tours and river cruises to choose from – full listings can be found on the tourist-office website *(see p231)* and at **http://paris.city-discovery.com**. For a low-key boat trip, take to the canal *(see p106)*. Some of the less obvious tour options are detailed below.

Fat Tire Bike Tours offers day- and night-time bicycle tours around Paris. Tours take 4 hours or more but are not strenuous, and children are catered for with tandems and child seats.

If you prefer posing to pedalling, join a **City Segway Tour**. These offer a unique opportunity to experience Paris by electric scooter – and you do get to practise before you hit the streets.

For stunning aerial views, take a helicopter tour with **Helifrance Paris**, or see the city the romantic way from a hot-air balloon (try one of the trips run by **France Montgolfiers**).

The flexible option is **AlloVisit**'s tour – this can be taken at your leisure, guided only by your mobile phone. Or, if your French is up to it, try one of **Urban Safari**'s SMS tours. And if you're feeling self-indulgent, order a tailor-made itinerary from **Edible Paris**: any-thing goes, as long as it is food-related.

Directory

ADP (Aéroports de Paris)
01 49 75 15 15 • www.adp.fr

Airport Connection
01 44 18 36 02
www.airport-connection.com

Airport Limousine Service
01 40 71 84 62

AlloVisit
04 95 04 95 32
www.voxinzebox.com

Bus de Nuit
08 10 02 02 02

City Segway Tours
01 56 58 10 54
www.citysegwaytours.com

Edible Paris
01 64 81 14 70
www.edible-paris.com

Eurostar
www.eurostar.fr

Fat Tire Bike Tours
01 56 58 10 54
www.fattirebiketoursparis.com

France Montgolfiers
08 10 60 01 53

Helifrance Paris
01 48 35 90 44

Paris Airports Service
01 55 98 10 80
www.parisairportservice.com

Paris à Velo c'est Sympa
01 48 87 60 01
www.parisvelosympa.com

PariShuttle
01 53 39 18 18 • www.parishuttle.com

RATP
01 58 78 20 20 • www.ratp.fr

SNCF
08 25 84 58 45 • www.sncf.com

Thalys
08 25 84 25 97 • www.thalys.com

Urban Safari
01 49 52 07 25
www.urbansafari.com

Practical Information

Paris is not a difficult city for most visitors, although people with special needs can find it tricky to access information and get around. The city's Office de Tourisme has an excellent website packed with useful information and suggestions and several welcome centres dotted around the city, which increase significantly in number over the summer months. The following is some essential practical information; for further tips and information, check www.eparis.dk.com.

Disabled Travellers

Unfortunately, much of Paris's public-transport network is inaccessible to wheelchair- (and pram-) users, though wheelchair-friendly buses are gradually replacing the old stock. On the Métro, only line 14 has stair-free access at all stations. Station staff rarely go out of their way to help, but leaflets about disabled facilities are available at main stations, and there is a **Compagnons du Voyage** service to accompany disabled people on public transport (25E per hour). Guide dogs can ride on public transport, but owners must pay 50% of the fare for them. A Braille Métro map can be ordered from **Service des Ventes**.

Taxi drivers are bound by law to assist disabled passengers and accept guide dogs, but not all cabs are equipped to carry wheelchairs.

The French **Tourisme & Handicaps** association has a list of disability-friendy accommodation, restaurants, cultural sites and leisure facilities, which is also posted on the tourist office website. There are separate criteria for those catering to physical, mental, hearing and visual disabilities.

There are several organizations that specialize in guided tours of the city for disabled people – check with the tourist office for information.

Emergencies & Health

French pharmacists are highly trained and therefore authorized to sell some medicines that are not available over the counter at home. As they can also usually direct you to the nearest doctor, they are always a good first port of call for minor ailments. After hours, a note on the door will direct you to the nearest late-opening pharmacy; alternatively, try the 8ème's **Dhéry Pharmacy** – one of the few that stay open all night. Paris's hospitals all have A&E departments, but if your French isn't up to scratch, you may prefer to try the **American Hospital in Paris** or the **Hertford British Hospital**. Both are private, so check beforehand that your insurance will cover the cost. Check **www.magicparis.com** for a list of English-speaking doctors.

Gay and Lesbian Travellers

The legal age of sexual consent is 16 and Parisians are generally very tolerant of same-sex relationships. The most openly gay areas, with lots of gay bars and clubs, are in the 1st–4th arrondissements. The **Lesbian & Gay Centre Paris** is on hand for support.

Left Luggage

Paris's six main stations all have left-luggage facilities. The airports do not.

Listings/What's On

Pariscope and *Officiel des Spectacles* are well-known, comprehensive listings magazines. The tourist office also publishes a free monthly guide called *Where: Paris*, available from information kiosks across town. The website **www.novaplanet.com** gives a more underground perspective on what the city has to offer.

Money

If you need to exchange cash, banks usually offer a better rate of exchange than the *bureaux de change* that are clustered around the tourist hotspots and along the Champs-Elysées, even once you have taken commission into account. Withdrawing cash from an ATM is a much simpler – and usually cheaper – way of getting your euros. Your bank will usually offer a competitive exchange rate, but may charge more commission for small transactions, so it is best to withdraw larger rather than smaller amounts. Check with your bank before you leave home.

Opening Hours

Most **restaurants** close between lunch and dinner, while **cafés** typically stay open from the morning until the end of the afternoon, when restaurants re-open. **Brasseries** often remain open until very late. **Bars** (and bar-like cafés) tend to open from mid-afternoon until the early hours. Some late bars stay open until around 6am.

Shops and **restaurants** are generally closed on Sundays – though some shops (typically tobacconists and general stores) open briefly on Sunday morning. The exceptions to this rule are generally found in the Marais and along the Champs-Elysées. Late-night shopping is on Thursdays until 9pm.

Most **museums** and many **shops** are closed on Mondays. Small shops may also close for lunch, as do many local bank and post office branches. Parks tend to open from dawn to dusk daily.

Public holidays are 1 Jan, 1 May, 8 May, 14 Jul, 15 Aug, 1 Nov, 11 Nov, 25 Dec, Easter Monday, Ascension and Whit Monday. Paris closes down on these days, and anywhere that does open will usually keep Sunday hours. The city also practically shuts down in August for the summer break; during this month, it is always best to phone ahead to check that your restaurant, bar or boutique of choice is open.

Phones and Communications

Many public telephone boxes are falling into disrepair and, given the rise in use of mobile phones, they are often left unrepaired. If they do work, you will most likely need to use a phonecard (available from Métro stations and *tabacs*). Some cafés and bars have public phones.

Non-residents cannot buy a French SIM card, though if you know a resident, they can buy one on your behalf. Phone-hire companies advertise at airports, but they rarely offer significant savings over a roaming contract.

Internet cafés are springing up all over the city – especially along the Champs-Elysées. Small local places offer good deals but little availability, and have a habit of closing down at

short notice. Visit **www.pidf.com** for an up-to-date list, or try La Flèche d'Or *(see p126)*, **Café Orbital** or **Paris-Cy** if you're having trouble getting online elsewhere.

Stamps are sold by many *tabacs*, some hotels and most postcard vendors. Post boxes are yellow and are marked "La Poste".

Security

Everyone must carry ID (passport or EU identity card) at all times. Police may – and in the case of ethnic minorities, frequently do – ask to see it. Certain areas in the north of Paris – La Goutte d'Or *(see p158)* in particular – are best avoided after dark.

Tipping

In restaurants, cafés and bars, service is usually included, but most Parisians will round up their drinks bill to the nearest euro, and leave a couple of euros for good service in a restaurant or café. Where service is not included, you should leave around 15%. Taxi drivers and hairdressers expect a similar percentage, and in hotels you should tip porters a couple of euros per item, and other hotel staff the same amount per day.

Tourist Information

The tourist office has moved to 25 rue des Pyramides, 1er (Map 10 E3) – the location of one of seven permanent welcome centres. In addition, there are numerous seasonal welcome centres that are open from June through August. Check the website *(see directory)* for details.

Directory

Ambulance (SAMU)
15

American Hospital in Paris
63 bd Victor Hugo, Neuilly-sur-Seine
Métro Pont de Levallois-Bécon
01 46 41 25 25

Café Orbital
13 rue de Médicis, 6ème
01 56 24 09 04 • www.cafeorbital.com

Compagnons du Voyage
01 53 11 11 12
www.compagnons.com

Dentist (SOS Dentaire)
01 43 37 51 00

Dhéry Pharmacy
84 ave des Champs-Elysées, 8ème
01 42 25 49 95

Directory Assistance
12

Doctor on Call (SOS Médécin)
01 47 07 77 77

English-language Help (SOS Help)
01 47 23 80 80

Fire Brigade (Pompiers)
18

Hertford British Hospital
3 rue Barbès, Levallois-Perret
Métro Anatole France
01 46 39 22 22

Lesbian & Gay Centre Paris
3 rue Keller, 11ème
01 43 57 75 95 • www.cglparis.org

Office du Tourisme de Paris
www.paris-touristoffice.com

Paris-Cy
8 rue de Jouy, 4ème
01 42 71 37 37 • www.paris-cy.com

Police
17

Service des Ventes
01 44 49 27 37

Tourisme & Handicaps
tourisme.handicaps@club-internet.fr

Yellow Pages (Pages Jaunes)
www.pagesjaunes.fr

General Index

General Index

General Index

General Index

Contributors

Maryanne Blacker, a Paris-based journalist specializing in food and travel, has written for magazines including *Australian Gourmet Traveller*, *Qantas magazine*, *Vacations & Travel* and *Elle Cuisine*, and is a regular reviewer for the *Paris Time Out Eating & Drinking Guide*. For this guide she co-wrote the chapters on **Restaurants** and **Shopping,** and contributed the **Havens** and **Top Choices – Morning, Afternoon** and **The Year** chapters.

Rosa Jackson has been writing about Paris's restaurants, markets and food shops since 1993, and is the editor for the *Paris Time Out Eating & Drinking Guide*. She offers custom-designed food itineraries with www.edible-paris.com, and teaches cooking classes in Nice (www.petitsfarcis.com). For this guide she co-wrote the **Restaurants** and **Streetlife** chapters.

Britta Jaschinski was born in Bremen, Germany and has lived and worked in London since 1993, after completing her photography degree. She has received several **photography** awards and her work features in newspapers (such as *The Sunday Times*), magazines (such as *Time Out*) and books – including her own titles, *Zoo* (Phaidon Press) and *Wild Things* (Thames & Hudson).

From cocktails to concerts via strikes, shopping and singles nights, **Katherine Spenley** writes about all aspects of the Parisian experience. She is a regular contributor to several guidebooks and her work has been published in newspapers around the world. For this guide she co-wrote the **Streetlife** chapter, and was the sole contributor for the chapters on **Bars & Clubs**, **Hotels** and **Top Choices – Evening** and **Night.**

Based in Paris since 1989, **Julie Street** has written for *Wallpaper**, *Elle*, *The Guardian* and *The Independent*. She also works as a presenter and producer at Radio France Internationale and writes a regular Paris shopping column for *Where magazine*. Julie co-wrote the **Shopping** chapter for this guide.

British-born **Richard Woodruff** moved to Paris in 1999. Ever more at home in France, he now lives in the up-and-coming 13th arrondissement, and works as a copywriter and journalist, specialising in film, culture and travel. For this guide he contributed the chapters on **Art & Architecture** and **Performance.**

Produced by Departure Lounge
Editorial Director Naomi Peck
Art Director Lisa Kosky
Assistant Editor Debbie Woska
Designer Bernhard Wolf
Proofreader Sylvia Tombesi-Walton
Researcher Laurie Gabay
Indexer Hilary Bird

Published by DK
Publishing Managers Jane Ewart, Vicki Ingle and Anna Streiffert
Senior Editor Christine Stroyan
Senior Designer Marisa Renzullo
Cartographic Editor Casper Morris
DTP Designer Jason Little
Production Coordinator Shane Higgins

Acknowledgements

PHOTOGRAPHY PERMISSIONS

The publishers would like to thank all the churches, museums, hotels, restaurants, bars, clubs, shops, galleries and other sights for their assistance and kind permission to photograph at their establishments.

Placement Key: t = top; tc = top centre; tca = top centre above; tcb = top centre below; tl = top left; tr = top right; c = centre; ca = centre above; cl = centre left; cla = centre left above; clc = centre left centre; cr = centre right; crc = centre right centre; crb = centre right below; b = bottom; bl = bottom left; br = bottom right; l = left; r = right.

The publishers would like to thank the following companies and picture libraries for permission to reproduce their photographs:

32 Montorgueil: 163cl

Aero Paris/Olivier Roux: 16br

Brontibay/Jérémy Fournier: 70bl

Cinq Mondes: 166br

DK Picture Library: 12tr, 94cl, 113tr

Fondation Cartier pour l'art contemporain/Fabien Calcavechia: *Nomadic Nights, Suicide 2002*: 16tr

Four Seasons Georges V: 166cl

Helmut Lang: 61tl

Britta Jachinski: 154bl/cl, 156br

Kong/Patricia Bailer: 34bl/br

La Bistrot d' à Côte Flaubert: 44cl

La Suite: 144cl

Lavinia: 64bl

L'Espandon: 24br

M.A.N. de Saint-Germain-en-Laye: 106tl

Musée départmental Maurice Denis "Le Prieuré": 106cl

Nickel: 163tr

Paris Tourist Office: Catherine Balet/10br/tr, 12cr, 16cr,19cl/tr, 116cb; Angélique Clément: 157cr; Henri Garat: 17tl; David LeFranc: 8–9, 11tr, 18tr/cr, 156tr

R'Aliment: 28cl

Renaud Pellegrino/Béatrice Drumlewiez 83cl

Ritz Paris: 13br

Maison Blanche: 40tl

Ventilo: 63cr

Zefa Visual Media/G. Rossenbach: 1c, 6–7

Jacket images Front: Getty Images/Philip Lee Harvey (cr & spine); Steven Rothfeld (crc); Photolibrary.com/ Bragg John (cl); Topfoto.co.uk (clc); Zefa Visual Media/G. Rossenbach (background).
Back: Steven Rothfeld (tr); Zefa Visual Media/ G. Rossenbach (c).

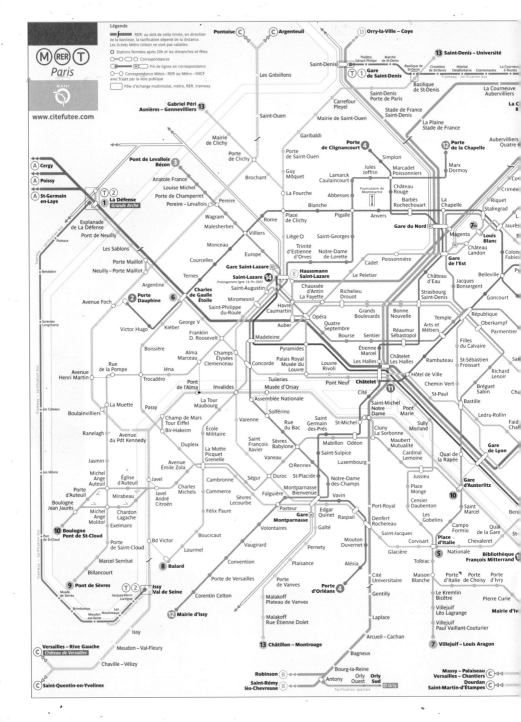